Susan Sellers is the editor of the much-loved and bestselling *Delighting the Heart: A Notebook for Women Writers* (The Women's Press, 1989), a companion volume to *Taking Reality by Surprise*, and *Instead of Full Stops: A Guide to Writing and Publishing Non-Fiction* (The Women's Press, 1996). She has published widely in the areas of literary theory and women's writing, and is Professor of English and Related Literature at the University of St Andrews.

Also edited by Susan Sellers from The Women's Press:

Delighting the Heart: A Notebook for Women Writers (1989)
*Instead of Full Stops: A Guide to Writing and Publishing
 Non-Fiction* (1996)

Taking Reality *by* Surprise

Writing *for* Pleasure *and* Publication

edited by **Susan Sellers**

First published by The Women's Press Ltd, 1991
A member of the Namara Group
34 Great Sutton Street, London EC1V 0LQ

Reprinted 1994, 1999

British Library Cataloguing-in-Publication Data
Taking reality by surprise: writing for pleasure and publication.
1. Authorship
I. Sellers, Susan
808.02

ISBN 0 7043 4267 7

Typeset in 9.5/11.5pt Times Roman by AKM Associates (UK) Ltd, Southall, London
Printed and bound in Great Britain by Cox & Wyman Ltd, Reading, Berkshire

'Art must take reality by surprise.'
Françoise Sagan

Contents

Finding a Subject

Finding a Voice

Openings

Continuings
Deciding Which
Genre to Write In

Endings
Finishing

Publication

Appendix

Acknowledgments

I would like to thank the following people and institutions for replying to correspondence, forwarding mail and suggesting contributions: Fleur Adcock; Rukhsana Ahmad; Linda Anderson; The Arvon Foundation; Margaret Atwood; R.V. Bailey; Sally Basto; Brenda Beaghen; Alex Bennion; Alison Brackenbury; Anita Brookner; Carol Burns; Camden Institute; Centreprise; Caryl Churchill; The City Literary Institute; Clapham–Battersea Institute; Diana Coben; Jeni Couzyn; Sarah Daniels; Louise DeSalvo; Julia Dinsdale; The Drill Hall; Carol Ann Duffy; Sarah Dunant; U.A. Fanthorpe; Fulham and Chelsea Institute; Penelope Farmer; Sue Gardener; Lynne Garrett; Shirley Gee; Goldsmith's College; Susan Goldstein; Hackney Institute; Hammersmith and North Kensington Institute; Gillian Hanscombe; Angela Holdsworth; Sarah Hopkins; Islington Institute; Olga Kenyon; Paddy Kitchen; Lambeth Institute; Maureen Lipman; Liz Lochhead; Shena Mackay; Rhona Martin; Anita Mason; Mary Ward Centre; Philip Mercer; Toni Morrison; Morley College; Suniti Namjoshi; Bridget O'Connor; Imogen Parker; Linden Peach; Jean Plaidy; Putney and Wandsworth Institute; Ravensbourne Institute; Ravinder Randhawa; Carol Rumens; Gillian Slovo; South Greenwich Institute; South Lewisham Institute; Southwark Institute; Streatham and Tooting Institute; Elizabeth Summers; Emma Tennant; Thamesside Institute; Sue Townsend; Tower Hamlets Institute; Deborah Warner; Marina Warner; Carol Watson; Fay Weldon; Westminster Institute.

Particular thanks are due to my editors, Hannah Kanter and Christine Considine, for their help in preparing the final typescript.

Acknowledgments

I would like to thank my mother, Shirley Sellers, for numerous 'secretarial' services, and Joyce Evans for help with photocopying.

I would also like to thank Rhona Tibber for her involvement with the project.

Grateful ackowledgment is made to the following:
Janet Beck, Cheryl Robson, Vania Georgeson and Aurora Metro Publications for 'Self-Assessment', 'Self-Censorship' and 'Fear of Failure' published in *The Women Writers' Handbook*, Beck, Georgeson and Robson (eds), Aurora Metro Publications, 1990; Alison Brackenbury for extract from 'Portland'; Liz Cashdan for extract from 'The Mariner's Tale'; Maura Dooley for extract from 'Mansize'; Carol Ann Duffy and Anvil Press Poetry for 'Boy' published in *The Other Country*, Anvil Press Poetry, London, 1990; Nicki Jackowska for 'Bulb Seller'; Marion Lomax and Bloodaxe Books for 'The Father's Story: A Pre-Raphaelite Dream' published in *The Peepshow Girl* Bloodaxe Books, Newcastle Upon Tyne, 1989; Medbh McGuckian for extract from 'The Rose-Pirate'; Sue Roe and Harvester Press for extract from *Women's Writing: A Challenge to Theory*, Moira Monteith (ed.), Harvester Press, Brighton, 1986; Peter Owen and Elizabeth Rokken for extract from *Alberta and Freedom*, by Cora Sandel translated by Elizabeth Rokken, The Women's Press, London, 1980; Penelope Shuttle for extract from 'Silver'; *Strawberry Fare* for Sue Stewart's 'Lucinda's Act'; Ruth Thomas and Hutchinson for extract from *The Runaways* (Hutchinson Children's Books, London, 1987).

Introduction

Taking Reality By Surprise: Writing for Pleasure and Publication is a collection of articles and writing exercises by women novelists, poets, songwriters, playwrights, journalists, writing tutors, editors and agents spanning the range of writing from initial idea to publication. Devised partly as a companion to *Delighting the Heart: A Notebook by Women Writers* (The Women's Press, 1989), the volume comprises suggestions and advice on the various stages of producing and publishing a piece of writing.

The volume is divided into three parts. 'Beginnings' explores the difficulties of putting pen to paper, suggests strategies for freeing the imagination, addresses the issues of subject and voice, and considers the importance of opening lines. The articles and exercises in each section are organised according to theme; the exercises are numbered consecutively for easy reference and prefaced with a statement of their aims.

'Continuings' opens with a series of articles on genre. Writing fiction, writing poetry, writing feature articles, writing for children and playwrighting are covered in this section. A problem area for many writers is keeping the momentum going through a long piece of writing, and this is the subject of section two. Writing skills – such as plotting, characterisation, creating an appropriate context and editing – are addressed in the final section of 'Continuings'.

In 'Endings', contributors confront the difficulties of ending. How does a writer arrive at her ending? How open should the ending be? Finding a publisher and presentation are discussed in the final section, and there are suggestions for alternative forms of publication outside mainstream channels.

The 'Appendix' includes articles on forming a writing group. A number of the exercises are intended specifically for group use and this is indicated in the aim prefacing each exercise.

No writer works in a vacuum. Despite the myth (a vestige of the Romantics?) that the true writer is born to the art, we all draw on and learn from the experiences of others. How has this writer dealt with characterisation? When should I use poetic form? What are the requirements when writing for radio? How can I turn my ideas for a television series into the kind of selling document that will ensure my proposal does not end up on the editor's slush pile? We would not expect a painter to paint without knowing something about the medium. Even the divinely inspired Keats used a thesaurus. The contributions in this volume aim to answer these questions, not because technique or inside information guarantees good writing, but because the suggestions of others offer a starting point from which to shape the connections between language, ourselves and the world more effectively.

Susan Sellers
August, 1990

Beginnings

Starting

Breaking New Ground
Sue Roe

At the beginning, you will find you need to go quite slowly. Very tentatively. It will feel very odd, like dancing or playing tennis after a long rest. All the muscles will ache. But of course: you are bound to feel different, you are inventing something. Everything will feel as if it is changing. You can chant a mantra to yourself, if it helps: 'speed kills', or, 'everything has got to change.' I suppose it's rather like having a baby: you will have to do some major re-organisation to give it space. You will have to be prepared to accommodate it, once it arrives.

You will need to prepare yourself for this change in your life. Go for a drive, perhaps: get in the car and drive up and down the motorway. That's what I do. When I get past the bit with a mental ring round it marked 'home territory', I begin to panic. I glance at the clock and realise I am going too fast. There is a police car on the bridge ahead. Slow down. Panic kills. Speed kills. But I don't know where I'm going! you protest. Of course not. This is fiction you are writing: why d'you think it's called a 'novel'? You are going somewhere new. (You might, of course, be writing a play or a poem, but you will know what I mean.) You are breaking new ground. Everything will feel as if it is about to change. Be prepared for this, but at the same time, take it gently. Don't be too hard on yourself.

Start. Anywhere. Right. There is a little girl in a room. (Can you see her? Good. Go on . . .) Her mother is there, too. The mother is wearing a black coat. Her lipstick is red. What year is it? When is this going to be set? (Don't worry about this, yet: just keep going . . .) There is a line of apricot-coloured powder gathering in the crease at the side of the mother's nose . . . Wait a minute, haven't I read that somewhere? Am I sure that that's original, that it is mine. Keep going. If it isn't your material you won't be able to get very far with it. See where it leads. Remember what my driving instructor used to say: 'Keep your eyes on t' road ahead.' He was from Yorkshire. But don't digress. Keep going. Go *on* . . .

Something else has come into my head: a coffin, and a silver incense-shaker. I can hear something: a bell, a flurry of rings: once, twice . . . a funeral perhaps? (Don't ask whose. Don't ask where this image comes from, what it is you may be remembering. Let it detach itself from its source. It is going somewhere new, now. Let it unfold, slowly. Write it down. It feels odd, strange, unrelated to anything you know? But of course: you are beginning to create the atmosphere for your fiction.

There is a death. A funeral. A missing person, perhaps. To be discovered later? Yes? (I don't know. Just keep on.) This person is hovering in the background, while in the foreground the little girl is asking where her Daddy is. (Let her ask. Write her words. Give them plenty of space on the page. Get them down.) Is this a story about a missing father? *Don't ask* (yet). Just write it down.

Remember: take it gently. Everything is changing. The world is beginning to look different. Something new is evolving. For the time being, just get it down.

Exercise 1: A Ten-Minute Exercise on Time-Wasting
Nicky Edwards

Aim

To speed the writer from bed to computer, eliminating all forms of procrastination.

Method

1 Get up, clean teeth, feed cat, etc.
2 Sit at desk, confronting blank screen, or sheet of paper.

3 List all the activities you undertake before getting on with any writing.

4 Award yourself marks, in the manner of a women's magazine quiz, as follows:

a Minor distractions which do not involve getting up: cleaning spectacles; filing nails; reading the dictionary; removing ink from typewriter keys with small blob of blue tack. 1 point each

b Fidgeting: making cups of tea; watering houseplants; catching the post before it lands on the doormat; pasting the first-prize-choice stickers on to the promotional literature of mail-order catalogues. 2 points each

c Major distractions: unnecessary phone calls; going to the shop for a pint of milk; reading the newspaper; hoovering. 3 points each

d Trance-like states: staring out of the window; giving way to despair; thinking with the eyes shut for more than ten minutes; falling asleep. 4 points each

Your score:

0–4 Were you really telling the truth? There's more to life than work you know.

5–9 A perfectly normal amount of dithering, but beware if you find your work-avoidance techniques becoming more elaborate.

10–14 Remember to finish your personal grooming before sitting down to work. Clear all books, papers and advertising flyers from the room before starting, in case you are tempted to read them. If these dilatory habits persist, get a job in an office, where they will be part of the normal working day.

15+ What a time waster! Have you tried cold showers, press-ups and artificial stimulants? There are religious orders for people like you.

5 Having listed all the ways in which you postpone having to write, you are now in a position to cut out the time-wasting devices which you have hereto employed.

Caution

Making lists is a prime displacement activity.

Exercise 2: Self-Assessment
Janet Beck and Cheryl Robson

Aim

To identify skills, blocks and support systems.

Method

1 Take four sheets of paper. Give each page one of the following titles: skills, problems, support systems, ambitions.
2 Under each title, list your own:
Skills – talents, things you're good at, qualities.
Problems – obstacles, difficulties.
Support systems – things that keep you going, stimulants, inspirations, good friends/family, etc.
Ambitions – hopes and dreams.
3 Study your lists and write down three conclusions about whether you are managing to use your skills to achieve your ambitions. For example:
You may have found it very hard to identify your skills, which may demonstrate a lack of confidence.
You may find you have very few support systems and consequently have little help in dealing with problems.
You may have written the same thing on two lists – a relationship is both supportive and problematic, or alcohol might be a support system and a problem.

Note

This exercise is designed to help identify those areas which may prevent us as writers from using our talents to the full.

Exercise 3: I've Always Wanted to Write But . . .
Sheila Yeger

Aim

To confront and (hopefully) dismantle the blocks we put in the way of our own creativity.

Method

1 Complete the sentence 'I've always wanted to write but . . .' For example 'I've always wanted to write but . . . I'm too busy.'
2 Try to look honestly at the excuse (because it *is* an excuse!). What are you 'too busy' doing? Are you inventing things to do rather than getting involved in writing? If you were to make writing your top priority, would you still be too busy?
3 Try a more *honest* statement. (This will be difficult, but worth attempting.) For example 'I've always wanted to write but I'm afraid that if I do I shall: neglect the housework/the children/my husband/my lover; go mad; find it too painful; be a total failure; not be able to earn a proper living; look silly; never finish anything; be disapproved of by my mother/my father/my husband/my children/my friends.
4 Take a long, calm look at all your fears, misgivings, self-doubts. Perhaps you could overcome them? Perhaps your husband/the housework, etc. could survive a little neglect? Do you, a grown-up woman, really need the approval of your mother? Should pain necessarily be avoided? Is madness the worst thing that can happen? If your desire to write is strong enough, nothing will stop you. All the things you feared *will* happen, and more besides. But you will consider it was worth it, most of the time. And you will, eventually, feel there is no real alternative.

Note

So many courses for 'beginning' writers work from the premise that writing is something that can be learnt, like French or car mechanics: simply absorb the rules, do the exercises, practice makes perfect.

But whenever I lead a workshop, I ask the women to put away their notebooks. I say 'Nobody can *teach* you to write, because you are already a writer. All I can do is to help you to confront and hopefully overcome the fears and inhibitions which have so far prevented you from expressing yourself in writing.'

Fear is a word I often use in this context. Pain is another. At first most students have little idea what I'm talking about (or pretend to have little idea). Later, as they begin to dip deep into their unconscious, to see all the dreams and nightmares waiting to be raised to the surface, they come to understand.

This, inevitably, is when one student leaves the workshop. She has, of course, an excellent excuse. She suddenly discovers other commitments. Her father/child/lover is sick. Her husband is away on business/angry/hungry. The house needs decorating/cleaning/moving. The garden demands to be dug/weeded/rotovated. We all know the excuses ... we've used them often enough. This is a writer not yet ready to be born.

Then there are the rituals. (I'm personally guilty of almost all of these.) First I'll sharpen my pencil/fill my pen/make the bed/hoover the room/walk the dog/feed the cat/make a patchwork quilt/phone my mother/bake a cake/research a thesis on women in the nineteenth century. *Then* I'll start writing. Excuses and rituals all come back to the same root cause. You are afraid, and rightly so. But only by naming that fear and confronting its causes, can you hope to overcome it.

As women, we have been conditioned not to cause offence, to 'do a dance for daddy', not to upset the patriarchal applecart. As women, we can so easily become afraid of our own energy, our own power and potential. We have been taught to curb that power, to be 'good girls', fulfilling those roles considered suitable for us, and no others. Is it surprising, therefore, that we are frightened of those aspects of ourselves we have suppressed, repressed or even killed – our 'dead babies'?

You, dreaming of being a writer, know instinctively that once you begin the journey, there will be no turning back. Pandora's box will spring open, and everything will be terrible and wonderful, life-enhancing, overwhelming and totally revolutionary. Your journey will lead you away from the safe, the predictable, the structured, the organised, into a landscape which is both utterly familiar and terrifyingly strange. Powerful and painful. Others may call you mad. You may even call yourself mad. Nothing will ever be the same again.

Is it any wonder that you sharpen pencils, tidy drawers, clean, cook, sew, use any excuse rather than pick up the pen and *write*? But ... admitting the fear and trying to analyse what lies behind it could be the first step on the journey ...

Starting Where We Are: One Way of Warming Up
Valerie Hannagan

Like me, you may occasionally find yourself wrestling with the notion that you have nothing to write. At least, nothing 'important'. As you know, there is no greater turn-off than that. It's awful: there we are, aching to write, aware that somewhere inside us lie whole continents of meaning, always beyond our reach because we cannot bring ourselves to value them. We stare, discouraged, at rows of books written by others and a horrid little voice inside us says 'They count: you don't. Why don't you give up the whole idea? You'll never be a writer.' Not surprisingly, we freeze.

I would like to suggest one of the many ways in which we can make friends with that seemingly impossible, life-arresting voice, and gently ease ourselves into writing.

Start where you are. Do not seek out special places, special times. Just get out your writing materials, whatever they may be, and keep them close to you. It may help if you can have silence; but if noise is where you are, do not attempt to shut it out. A dog barks in a neighbour's garden. Without thinking too much, try to get hold of that sound. Perhaps it embodies your frustration, your despair – you think of the cooped-up animal trying to get out; or else you are afraid of it – the dog wants to attack you. Maybe the barking is pleasurable, reminding you of a beloved childhood pet. Whatever it is, *write it down*, and if words refuse to come, then draw, doodle or scribble. Find a simple title: 'This is the dog barking; this is where I am'. Write the date, the time, the place. Perhaps your starting point will be visual: you may find yourself drawing the outline of your hand, or copying in words and pictures the grain of a wooden object. Or you will close your eyes, recapturing a fragment of conversation. The important thing is not to expect artistic miracles, but to meet yourself as you are now. If the horrid voice is uppermost, write out what it says, then draw a wavy line around your words and decorate them in any way you choose. Play with them, mix them up, cut them out if it helps, or contain them within other words. Once, when very depressed, all I could produce was a vertical line. But that was already something; the terrifying blankness of the page was split, I had created two spaces out of one – an early life form. Once you put yourself on the page, however simply, you can tell the bad voice 'I am writing'. And you may find the voice ceases to be bad, that, like a child coming out of a tantrum, it is relieved: it did not injure you after all, because you were able to hear its desire as well as its frustration.

Exercise 4: Timed Writing
Rosalind Brackenbury

Aim

To catch the first thought and see where it leads. To improve the skill of writing. To make the most of otherwise pressurised or wasted time.

Method

1 Sit at home or in a café or at the bus station, alone or with someone else, and begin writing – in a notebook or on a sheet of loose paper – about anything.
2 Stop after 20 minutes.
3 Repeat every day.

Note

This is rather like letting a bucket down into the well of your unconscious mind in order to bring up all the memories, impressions, thoughts and dreams that we carry around all the time. Twenty minutes is long enough to begin writing beyond the original thought (which may be something like 'I can't write') but not long enough to arouse the censor in our head. If you write for 20 minutes a day there are 23 hours and 40 minutes left over for everything else, which helps disperse the feeling that you need immense self-discipline to write.

This exercise can also be tried in spare moments, for example in doctors' surgeries or waiting for or on trains. A small ring-bound loose-leaf notebook, which keeps pages of writing together, and which can be carried, makes writing possible to do anywhere. This writing becomes the raw material for fiction, and is significantly different from keeping a journal because it is rarely connected with the day to day. I sometimes use this notebook for roughing out poems too. If you have your writing with you, you also stop worrying about getting back to your desk and 'getting down to work'. Life appears a lot less frustrating!

Exercise 5: Mental Filming
Caeia March

Aim

The exercise is strongly structured, timed to show how it could work. It can be adapted in many ways to suit many needs. I use it myself at many different points during novel writing. Its aims are:

i   To nourish the whole writer.
ii To acknowledge that other needs often conflict with a woman writer's urgent desire to write.
iii To sustain a woman writer when she's faced with short time, emotional demands, and a terrifyingly blank page.
iv To help a woman writer prepare to bridge disconnected periods of writing.
v   To protect a woman writer from panic and dismay at the closed ending of her writing time, to hold her concepts and words until she can sit to her writing again.

Method

This exercise is designed for women having to 'write against the clock'. The exercise itself takes two hours, and can be done in any two hours, any time of day/evening.

Beforehand you need to prepare by: collecting thick felt pens or wax crayons, plain (scrap) paper and your choice of writing paper; clearing the table in the room/corner/alcove where you write; purchasing a couple of cheap white candles and matches;

reading or re-reading a letter from a friend/a newspaper or magazine article/a favourite poem/ a chapter from a book.

The following are some women in writing groups I've tutored who have enjoyed this exercise and found it useful for focusing ideas and validating the desire to write, amidst competing demands on their time.

a A mother with young children. She takes one to school, the other to a friend. She arrives home frazzled, doing the shopping *en route*. It's 9.30. One child arrives home at 11.30. The house needs hoovering.

b A disabled woman with post-viral fatigue syndrome. It's 10.30. She is exhausted though she slept soundly. She has two hours up out of bed by which time she'll collapse, wiped out by the activity.

c A pensioner with a depressed husband. He's gone to his allotment for two hours. The washing needs doing. When he comes home he'll want 100 per cent attention.

d A woman who works full time and lives alone. Arrives home 6.30 desperate to write having held it in all day. At 8.30 she's going out to a meeting, eating a takeaway *en route*.

e A lesbian mother with two teenagers. Her lover takes them out on Saturday afternoon, but there's a pile of ironing to do. They'll be back at five o'clock.

9.30 Disconnect the phone. Everything can wait two hours: your child, partner, friends, housework, work crises.

9.31 Make tea/coffee/a drink. Take it to the bathroom, run a bath. Shut out the light. Light the candles while the bath is running. Sit on a stool (or loo-seat lid!). Slow your breathing. Count while breathing in and out slowly. You are now writing. Think back to the letter/poem/article/chapter/piece of your own writing. Recall the feelings as you first read it. Recall the ideas/phrases/jokes that affected you.

9.40 In the bath. Candlelight. Forget external demands. This is your time, your writing time. Forget that you're supposed to dash out of the bath to attend to everyone else's needs. Forget that you 'should be at your table getting on with *the* writing'. This *is* writing time. Time now to connect to the quiet writer inside who has been waiting. She needs to be *slow*. Relax your shoulders, hips, legs. Watch the candlelight. Recall the concepts, images, phrases of your chosen reading. In the water, think your way into an inner space from which writing comes. Trust that it will. Connect heart and mind to arm and hand. Relax your arm, your hand. If they are tense, agitated, your writing cannot flow through them to the paper. Say aloud, 'I have the right to be creative. I am writing.' Forget that writing should be on paper. Say, 'I am writing.' Say it aloud.

9.50 Out of the bath, in a warm robe or jogging suit, comfortable clothes, easy to put on. Don't delay now, but do all actions smoothly, steadily, without tensing.

9.55/10.00 At your table. Write whatever comes into your head. Don't determine what form, concepts, images. Let them happen. If you pre-plan this stage you may miss the chance for flow, continuous from your hydro-therapy, your earlier word-work.

Perhaps snatches of a poem arrive. Perhaps disconnected ideas, words, feelings. Perhaps odd bits of dialogue. Perhaps a woman (or man) with a name arrives on paper saying or doing something you didn't expect. S/he may be 'real', taken from the newspaper article, poem or chapter. Or s/he may be derived, similar to but not identical to what you read – a bridge to fiction. Let the writing flow or jump in whatever way it comes. Keep the pen on the page/fingers at the keys if you're typing or word processing. Don't move away. Stay there with the paper.

11.15 Suddenly the time has come round. You have to stop soon. You're mid-flow, mid-phrase, mid-sentence. Panic sets in. *Stop*. Take a deep breath. Close your eyes. If it helps, put your face in your open palms, elbows resting on the table. Concentrate your breathing, deliberately slowing it. Count if necessary to accomplish this. There are pictures in your mind, from your writing. Hold them. Fix them. Now run them again, like a film. Keep your eyes closed. Hold them. Fix them. Open your eyes. Pick up your felt pens. Scrawl picture after picture on to paper, however crudely. Often it is easier to fix pictures and carry them over to your next writing period than to fix the actual words. Practise this technique of inner filming wherever you are. It is part of your writing. Practise on buses; in public; just before falling asleep; in the bath; next time you're alone. This internal world is a resource, a retreat from external demands. It is a place where you can build a memory bank of pictures to return to when you next get chance to convert them into words.

It takes practice to film like this but it is useful when creating fiction and a most powerful/empowering compensation for a woman writer whose writing time is constrained.

11.28 The drawings might be naff – you may be sceptical about their value. But next time you come to this exercise they are proof of today's session, and a bridge/a starting point.

11.30 File them carefully, with the date on, with your writing.

Note

The same technique (drawing) can be used for recalling dreams, if felt pens are ready just in case. When I'm writing, I dream bits of the work, which would be lost if I waited to write them. Also, during illness and invalidity, I practised filming, editing and re-running my new novel, in my mind. Later, when I was physically able to write, the novel came through almost in final draft: dialogue, images, journeys, characters, interactions, structure and sequence. It was well worth the practice.

Beginning to Write
Joan Riley

How to get started?

The question I am most frequently asked in discussions and workshops is 'where should I start writing?' My answer is usually that trite cliché 'Why not at the beginning?'.

This, however, begs the question of *how* one starts.

How does one start putting pen to paper?

You have a yen to write but probably have never written anything creative since doing English language at school. The idea of a novel is great but you secretly wonder if even a short story is within your capability. Practically all the writers you have read about or listened to seem to have started at an incredibly early age. The route seems to have been the same for everyone: discovering Shakespeare and the classics by the age of eight and graduating to general adult fiction by eleven.

Thankfully, this is no more the case than the British being a nation of shopkeepers. Many people who were precocious early readers never write a single creative thing beyond school and many copious writers had as normal a development as you and I.

So how do you start?

Probably with a blank piece of paper or a notebook.

The problem is, nothing can be so intimidating as a blank piece of paper, especially when you approach it in the knowledge that it has to be filled. There are a million and one reasons why you can't do it today. A hundred and one things keep cropping up every time you sit down and try to find something interesting to fill it with. Or, worst of all, just thinking about writing in such a cold-blooded fashion makes your mind go blank.

This is certainly a normal reaction. Why not try writing about a situation you were in recently? Perhaps a traffic jam, a checkout queue, waiting for a bus, a train, that didn't turn up. What were your feelings? Were you in a hurry, late for something? Were you cold? Tired? Did you have children with you? Were they irritable? Had it been a long day? Maybe you could write something about where you were waiting. The place, what it was like. If it was a train station, for instance, did you find yourself pacing up and down? Did you read the advertising posters? Why? What was going through your mind?

Already the answers to these questions should have given you a fairish amount to write down. Maybe these answers will even suggest other questions, or jog your memory about some particular aspect of the incident you may have forgotten. Maybe within the context of that one scene several incidents happened. What were the other people around you doing? What was your reaction to them? How might they have been reacting to you?

Don't worry if you seem to be writing a lot about one small thing, or if certain sentences don't come out exactly how you want them to. Those are details that can be adjusted later. Sentences can be trimmed and altered and details inserted or deleted. What is important is getting something down – a pool of words that can become your raw material to work with.

Asking yourself questions is a good way of jogging your memory about things. You will probably find that once you begin to remember and write down an incident, many details start coming back to you.

Once you have collected a fair number of episodes, and have started to become more confident about your ability to explore a situation or occurrence, you might begin thinking about writing something with more structure and more point to it. You might decide you want to write a story or a longer piece of fiction. But before you start, there is one more thing it might be useful to give some thought to: the *story-line*.

Where to begin?

If you think of your story or fiction as a lot of different episodes joined together into a continuous movement from beginning to end, a useful way to think of your story-line is as a thread running through and linking all the episodes into a recognisable whole.

The first thing to decide is who this story is about – the *main character*.

This is where you come in. The character does not necessarily have to be you, but you can draw on your own experience to make her believable.

Alternatively, a starting point might be the people you know.

But what about your story-line? A series of unrelated episodes or vignettes do not make a story. There has to be some common thread or progression running through them which locks together into a whole. What time-scale, what dilemmas and what resolutions will your story have?

Suppose, for instance, you are writing about a specific thing, perhaps the first day on a new job. You might decide to take your story-line from the point of getting the job offer to the point of starting the job. What things will you incorporate? Let's suppose our character did not expect to get the job. More than that, she has been less than truthful about her quali-fications. Already there is an element of drama, an ingredient from which a tension can result. What will the character's feelings be, having accepted the job knowing she has less than the required skills and experience? What kinds of fears, tensions, apprehensions will she have? How will she feel that first morning? Might she dress a particular way to aid her confidence? Once she gets to the new place of work will she feel out of her depth? Will she try to disguise her uncertainties?

What will she do if confronted with some aspect of the work she can't tackle? Will she come clean or try to stall for time?

You could begin this story at any point in its chronology.

Some useful tips

1 Don't think of the first sentence you write as the only possible beginning. Everything you write is negotiable and nothing is set in stone until it is in a published form. The beginning is often a way of getting into the flow of the story, so be prepared to revise it at a later point once the story is in flow or finished.
2 Don't spend hours trying to get the perfect beginning. As the story evolves and the characters become more focused, new ideas for the beginning will often occur. Putting too much effort into getting the first page right could end with you losing the spark and freshness of the idea.
3 Don't worry about correcting grammatical errors at the drafting stage. This will bog you down and shift your focus away from the creative process.

Fiction in all its Forms
Ursule Molinaro

'Fiction in all its Forms' is the name of the creative writing workshops I conduct at various American universities, as a visiting writer, or a writer-in-residence, depending on the length of my stay. Students range in age from the early twenties to 60 plus.

I usually start the course with a few words of discouragement.

Don't count on your writing to support you. At least not at the outset. You need to have another job to support your writing.

Be aware that few people are as eager to read a book as they are to: look at a picture   drive a car   go for a swim   watch TV   go to sleep.

There are no breathless readers bending over your shoulder to catch your next *mot juste*. Not even in your circle of family & friends. Writing is solitary confinement.

You've got to seduce your readers from your first sentence

on. Whether you shock them, elate them, or merely interest them by the newness of your approach.

Yet, the effect you wish to produce on potential readers must not influence your story while you're writing it. Not until it is completely finished, when it becomes a marketing problem.

My students are free to write stories, novels, or plays of any length, & in the style of their choice, or of their invention. They set their own rules, & are held only to consistency. Everything is criticised strictly within its own context.

There is only one condition that all, even the shyest, must accept: all *must* read their work in progress *aloud* to the class & receive feedback. It is the only thing I insist on, & I strongly recommend it to anyone writing. Form a group. Meet once a week. Read your work to each other in rotation. As you read aloud, weak points jump to the fore, better words suggest themselves, flaws in the structure become apparent. Usually before a listener points them out.

Painters often hold their work up to a mirror to gain the perspective helpful for self-criticism. Reading aloud is a mirror for words. Unfortunately, though, you need an audience of at least one.

Reading aloud to yourself is also good. It helps with cadence, or finding a better word, but it's usually not enough to redirect a faulty story-line. You may find the redirection by yourself, before your listener points it out. & you'd probably find it in total silence at your writing place eventually.

Still—find someone to read to. A well-meaning, or at least neutral ear. Someone who will not use your self-revelations against you in a personal relationship. Because, if you're writing fiction, you're bound to reveal your inner self, whether your subject is autobiographical, or pure imagination. The choice of your subject reveals you. The way you depict & treat your characters reveals you. Your likes & dislikes become apparent. A writer of fiction is stark naked, unlike journalists who can cloak themselves in facts. Who reveal only the potential slant of the papers or causes they work for. Whose goal is objectivity.

—Reading aloud does *not* mean talking your story away before it has been written. Letting air to the foetus aborts it.—

Your language gets better if you like words well enough to dig up their roots, & understand the initial tangible meaning before the word acquired its abstract extension. (gauche sinister dexerity latent bias, etc.) & of course it's useful to know the basic rules of grammar & spelling before you break them. Any rule that is broken should be a conscious defiance.

Must a story have a beginning, a middle, & an end? Not necessarily. Or rather: it will anyway. One of my students at the University of Hawaii had trouble with middles. I suggested she write a number of beginnings, followed by an equal number of endings. She did. The result was a most enjoyable, publishable piece, dealing with relationships between couples. The repetition formed a pattern, from which the untold middles clearly emerged.

However, if you choose a conventional narrative form, you will need a conventional beginning, middle & end. But don't let your figures freeze on the keyboard, or around your pen or pencil, as you try to adhere to that sacred order. You can start your story at the end, if that is what you conceive first. You overhear a conversation that would make a perfect middle. Write it down, & fit it in later. Sometimes a glorious first sentence that triggered the whole story in your head needs to be discarded once the story is told. Cut it out. Put it on ice in a notebook. It might be perfect in something else. Be flexible. Don't put on a strait-jacket, unless your story deals with one. In which case, physically wearing one for a while might be a good idea.

& don't think only inexperienced or untalented writers rewrite! *Au contraire*.

What about the physical requirements? Should you use a pencil   pen   typewriter   word processor? Work at a desk   the living room table   in an office   in your bed? In a sidewalk café? X hours a day, every day? Or in spurts, preferably uninterrupted, when a subject grabs you? Shaw wrote on trains, in shorthand. Gide used narrow notebooks to jot down thoughts when he took walks. Proust wrote in bed. Virginia Woolf wrote standing, at a lectern, one and a half hours every morning.

---Virginia Woolf made an excellent suggestion that has saved me many times from getting stuck: don't end your work of the day with a well-finished paragraph. Always write a few sentences ahead. You have something to pick up on & grow from at your return. Even if the sentences themselves are eventually thrown out.

Should you work out a skeleton of the complete story/novel/ play & fill in the flesh when you know where you're headed? Or should you let your idea grow toward an as yet dim, distant goal? Let your characters surprise you, & polish each paragraph before you start the next.

Again, there are no rules. Try out what feels best to you. ---Which may not be the best for your next project.--- Use any tool. Sit/stand/lie wherever you feel comfortable, for as long as you can concentrate. ---Force yourself to push a little beyond comfort & concentration sometimes. Ideas often surface during less perfect conditions.

Now that everything has been set up, what are you going to put on that blank page in front of you?

You could start with writing your name. Tell us why you're called what you're called. Who named you; perhaps after whom.

Do you like your name? Does it identify you, also to yourself? Have you disliked it at any time in your past? How do you feel about people who misspell, mispronounce or misremember you?

There can be endless leads into stories, just thinking about your name. But perhaps you don't want to be that personal.

What about writing a Portrait of an Odious Person. Maybe you can't think of anyone you hate, but there must be character traits that annoy even the most tolerant among us. Make a list of them: nagging   a whiny voice   self-righteousness boasting   burping   a vicious tongue   pettiness transparent lies   tightness with money   ruthlessness yelling . . . etc. Pick the quality or qualities you resent the most, & create an Odious Person. Of any age, or sex. If you have someone specific in mind, who has been getting on your nerves, expand him or her. Don't feel limited by the facts.

---This is important for anyone drawing on autobiographical material: you're writing fiction. If something doesn't sound plausible in your story, change it. Free yourself from loyalty to facts, such as dates, places, chronological sequence. What you invent instead may turn out to be closer to the psychological 'truth' of the situation than what really happened.---

Take liberties. Play with your subject as you get to know him or her. Annoying people can be funny. Show your sense of humour. Quite often a successful Odious Person can become a character in a longer work.

Another amusing exercise is to establish a dialogue between a cup & a knife. Do anything that comes to mind, from a piece for children to a philosophical treatise.

Finally, you may have fun writing your own obituary. Fix the date of your death at any point, in the past, or way away in the future. Make your community regret/exalt/slander you. Describe your accomplishments. Don't stint on praise. A great deal of a writer's self-expectation can crystallise in such an obituary. It helps to remove the self-criticism that often hampers self-expression. It is also a challenge to immortality.

Another approach is through frustration:

1 If you know another language, choose a piece you like particularly well, & start translating it. Using no dictionaries. Your conscientious rewording of another writer's words will make your own dormant ideas wake up in rebellion. When they do, drop the translation, & start writing. You can go back to the translation for another push, if you get stuck.

2 If you don't know another language, choose a story you particularly dislike & reform it to your liking. Change the characters, make men into women, humour tragic, tragedy funny. Outrage the text. Have a ball. It's your hate-homage, that might readily turn into your own, totally original creation.

Ultimately, writing is learned by writing. & by reading other writers. Do not choke on what you feel people expect of you, as 'a writer'. The world is full of self-appointed critics. Don't listen to them. Except to put them in your story.

Freeing the Imagination

Exercise 1: Cloudburst
Sheila Yeger

Aim

To generate ideas/form connections in an organic, non-linear way.

Method

1 As an idea surfaces sufficiently to have some form, put it down in a 'cloud'.

2 When you get the next idea, put that in another cloud.

The woolly, vague shape suggests that nothing is fixed. It's all still very fluid. The non-linear arrangement reminds you that there is no order to these thoughts yet. (Or ever, perhaps?)

3 When you have quite a few of these clouds, you might begin to see some tentative connections between them. Don't hurry. Simply indicate connections by linking clouds in some way.

Keep it vague, fluid.

Keep asking yourself questions.

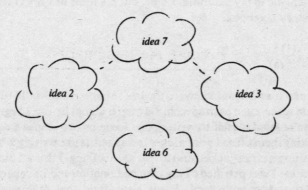

4 Looking at the 'cloudburst', you may begin to get a vague feeling about what is surfacing. Don't be in a hurry to name it, or organise it. Live with the uncertainty for a while. As new thoughts arise, just add another cloud.
5 Now the original connections you saw between your ideas may begin to seem out-moded. New connections arise. So draw another cloudburst which reflects these new connections. Don't destroy the first. It's still part of your work process.
6 Very slowly a theme, or themes, may begin to emerge (or what you take to be your theme at this stage). Still keep a very open mind. Do not expect or attempt to get it all 'worked out'. Be in tune with your own energies, and start writing when you feel ready, when the momentum feels right. Regard the writing itself as a process of 'working out', a solving of the mystery (or not, as the case may be).

Note

Women's work for the theatre is often criticised as being 'deficient in structure'. 'Great characters/dialogue. Shame about the structure' is a criticism I've often had levelled at my work. Eventually I began to ask myself whether women's work can or should be 'built' in the same way as men's work. After all, our bodies are different; our experiences are different. Is there, perhaps, an approach to 'structure' which is more distinctively 'female' and so more appropriate to the ideas we wish to express? When I first started to write plays I was rigidly schematic in my planning. I'd lay out my ideas like my O level History notebook:

   A
     (1)
      (a)
       (i)

I knew (or *thought* I knew) to the last comma, what would be in each scene, even each speech. I'd map it all out before I began, then commit myself to writing one scene or two scenes a day, ticking them off as I went along. It was a little like writing while wearing a strait-jacket, and about as satisfying. I think I did it because I was petrified of my own imagination and its capacity to run away with itself. I was also afraid that otherwise I wouldn't 'get through' the work, as if writing a play were like writing a school essay or a thesis. But, for all my order, chaos still prevailed. Characters would develop minds of their own and anarchically take over a scene. 4(a)(i) would spread messily into 4(b)(i) and my precious scheme would be disrupted. It took a while to see that I was trapped inside my own cleverness (developed through years of education in the ways of the 'system') and nothing, least of all a creative thought, could flourish in that repressive atmosphere. That's when I tentatively started working in a different way, terrified, but trying to let ideas grow organically, chaotically and unpredictably. A bit like climbing a mountain without equipment – exhilarating, frightening, dangerous, but potentially ecstatic.

You make a decision *not* to arrange, to prejudge connections but to regard the writing as a journey, destination unknown. It takes time, courage and a fairly distant deadline. But it feels natural, real.

Eventually you begin to trust the process. But it never loses its awful sense of danger. It can lead you into terrifyingly deep waters, or to peaks where the view is breathtaking. And these experiences will be communicated in your work so that the truth they speak will make connections with your female audience, who, of course, also know of these things, although they may not yet dare to articulate that knowledge.

Exercise 2: The Blindfold Game
Valerie Taylor

Aim

To highlight feeling sensations; develop a repertoire of descriptive words for touch.

Method

1 Prepare a tray of objects (not too many). The objects should have a variety of textures and temperatures, for example stones, wool, velvet, apple, bottle, foil.
2 If in a group, blindfold one member, who then describes an object. Someone in the group could write down what the blindfolded person says.
3 It is important to describe how the object feels rather than to say what it is.

Note

The fact that the sense of sight has been cut out should heighten awareness and produce unusual language.

Exercise 3: Sensing Metaphors
Gladys Mary Coles

Aim

To sharpen sensory awareness and facilitate the creation of arresting imagery.

This exercise can be useful as a 'limbering up' of word flow and mental alertness, like a physical workout, prior to getting down to the day's work, resuming the writing of our ongoing poems or prose. Often, too, it succeeds in triggering or unblocking the imagination. The exercise works by focusing the senses; the steps are progressive and can be applied to each of the senses in turn. Here, for an example, we will focus on the sense of touch.

Method

1 In the middle of your blank page, write down a list of half a
   dozen of the objects/things you most *dislike* touching, (e.g.
   liver, blood, cobwebs).
2 To the left of this list, write another list of adjectives or words
   which tell something more about the objects you dislike
   touching (e.g. the texture, feel, specific kind or type).
3 To the right of the list write a list of verbs which will further
   illuminate/add meaning to the objects and why you dislike
   touching them. These verbs should be very exact and energetic.
4 Now think of what each item on your list resembles/reminds
   you of . . . create a simile or metaphor. This is the important leap
   into imagery.
5 Following the same procedure, make another list of the
   objects/things you most *like* to touch.
6 Take one of your tactile images and use it as the starting point of
   a poem or story. Incorporate two more of your new images
   somewhere in the piece of writing. The images can perhaps be
   the nodes or hubs around which the piece is structured (and act
   as symbols) or alternatively they might be used simply to
   enhance vividness and originality.

Note

This exercise is an excellent stimulant, and best of all it brings
forward images from the centre of the writer's subjective
experience. When used for the other senses too, all the lists
being kept in a notebook or stored in a file, they become a kind
of imagery bank on which to draw in our writing.

Exercise 4: Writing with the Senses
Amryl Johnson

Aim

This exercise helps to improve the sensitivity with which we
approach writing in order to give it greater depth and quality.
Whenever you read a novel, short story or poem and it seems as

if the writing is truly alive, it is because the writer has brought to the task a high sense of awareness. Being more aware of all five senses and how they assist us in identifying and recognising things will sharpen our awareness as writers. Spend time concentrating on each sense and how it functions.

Method

Sight

Look! Look at the wallpaper. Notice the colours, shades, texture, where the paper joins. Look at the curtains and notice the weave, any irregularities in the pattern, colour, shades. These are just two examples. Notice corners, shapes, angles. Be aware of what there is to see in this room, this corner, this place which is your writing space.

Smell

After you have spent a few minutes looking, close your eyes. You do not need to start taking deep breaths to perform this exercise. There will be some smells which can be readily identified. What else? Any surprises? What about those smells you do not recognise? What do they remind you of? Don't be lazy. You are doing this for you. Stretch yourself when it comes to identifying this unknown quantity. Keep asking yourself, is this the closest I can get? Is there anything which comes closer to what it reminds me off?

Touch

Let your fingertips do the work. Touch anything you choose – with your eyes closed, if you wish. Touch your body, the tablecloth, furniture, flowers, carpet, curtains, anything. Be aware of how everything feels under your fingertips. 'Smooth' or 'rough' won't do. There are degrees of smoothness. There are degrees of roughness. Try to find the word or words which come closest to expressing what you feel.

Hearing

Close your eyes and listen. There may be a range of sounds both inside and outside the house which will reach you. Peel off each layer of sound as you go through the process of identifying them. That was . . . That one was . . . And this one is . . . Again, where you cannot readily identify a sound, draw a comparison.

Taste

This exercise (for obvious reasons!) may take place outside your writing space. Eat and taste. Even when we find ourselves with time to spare, we are inclined to treat the process of eating as if it were merely functional. Even those of us who are slow eaters or take time to chew each mouthful as many times as we have been taught we should, are not nearly as aware as we should be of how the food feels and tastes in our mouths. What about temperature? Has the food been under-cooked or over-cooked? Be aware of your tongue inside your mouth, its tip touching your teeth. As you sit in contemplation with both elbows on the table, chin resting on cupped palms or locked fingers, part your lips and let your extended tongue touch your hand. 'Hand-creamy' or 'salty' in describing the palm, finger or knuckle(s) will take you only part way there.

Note

Divide the time as equally as you can among the five senses. In everyday life, we depend heavily on our sense of sight. The other four senses, unless roused, often lie dormant. Practise this exercise each day before you sit down to write. Even if your time does not permit you more than a few minutes, concentrate on each. The senses are what we use to perceive things. Wake them up to the writing task ahead.

Exercise 5: Recording Sounds
Valerie Taylor

Aim

To increase awareness and move away from automatic sense responses.

Method

1 List all the sounds which can be heard in the immediate vicinity, as well as the more distant, background sounds.
2 If in a group, try recording different sounds – a baby crying, water, a biscuit being crunched, a fan heater, the sea – and then ask the group to note any word that comes to mind as they hear the sounds.
3 Write down any associations generated by the sounds. These could be stored in a notebook and used in a story or other piece of writing.

Note

There is a 'background' to everything, which puts action into context. Sometimes this background can intrude into the fore-ground. One of the sidelines of the tape-recorded exercise is that sensations which are not identifiable can spark different words.

Exercise 6: Slow Down
Christian McEwen

Aim

To accumulate information outside your usual run-of-the-mill activities. To teach yourself to *notice* and to listen.

Method

1 Think of something you do often: washing the dishes, perhaps, walking to work or to the laundromat.

2 Do that ordinary thing, but do it *slowly*, and pay attention to yourself doing it. Watch the bubbles on the knives as you rinse them under the cold tap, listen to the conversation as you stand in line to get change for the machines.

3 Hoard these details, slip them into whatever piece of work you have in hand, or let them go, confident that they'll re-emerge when you need them.

4 Allow yourself to continue to train this particular muscle of attention.

Exercise 7: Writing with Colours
Caroline Halliday

Aim

To use colour and visual imagery to help your writing. For in-depth focusing on a piece of writing, or getting started. You can use this exercise at the beginning of the editing process, to conceptualise a piece of writing, or at any blocked stage. Particularly useful for longer pieces of writing.

You can do it on your own, or with others.

Method

1 Select a piece of writing you want to think about, a piece you want to do more work on, or are not sure is finished, *or* think about a subject you would like to write about.

If you are doing new work, it may be useful to do this exercise in conjunction with (but before) another 'starting off' exercise.

2 Gather together some large-sized pieces of blank paper, preferably A3 or larger. You can use pale or coloured paper, or black if you have pale or white chalks, or use paint. Scrap paper or used computer paper is fine (particularly as the rain forests are disappearing), as long as you can't see too much through the paper.

Use finger paints/crayons/chalks/children's wax crayons/ charcoal/any kind of marker you prefer, or preferably a mixture of all of these. Finger paints are particularly recommended (you can buy them in Mothercare, Woolworths, or borrow them from a child you know!). Have some cloths handy. Use large-scale markers not pencils.

3 Loosen up. Either stand up and shake hands and legs, stretch, bend, *or*, in a group, lightly massage your neighbour's shoulders, and then swap.

4 *Remember*, working alone, no one but yourself is going to see or judge your work. This is not an exercise for artistic merit, but to assist in the writing process.

In a group, emphasise and encourage each person to see the exercise as fun, as a new departure and exploration to improve the depth of your understanding of your own writing. Everyone's work will be visible to a certain extent. You can try not to be overlooked as you work by finding a quiet/private place, but some of the fun of working in a group and encouragement to be spontaneous may be missing.

The best way in working as a group is to start with a group picture using finger paints, as this helps everyone to relax together. Focus on expressing anything you are feeling right now.

5 You are aiming to cover your paper with marks/colours/ shapes that suggest something to you about your writing. This is very definitely *not a picture*. Avoid figurative work, i.e. pictures of people or things, especially in your first attempts. This is very important, because figurative work will focus your mind too much on specifics and make you draw rather than *mark*.

Use marks that express the writing without words.

Start by using *both* hands together.

Use the hand you don't generally use.

Work with your eyes closed.

Work quickly or slowly but avoid thinking!

Use bold, free movements, especially to start with.

Use a variety of markers.

6 Colours: try not to be stereotyped about choosing colours. Either pick them fairly quickly without thinking too much about them or deliberately choose colours that are not stereotypical. Aim to let your mood flow easily on to the paper and let the subtleties of colour work on you. Avoid thinking in stereotypes of black or dark = bad, white = good, red = hot, green = nature.

7 Use more paper as additional space anytime you want to.

8 Use different pieces of paper or different parts of the same paper to focus on different aspects of your writing. If you are in a group, someone can mention different focuses as you go along. On your own, refer to headings you've already made.

Think about:

The main theme of your writing.

The atmosphere of the writing. Is it sad, angry, excited, mysterious?

Focus on the characters in the piece; express them as shapes, marks, colours, patterns. Put them in places related to each other, or far apart, as you feel appropriate.

Think about all or any of the following: the emotions shown; the place(s) described; flow or direction (fast/slow/every direction at once); where the writing ends/conclusion/final thoughts on the writing.

9 You can also indicate your emotions about the writing. Make sure you put everything in colours and shapes, marks and patterns, *not* drawings. If you have a block about the writing, express that difficulty visually too.

10 Towards the end you can, if you want, make shapes into stick people or quick faces etc., squares into house shapes etc., and use words, but limit these to a few. You can write all you want later!

11 If you've never done this kind of thing before, try taking a whole afternoon, or a couple of hours at least. Not only is it enjoyable, it will stretch and deepen your writing.

If you are very familiar with visual expression, it's advisable to throw out of the window all your notions of *right* and *good*. This exercise is for feelings and atmosphere, not artistic skill.

Once you've got used to the idea, you can use this kind of exercise as a quick aid to any part of your writing, taking 10 minutes, or with a pad and crayons beside you as you write.

12 Finally sit back and look at what's shown. Don't judge. We thought and experienced things visually before we used/learnt words, and many of us have lost touch with this dimension. See what the marks tell you. Allow yourself to be surprised and intrigued. Don't show your work to anyone you don't trust!

Note

Use the results to think in more depth about your writing. The visual technique should show you a more coherent image of your work, highlight the connections between disparate parts and emphasise pace, or atmosphere.

You can focus on particular problems, e.g. a character or a place. The technique can be particularly useful for longer pieces of work, as you can put marks, symbols, images for the whole concept of the writing on one piece of paper, and visualise the vast extent of your writing in one go. You can put the paper(s) on your wall and use them as an instant reminder of direction to keep your writing focused.

The value of the process is in expressing ideas non-verbally, exploring details and broader viewpoints, atmosphere, emotions, to loosen up when writing is feeling confused, or when you need to feel more detached in order to redraft/edit, or when you have a block about a piece of writing, or at the very beginning of writing something new.

Exercise 8: Sound Play
Michèle Roberts

Aim

To have fun with sounds.

Method

1 Find three language sounds that particularly give you pleasure at the moment and write them down, e.g. ess, ckl, ock.
2 Embody the sounds in as many words as you feel like, e.g. reckless, feckless, abbess, confess, tackle, suckle, buckle, frock, mock, block, etc.
3 Write three or four sentences using *all* the words.

Note

What you end up with is a short, surreal narrative full of wonderful sounds that demonstrates the play of the unconscious.

Exercise 9: Writing Spells
Gillian Allnutt

Aim

To focus on 'sound', as opposed to 'meaning', in language. To get back to the roots of poetry, which are close to music and dance.

Method

1 In Witch language, write a spell or chant for:
invoking the powers of the moon
laying the wind to rest
making the rain come
enticing your beloved to you
curing the common cold
making the walls of Jericho/Greenham fall down
or whatever else you choose to invent.

Then write the English translation.

Example First four lines from a spell for invoking the powers of the moon:

> Morlin, Morlin, Morlini,
> morka-mak, morka-mak,
> morka tu borklegrock mak
> shlarda-mik

It means:

> Moon, moon, little old moon,
> make light, make light,
> make your bent back of light
> stoop over me

2 Read out and/or perform your spell.

Note

In a group, this exercise requires a degree of trust and confidence both to run and to participate in.

If you are leading the group, saying 'then write the English translation' lets people know that they have to invent the language of the spell. I prefer not to be specific at the beginning, unless everyone looks completely blank in which case I might read a line or two from a spell I have written. Or I might ask someone what, for example, she would say to the wind if she wanted to lie down and be still. I might also say 'nonsense language' or even 'onomatopoeia'.

Doing the exercise myself, I've found that sometimes I write the spell then the translation, sometimes both together, and occasionally the translation and then the spell.

It is fascinating to hear what comes out of doing this exercise – one spell will sound like Russian, another like Italian, another like a Scandinavian language. This can lead to interesting discussion.

I do not suggest any spells that could be curses.

If you are working in a group and you have the space, performing the spells can be very interesting and also good fun. I usually ask each person in turn to use the group in any way she likes to perform her spell – so you get a director and chorus/chief witch and willing coven! What seems to happen is a kind of choreographing. It gets people working together, loosens inhibitions, and raises interesting questions about how we use our bodies in relation to our voices and the word.

Exercise 10: The Impossible Visitor
Nicky Edwards

Aim

To get off the straight and narrow.

Method

1 Place yourself on a desert island, inhabited only by you.
2 Observe that no boats, planes, submarines, parachutes, craft or conveyance of any kind have passed within 3000 miles since you have been there.
3 Despite this, another living being (human or otherwise) suddenly appears on the island.

4 Record the conversation you would have with this creature. Remember, there is no possibility of a rational explanation for the arrival of your fellow islander.

Note

You may not wish to deal with the fantastic every day, but it helps not to get stuck in the kitchen sink.

Exercise 11: Poppy Heads
Angela Brown

Aim

To free imagination and stimulate dialogue.

Method

1 Remind yourself of the technique for simple playscript (new speaker on each line, no need for 'She said', etc. . .).
2 Find two dried poppy heads with reasonably long stalks.
3 Study the infinitesimal differences between the two. Imagine that the seedheads are people, possibly with some of the differences noted, though this is not essential.
4 Without delay, write a simple dialogue overheard between these two.
5 If possible, share these with a group and enjoy the variety!

Notes

A very successful stimulus for writers nervous about starting dialogue and/or reading aloud to a group. The poppies impose just enough of their own qualities and engender a range of ideas in the person studying these. They also give a focus so that the writer does not feel so self-conscious. The configuration of poppies seems to encourage characterisation across a rich range of cultures, e.g. tribespeople, punks, posh ladies, ruffle-headed children, etc.

Other puppet stimuli could be used, such as nuts, stuffed

socks and tights. However, the delicacy of the poppyheads seems consistent with the intricate qualities of real people, and a subtlety of response is possible.

Exercise 12: Collective Dialogues
Gillian Allnutt

Aim

To stimulate the writing of dialogue in a group context.

Method

Before the workshop

1 Make two lists, one of things (e.g. garlic crusher, left hand, Cruise missile), and one of people (e.g. brain surgeon, Fanny Adams).
2 Write each one on a small piece of paper, fold the papers and put them in a hat.

At the workshop

3 Each person in the group should have an A4 size piece of paper and a pen.
4 Each person takes two bits of paper out of the hat. (You don't have to have a hat. I usually just shake them out onto the table.)
5 Tell the group that each person will now start writing a conversation between whatever two things or people they have picked out. Remind them to set it out in dialogue form, as in a play. Let them know that after ten minutes you will say stop and they will then pass the paper, without folding it, to the person on their right.
6 Then everyone writes for 10 minutes. You say stop and the papers are passed on. At this point remind the group that they have finished with the dialogue they were writing and must now continue the one in front of them.
7 After four or five bouts of writing, tell the group that the next

one is the last, and they should try to draw the conversation they have just been given to a close.

8 Pass the papers on once more so that each person reads the conversation they have, to make sure it is decipherable. Then read them all out.

Note

I invented this exercise because people so often say they 'can't write dialogue'. I have used it a lot and never found anyone unable or unwilling to join in. It works well as an ice-breaker with a new group. It is at the very least always good for a laugh! And I think it frees people into writing because, since you keep passing the papers on, no one has the responsibility for completing a whole piece of work. It is also about communication through writing in a literal sense – people see what happens if their writing can't be read. It forces you to think quickly and to be flexible – you have to keep adding to conversations you haven't seen before. And, as writing is mostly an isolated activity, this exercise has the advantage of getting everyone working together. There are always at least one or two dialogues that work surprisingly well as complete pieces of writing.

You could also do the exercise on your own, by taking two of the bits of paper and insisting to yourself that you produce a dialogue, whatever you've picked out.

The dialogues between two things are usually the funniest. My collection of bits of paper now has more things than people in it.

Exercise 13: Knocking Out Key Words
Valerie Taylor

Aim

A group exercise to illustrate the power of unusual juxta-positions and the importance of rhythm and idea.

Method

Write out a poem knocking out the key words:

> O Rose thou art _____
> The invisible _____
> That _____ in the night,
> In the _____ storm.
>
> Has found out thy _____
> Of crimson _____
> And his dark _____
> Does thy life _____

2 Ask group members to complete the blanks.

Note

Often with this exercise the words chosen are fairly predictable and highlight the need to be aware of rhythm. When the poem is revealed, the power of the unique choice of words comes over well. Also, the significance of the poet's choice of words shows up levels of meaning which a predictable choice of words lacks.

Exercise 14: Words that Unlock
Angela Brown

Aim

To use creatively the emotional resonance of a word.

Method

1 Search the dictionary and thesaurus to find a single word which has potential for emotional exploration. I have found words such as *after, lost, provoke, gain, displace, look, beginning* to be potent.
2 Outline some of the range of meanings within that word, ideally using the *Shorter Oxford Dictionary* to help.
3 Take plenty of time to assimilate the word and to let it work on your own life experience and imagination. A week is a good

length of time. Write a piece of poetry, dialogue or prose in which you apply the theme of the word to one fairly specific episode: what, for instance happened in the time 'After'? What did that 'after' moment feel like? The writing may be auto-biographical or fictional.

4 Share the writing if possible. If you have the resources in a group, collate the work for a display or booklet, especially if you feel that the group has uncovered and celebrated some emotional truths.

Note

It can be valuable to look at the writings of published writers to see how they use the word in their work.

For more experienced writers, these one-word titles can prove a useful starting point for experiments in strict form, such as the villanelle, triolet and sonnet. (See 'Continuings'.) In these there is often scope for the potency of repetition or the exploiting of different facets of the same word or experience.

Chambers Twentieth Century Dictionary is a rich source of meanings, idioms, dialect words and the usages of words. It makes an excellent adjunct or replacement for the *Oxford*.

Exercise 15: Jigsaw
Valerie Taylor

Aim

To free resistances and conditioned responses.

Method

1 Write snippets of a plot on cards and lay them out on the floor.
2 Juggle these around, trying out different endings, different beginnings.

Note

This exercise can also be done with work in progress. Write out the existing plot so far on cards and lay these out on the floor. Now write different possibilities and lay these against the original writing. Working visually like this can be very helpful. Sometimes moving the sequence around can release new ideas. Plot cards can also be used in a group as a basis for a short story. This frees the imagination by allowing us to work within an already established structure.

Finding a Subject

Exercise 1: Personal Process
Maxine Davies

Aim

To create a structure within which to focus on and explore personal experience as a source for writing.

Method

1 In a calendar which shows the dates of an entire month and which has enough space beside each date for your own entries, mark any significant meetings, as well as any important activities or events you have planned. Then mark each of these dates with an asterisk. As you live the month add entries relating to experiences which are vital or important to you. You may also wish to add brief notes about these as thoughts and feelings occur.
2 As the month ends you will have a structure outlining the movement of your personal process. Join up the asterisks with a continuous line so that each experience becomes one step in this process.
3 Settle in a comfortable seat. Close your eyes and take a few deep breaths. Be aware of your body relaxing against the seat. If, after doing this, you still feel tense, try contracting and then consciously relaxing the tense parts of your body. When you are completely relaxed, visualise a stream of water. The current is sweeping you onwards. Allow yourself to flow with the current which is carrying you towards an unknown destination. The

water is crystal clear and you can hear the sound of the water as it rushes and pours over the boulders strewn in its path. Allow yourself as much time as you need to feel yourself gradually becoming part of this water and natural energy. When you open your eyes you may wish to record any feelings or impressions which came to you during the exercise.

4 Now return to your own calendar process and imagine that this is flowing in a similar way to the stream, over and around the stepping stones of the various experiences and events.

5 Choose one or more of these experiences to explore through writing, using your new energy to re-enter and elaborate on the association of experiences. You might choose an experience further back in time, returning to unfinished experiences to reposition yourself in your current life. Or you may choose a turning point, an event marking a time of change. Whatever you choose to write about, do so in your own way. I suggest you focus on feelings, atmosphere, people and places. If very strong feelings arise which seem to signify more than a recent happening, try asking yourself when you had similar feelings in the past. You may wish to make a list of those experiences in the past which influenced you in a similar way, and then choose one of those experiences to explore in writing. If you feel stuck or unclear in your writing try allowing some time to elapse before you continue. Usually a new clarity will emerge in its own time. If this does not happen, you may find it helpful to talk to someone else, or to seek the support of a group of writers.

Note

One of my earliest experiences as an evacuee in Somerset led me to spend long periods alone or fishing with my brother. My favourite place was Moore End Spout, where I sat on a small stone bridge watching the continuous flow of the water. Later in life I found myself drawing on this experience. Giving expression to life experiences has led me to value day-to-day activities more highly. The calendar exercise has also been used by journal students as a way of becoming more aware of their own experiences as a source for writing.

Exercise 2: I Can So Tell . . .
Christian McEwen

Aim

To open up new areas of your past to write about. To give
yourself permission to describe other people's past lives.

Method

1 Make a list of all the things 'I'm not supposed to tell . . .' either
   because they are too painful or too embarrassing or too difficult
   in some way. This list might include incest, abortion, a parent's
   drinking and other family secrets.
2 Take some time when you know you won't be interrupted, and
   make whatever constitutes a 'safe place' for you. Some people
   will draw the curtains and put soothing music on, perhaps light
   incense. Others will go off into the woods. Others will simply
   lock the door.
3 Get in touch with the strongest and wisest part of you, or with
   some person who loves you, and whom you know you can trust
   completely. Feel that strength, remember that person.
4 Look at your list and choose one of the subjects to concentrate
   on. Take some time just remembering it: who was involved,
   when, how old you were, or who told you about it (if you
   weren't personally involved).
5 Start to write. Write as much as you can in whatever form feels
   comfortable to you. Whenever you need to stop, stop. Take the
   time to breathe, and to make contact again with that wise self,
   or that person you know you can trust. Don't be afraid if you
   need to move about or to cry.
6 Keep coming back to the writing, but don't expect to complete
   this exercise in one session.

Note

Over the years we have all encountered a lot of information we
are 'not supposed to tell'. There are real and important stories
hiding under that prohibition: women's stories, lesbian stories,
outsider stories. Telling them can change the world! I first

learned this exercise from Gloria Anzaldua and Cherrie Moraga, editors of *This Bridge Called My Back*, and use some version of it in everything I do.

Exercise 3: When I was Ten
Rebecca O'Rourke

Time Taken Two and a half hours, plus homework and further sessions to read and respond to work generated.
Ideal group size Eight to 14
Preparation Summary of schedule on handout/flipchart
Materials Board/flipchart, pens and paper

Aims

This is one of my favourite group writing exercises from a repertoire developed over many years working in adult education and as a writing development worker for a community publisher.

It draws on knowledge of our own lives and reveals to us just how much skill we already have in selecting, ordering and recounting stories. Through a process of group discussion, individual reflection, talking and writing, these skills are extended to generate rich and varied sources for writing. The exercise moves between talking and writing. This does two valuable things. Firstly, it minimises the anxiety some women have about committing work to paper, as the progression towards writing is gradual and cumulative. But perhaps even more importantly, it begins to show that writing itself is a process rather than a gift.

A lot of the session involves listening to others, as well as thinking about our own lives and finding means and words to communicate those aspects which seem important. The pleasure, and value, of working co-operatively rather than competitively develops as the exercise proceeds.

Method

1 Introduction (10 minutes). This exercise needs strict time-

keeping. The sequence of different activities can get confusing, so a schedule on the board or as a handout is a help to everyone.

An introduction needs to tell everyone what they are being expected to do and why, and also give some indication of what it is reasonable to expect from the session. I also use it to talk about how members of the group should respond to each other's work, and also to reassure them that if they experience problems of any kind they can come and talk to me about them rather than feel they have to suffer in silence or leave the group.

In introducing the exercise I would say something like this:

Today we are going to work towards some writing by doing something we can all do already: tell stories about our lives. Think about all the times you've enjoyed being told a story, and what you've learnt from it. Did you enjoy hearing about your parents' and grandparents' lives when you were small? Do your children now ask you to tell them about the things you did when you were their age? Telling someone the story of your life is an important step in getting to know them. It is what we do with our friends and lovers.

Getting hold of our whole lives is too daunting an undertaking to begin with so I'm going to ask you to focus on a particular time. We've all been there, all we have to do is remember, and one of the beauties of this exercise is that we all benefit from each other's memories as they spark off associations and reminders of our own.

I want you to think about that time around the age of 10 or 11, just before or as everything starts to change for us. We were still children but starting to realise that we wouldn't always be, and often swung between desperately wanting to grow up and hating the idea of it. We went from being the 'big girls' of junior school to the new girls at secondary school. We began to have a sense of living in history; events in the outside world started to register with us for the first time. Our bodies started to change, and those changes weren't always explained to us. Looking back, it sometimes seems like the last time we were really able to enjoy our bodies or feel they belonged to us before the restrictions of adolescence descended.

It wasn't always a happy time. It may have marked the

beginning of unwanted sexual attention, or be remembered as the anniversary of a parent's death or of forced immigration into this country following war or poverty at home. We each have many stories to tell, some happy, some not. You choose what you say: don't feel obliged to be cheerful for the sake of it, or feel nothing really happened to you because you enjoyed your childhood. I want us to build up a rich and complex picture of the detail of our lives and the people we were then, as well as the things that happened to and around us: what you saw out of your bedroom window as well as the thing that most frightened you; your favourite food and toys; your ambitions; the name of your best friend and the teacher you hated most.

Initially we will be talking and listening as we gather together ideas and possibilities for writing. Try not to worry about writing at this stage. If you think, 'But talking isn't writing, anyone can tell a story', you are half-way towards what I want this exercise to do for you. I want all of us to be able to see and discuss what it is that we do almost without thinking when we tell a story. That will help us see more clearly what we have to work harder at when we write it down. How do we capture and keep people's interest in what we say? How do we create the atmosphere and effects we want? What is the best way to put our ideas across? All that will emerge through discussion this week and in the following weeks. Talking can sometimes be an evasion of writing, but here it is a way of moving towards it, interleaving each other's memories and images, testing out what works and doesn't. It gives you a rich store of ideas and threads to start from and return to.

Concentrate on listening and remembering to begin with. You will each be interested in what the others have to say: you will want to know what happens next and who these people are that everything is happening to. I want you to take that away with you. It will sustain you when it is just you, the pen, the paper and the searching for words. You will feel that there really are people wanting to hear your story, just as you want to come back next week and hear theirs.

2 Discussion (25 minutes). Go round the group with each

woman saying in what year she was 10/11. Then go round again, this time each woman takes up to two minutes to describe her life at the time. Say whether it was basically happy or not and give some pointers: e.g. where did you live? What sort of house was it? What jobs did your parents do? Where did you go to school? What was your hair like? Did you have brothers and sisters at home? Did you have a pet? What was your favourite pastime?

3 Writing and discussion (10 minutes plus 15 minutes). Introduce the five senses: taste, touch, sight, smell, hearing; and say how important it is to make writing sensually expressive. Each woman individually completes these as sentences or word lists:

The taste of being 10 is . . .
The smell of being 10 is . . .
The sound of being 10 is . . .
The touch of being 10 is . . .
The sight of being 10 is . . .

These are then read out and collected on the board. Talk about them. Say which senses are easy to recall, and which difficult. Discuss which have immediate resonances for other people and why. Talk about how best to express the images collected.

4 Ten to 15-minute break. This is important, even if you are feeling pushed for time.

5 Discussion (30 minutes). Go round the group, with each woman taking two to three minutes to describe a particular incident which happened to her during that period of her life. It is often dramatic incidents which stand out in our memory, but emphasise that women may tell any kind of story they like.

6 Writing (15 minutes). Each woman lists seven things which she especially identifies with that period in her life, and writes one sentence about each. She chooses three to read back to the group as a whole, without discussion.

7 Paired discussions (15 minutes). Divide the group into pairs. Explain that they are going to discuss the work they've done and heard so far with a view to deciding on a piece of writing to work on at home. These pieces will be read and worked on in the group over the following sessions.

In introducing the types of writing they could do, try to give as broad a choice as possible. Remind them of the range of poems, prose, drama, but also make more specific suggestions, e.g.:

A general overview of your life at the time.
A particular incident told from your point of view or from that of someone else – a teacher, parent, friend.
An extract from your diary of the time.
Write as comedy something that was tragic.
Imagine a meeting between your 10-year-old and current self.
Write about yourself as if from your mother's point of view.
Write out an incident entirely in dialogue.

8 Evaluation (15 minutes). It is always worth taking a few minutes at the end of a session to draw things to a close and focus on what has been gained from the day. It is particularly useful to tutors to get a sense of what they are doing well and not so well, and for students it reinforces the learning they have done.

Come back together as a group and ask students to pick one of three coloured paperclips from a box. They then speak as follows:
Green – says something positive
Blue – says something negative
Black – says whatever she likes.

Note

This exercise sparks off the best sort of curiosity about other women's lives and leaves everyone with a sense that much more has happened to them than they have ever given themselves credit for. It gives us a lot of space to be our own selves with our special pasts, but it also connects us into history by increasing our awareness of and respect for the differences between us based on age, class, race and other social factors as well as indicating the points of connection between women.

You can pick any age to work from, but there is something very powerful about the transition from childhood into puberty, and this has consistently generated excellent discussion and writing in the groups I've worked with. I have also had good work from concentrating on the ages of 5 and 16.

It is an excellent way into writing. All students will be able to contribute to the session itself, which relies on talking and listening. Individual and group memories are stirred and spark off from each other by contrast or reinforcement of shared experiences. Students can then take this as far as they like in recording, expressing and re-ordering some of those experiences in writing.

The way it combines talking with writing has always appealed to me. I first used it working with literacy students who wrote slowly and with little confidence. It was wonderful there in showing how a lot of the work of writing happens well before pen gets to paper: decisions about what to include or exclude, decisions about pace, suspense, characterisation and plot. These sessions are also good writing lessons for more experienced writers and it has always been easier to get to the 'how' of expression and communication from this writing exercise than from many others.

It does need plenty of time to work properly and you need to do all of it to get the most from it. It works best as part of a day school. This is because the effect is a cumulative one arising out of a deep immersion in your own and other women's memories. If more time is available, then women can spend 30 to 45 minutes writing and read this back, either to the group as a whole or in groups of three or four. I have sometimes split the exercise over two weeks and then spent a further two to three weeks reading and discussing the work produced. This works quite well, but there is something very special about the momentum of one full day.

Once you've worked through the exercise you will develop your own ideas about how to adapt it, particularly from the point of view of time. If I have to do it in a shorter period, I ensure we do all the work, but divide the group into two or three for some of the time so that we save reading round and listening time. If you have to do this, it is important to start and finish as a whole group and to try to mix the groups up for the various exercises.

Exercise 4:   Names
Sue Habeshaw

Aim

This group exercise focuses on names. (It is a good exercise for introducing new members of a group to each other.)

Method

1 Group members speak in pairs about their names. One tells the other what her name is and something about it: why she was given that name, what it means, whether she likes it, what different names – and nicknames – she has had in the past, etc. (This could take about 10 minutes, with each member of the pair speaking for about 5 minutes.)
2 Members spend a short time (say, 10 minutes) writing poems or pieces of prose about their names, based on the conversation with their partners. For example:

My Name is Susan

Before I was born
My mother called me David
Because she knew I was going to be a boy
And today
With my long hair and flowered skirt
I'm still a disappointment to her.

The day before I was born
My mother came home from the public library
And she said to my father,
'I've borrowed lots of books
Because I know David won't be born this week.'
Afterwards, she blamed me for being born the next day.
'I never read those books, Susan', she used to say to me.

When I was a little girl
My mother gave me the doll which had been hers.
'This doll is called David, Susan,' she said.
I refused to play with it.

Note

The topic of names is one on which most people have plenty to say.

Exercise 5:   Family Stories
Christian McEwen

Aim

To start to get a sense of your own material: the gold inside the dross of what you *already possess*. To begin to listen to the voice of your family with the interest and attention of an outsider.

Method

1 Make a list of the family stories that were 'always' being told: 'When Grandpa fell into the pond . . .'; 'When the car got stolen and was used by the thieves in a jewel-bust . . .'; 'When Una tried to sell her hair . . .' etc. Write as fast as you can. Don't censor.
2 Choose from the list a title that especially interests you, and try to write it in the voice of the person you heard it from most often. Leave gaps for the details you have forgotten, or allow yourself to invent.
3 Read it over and decide what you want to do:
   (a) make it your own, shaping and changing it in whatever way you prefer or
   (b) go with a tape recorder to visit your family, and ask the person who used to tell that story to tell it again. (If they have died in the meantime, ask the next best person.)
4 If (b), transcribe the tape and use it as the basis for an interview, a dramatic monologue, a scene in a story or a play.

Note

Writers as a breed are addicted to reading. This is of course a good thing. But it has its dangers, the main one being that writers don't always pay attention to what is going on around them. This exercise brings you back to the particular riches and idiosyncrasies of your own home dialect. It reminds you to listen and ask questions. It gives you a healthy respect for all the different versions of a story. It ensures (bottom line) that you will never be short of things to write about.

Exercise 6: Private Myths
Caroline Natzler

Aim

To help recognise that however painful, or dull, our lives are, they can be the source for stories with movement, form and value.

Method

1 Lie down and listen to a relaxation tape or music that you find soothing.
2 Think about your life and picture it as a simple story, something concrete, which could be enacted. Perhaps think of it as a myth or a fairy-tale or parable. Think of the symbols with which most people in your culture are familiar.
3 If you are in a group, act out each other's stories. The person whose story is being told will direct and will also enact the protagonist. Enact not just people but all the significant objects and the environment too. Use props if you like.

   If you are on your own, draw the story before writing it, if this helps.

Note

Pain is always a potential source of creativity and if pain is part of what you express in this exercise, it will be given a simple, accessible form. The exercise is designed to help you avoid the over-frantic, gothic style we sometimes tend to use when writing to work through pain, a style which may express how we feel but which will probably alienate the reader.

Exercise 7: The Chinese Bowl
Christian McEwen

Aim

To recover detailed memories from childhood. To furnish and

populate drifting half-remembered scenes.

Method

1 Think of some object you remember from when you were little: your father's shoe with the heel worn half away, a Chinese bowl filled with pot pourri.
2 Describe this object in the most scrupulous detail you can muster, as if someone's life depended on your accuracy. Turn it around in your mind, and *keep* describing it, even after you think you've said everything you could possibly say.
3 Come back to that description three and four and five times.
4 Begin to notice the other details which suddenly appear: the corner of the fireguard where the shoe rests, your grandmother's hands idly turning the pot pourri.
5 Let these pictures come to you in odd, unconnected snatches. Don't push too hard. Watch the scene as it unfolds.
6 Write down whatever you have been able to salvage. Ground your poem or story in the precision of those memories and feelings.

Note

I have used this exercise often in my teaching. It is astonishing how the concentration on one thing releases all sorts of other information, and how rich the final result can be.

Exercise 8: The Furniture Game
Sue Habeshaw

Aim

This exercise is based on the so-called 'furniture game', one stage of which involves the players in choosing animals, items of furniture, etc. to describe the other players. As a writing exercise it not only gives participants in a group practice in working with metaphors, but also offers insights into how they are perceived within the group and encourages reflection on our perceptions of ourselves.

Method

1 The exercise begins with all the group members listing the names of everyone in the group and then choosing an animal, piece of furniture, etc. to describe each person.
2 These are then communicated to each group member, who writes down her personal list.
3 Each person selects one of the items from her own list and spends a short time (say, 15 minutes) writing a poem or a piece of prose about it. For example:

Zebra

A parquet floor, a pot of tea and a chiming clock
And in front of the fire
A zebra skin
Stretched on a blue felt base.
'Isn't it marvellous', she said,
'How the hair changes colour to make the stripes?'
'I shot her myself,' he said,
'In South Africa. A group of zebra were running by
And I picked her out for her glossy hair
And the beautiful way she moved.
More tea?'

Toy Cupboard

I'd like to show you my room.
It's quite formal in some ways: look at this standard lamp and the modernist black chair, for instance.
But in the corner there's a toy cupboard which is so full that things fall out whenever I open the door. There are cheerful coloured wooden bricks, musical instruments, puzzles, dolls and teddy bears. Most of the toys belonged to my children though this stuffed lion cub is mine. It's silly really: I could put that cupboard to a better use now the children have left home. But the toys wouldn't like it.

4 Group members read out their pieces (if they want to) and say a little (again, if they want to) about what their piece seems to say about them. The writer of the pieces above, for example, noticed that she tends to represent herself as an object on show,

even a victim, and maybe a political victim. She also realised that she had chosen to distinguish between formal and informal aspects of herself by selecting from her list of pieces of furniture not only the one she liked best but also two others (standard lamp and chair) which described the self she often presented to others.

Exercise 9: Inspiration from Dreams
Caroline Natzler

Aim

To randomise ideas for stories. This is a group exercise.

Method

1 Each person writes brief notes on an incident in a dream they have had.
2 Each person takes someone else's dream and writes what happened just before and just after the incident given.

Note

This is a simple and thought provoking way of inspiring stories.

Exercise 10: Writing from a Given Plot
Valerie Taylor

Aim

To have, to begin with, a ready-made plot as a structure to work from.

Method

1 Choose a human interest story from the paper or a magazine.
2 Write out the plot in the form of events.
3 Write the story of the plot.

Note

It is important to find a story that has a certain obsession value. It is important to recognise where our own interests and obsessions lie, because this is where our real emotional energy lies. In a group, members might work on the same story separately in order to observe the variety of possiblities that come out of one story.

Exercise 11: Coloured Runes
Joan Downar

Aim

To bring disparate elements together to make a story. A group exercise.

Method

1 Have ready a number of coloured cards according to the number of people in the group. Red cards will have a character marked on them, blue a situation, green a place, yellow a time, white a theme.

   Alternatively, each group member could write her own selection of character, situation, etc. on blank cards to be shuffled and redistributed.

   The information can be quite simple, e.g. a tramp, an accident, a fairground, morning, regret, or it can be much more detailed, e.g. a middle-aged woman on a housing estate contemplating divorce, etc. It will depend on how experienced the group is, and how much preliminary discussion has taken place, and whether, for instance, examples of stories have been read for ideas. Not every group likes being tied down to too much detail.

2 Each group member picks five cards at random, one of each colour.

3 They then have to construct a story using their given elements.

Note

This challenge is always enthusiastically taken up. I usually try to have something different on each card but you can of course repeat some if you wish. The results will always be different.

Exercise 12: Cinderella
Kara May

Aim

Do you feel the urge to write, but your mind is a blank, awhirl with shadowy characters or half-formed plots? If so, this exercise can help. Tell yourself you'll sort out these phantoms some other time and cast them aside. Then . . .

Method

1 Take: a pen and a newspaper or magazine.
2 Open the magazine or newspaper at random, shut your eyes and make a dot on the page.
3 Find the first name nearest the dot and write it down.
4 What sort of person does that name conjure up for you? As quickly as you can, *in note form only*, write a total of 10 characteristics and/or aspects of his/her life and circumstances. For example:
   William
   an aristocrat
   mid-fifties
   marries for money when first wife dies
   likes good claret
   devoted to daughter by first marriage
   good-natured but ineffectual . . . anything for a quiet life
   etc.
5 Conjure up a person – B – associated in some way with Character A (above) and write in note form only, seven characteristics etc. as above. For example:
   Cinderella
   passive

gentle hearted
abused by stepmother
cruelly tormented by stepsisters who are jealous of her
beauty and place in father's affections
unknowingly protected by benign supernatural power
small feet

6 Conjure up a person C associated with A above and repeat
note-making process. For example:
  William's second wife
  married for status
  socially ambitious for daughters
  etc.

7 Take a moment or two to get the feel of your characters. Decide
which of the three interests you the most, and write his/her
name on a fresh piece of paper. For example:
  Cinderella
  This will be your principal viewpoint character, i.e. the
character through whom the reader experiences the story.

8 Choose the characteristic or aspect of his/her life or cir-
cumstances that you find the most interesting. Write it down.
For example:
Unknowingly protected by benign supernatural power.

9 Construct a plot which pivots around Step 8.

Note

1 In Step 3, don't be tempted to look for another name you like
better or you may find the day has been spent doing precisely
that. Stick with the name that chance offers and you'll make the
creative leap that forges something positive out of the most
unpromising material.

2 Write Steps 4 to 6 as swiftly as possible, and don't try to be
clever. Allow your unconscious to flow unfettered and
uncensored. Trust it knows where it's going, like a river making
its way to the sea. Save your ingenuity and discrimination for
constructing the plot.

3 Don't write yourself out in Steps 4–6! Keep to notes only at this
stage.

Exercise 13: Finding a Character
Sheila Yeger

Aim

To discover a character; to try to understand her in depth; to find an authentic voice for her.

Method

1 Go out and look for a character. Look in shops, pubs, parks, railway stations. Observe her closely. Eavesdrop. What is she wearing? How does she walk? What sort of voice/accent/language does she use? Is there anything incongruous, sad, funny, strange about her?

2 Go away and write an external description from memory, i.e. what you were able to *observe*. Make it as specific as possible.

3 Now write an *interior* monologue for your character which is based on what you observed. This is where your imagination takes over. Do not just report what you heard, though you may incorporate it, explain it, explore it. If she was wearing a heavy coat on a hot day, ask yourself why. Think of the most bizarre reason you can. If she looked tired, ill, angry, fraught, look for possible explanations and express them in her monologue.

4 Collect characters and put them together in situations you create. Invent connections between them. Devise opportunities for them to clash, argue, fall in love, accuse each other, tell lies, confess crimes . . .

Exercise 14: Creating Characters
Jill Hyem

Aim

To help build characters in depth.

The success of the series *Tenko* (which I co-wrote with Anne Valery) was based mainly on the fact that the audience became totally involved with the characters and their development over the three years of their imprisonment in a Japanese camp.

To me, getting to know my characters is the first and most essential part of my preparation for writing a play for any medium. The following are some of the 'exercises' that I use in the process of creating characters.

Method

1 Write a detailed biography of your main characters: their background, appearance, where they were born and brought up, their education, their relationships, personal idiosyncracies, everything of importance that has happened in their life up to the moment your play begins.
2 Write a monologue for each of the characters. Let them talk about themselves and their lives. In this way you will soon find out not only how each one speaks but also their attitudes to each other.
3 Invent an incident in which all your characters are involved, a tube train stuck in a tunnel; a road accident; a bomb scare. Imagine how each of your characters will behave in the situation and how they will inter-react.
4 (For a play or series with a large cast.) Having written your first draft, select a scene that includes a number of characters. Block out their names at the side of the script and see if you can still tell who is speaking.
5 Choosing the right names is an important part of building a complete picture of your characters. Spend some time browsing through 'Name the Baby' books and *The Guinness Book of Names*.

Note

I would emphasise that these exercises are intended as an aid and not a restriction. If a character takes off in a different direction, go with it.

Otherness
R.M. Lamming

In fiction, it is of great importance for a writer to 'know' the characters and situations she is writing about. However, there can be a danger of 'overknowing', so that every trait of the characters is exactly, flatly 'right', quite predictable in fact, and every situation has utter, indisputable appropriateness.

In reality, I suggest that people and life are odder than this. Motivations and happenings, reactions and circumstances all have an aura of 'otherness'; minds wander; people have bizarre, intensely private subcurrents to their thoughts; very few people are 100 per cent certain why they do what they do; and so on. In other words, people and events are not confined within our explanations. They are 'other' and so contain within themselves the potential to be irrational, surprising, outside and contrary to expectations.

Something of this 'otherness' needs to be conveyed in fiction if the writing is to have the charge of life and be convincing. Otherwise it may be reduced to surgical, or even blatantly manipulative narrative; we can only supply this 'otherness' which is, by definition, outside the author's own grasp of a character or situation through intuition.

Exercise 15: Whose Reality Is It Anyway?
Julia Casterton

Aim

To question the notion that there is one legitimate way of representing an event, a character, or a setting. To develop new ways of telling in a group context.

Method

1 Meet together with two or three writer friends.
2 One of you chooses one moment, one event, or one person in her life that is perceived as especially significant.
3 You describe that moment/event/person to the other people in the room.
4 Staying together in the same room, you all sit down and write down what you heard. You attempt to make as accurate a record as you can.

Note

You may be shocked by the disparities in the different accounts. Some may be unrecognisable, not apparently about the same thing at all. They may all concentrate on different aspects of the thing described. It will open up several new ways of seeing for the person who made the description in the first place.

You can take it further by using a particular event as the focus for a story or a poem, and then dreaming yourself into the thoughts of the two or three different characters to whom it happened. The event will become like a diamond, multi-faceted, heavy with more meanings than are possible from a single viewpoint.

Alternatively you can take a novel or poem that is obsessively from one point of view, like *Lolita* or one of Yeats's poems to Maud Gonne, and write it from the *object's* point of view. Beatrice's account of *The Divine Comedy* could be fun.

Finding a Voice

Exercise 1: The Writer–Reader Relationship
Frankie Finn

Aim

To explore the concept of audience.

Method

1 Select a scene from your day: a bus journey, shopping, taking children to school, etc. Recount this scene as though it were a story (or part of one) to a reader whom you do not know. This unknown reader can be an imagined person (if so, spend some time getting a picture of her or him in your mind), or they may be someone you have noticed on the street or in the tube. Aim to interest your reader. Allow 15 minutes.
2 Continue your story, only now your reader is a friend or someone who knows you well. Decide who this reader is, tell your story as you would write or talk to this person, including familiarities, in-jokes, etc. Allow 15 minutes.
3 Compare your two pieces of writing. Does your tone change? Which one did you enjoy writing most?

Note

Writing in a vacuum is intimidating. When I started writing I quickly came to question who I was writing for or to. Was I writing for myself', or was I attempting to communicate to somebody?

I notice that in conversation I talk on different levels, from different parts of myself, and this depends to some extent on who I am talking *to*. Is this difference in tone also true of my writing? Do I imagine my reader to be someone I like? Is she someone with whom I laugh a lot, or is our relationship characterised by argument or serious discussion? Sometimes I've caught myself writing for the wrong person. I realise I'm trying to please some authority figure, impress a publisher for instance, and a form of internal censorship is taking place; the writing goes flat and feeble. At this point I struggle to remember that I am free to write to whoever I like.

Exercise 2: Getting to Know a Character
Frankie Finn

Aim

To distinguish between first and third person narrative, and to explore the advantages and disadvantages of both modes of narration.

Method

1 (Before you set pen to paper.) Imagine you are in a café. Decide what sort of a café it is. Is it crowded or empty? Is it seedy or genteel? Are you in the country or the town? Give yourself enough time to get a clear picture in your mind. When you have done this, jot down a few details under the heading: *Café*.
2 *Writing in the third person.* Sitting at a table in a corner, on her own, is an old woman. You might have to rearrange your picture slightly to accommodate her; allow the picture to settle in your mind. Give the woman a name and write it down as a new heading. Now write a description of your character. Your description may include clothing, gestures, size, shape, particular features, etc. Pay attention to detail, aim for precision. Allow 15 minutes.
3 *Writing in the first person.* Read through what you have written. Now step into your character's shoes. Become her: How does it feel in those clothes you have given her? Are they

comfortable or uncomfortable? What is her mood? Look around and decide what she sees. Write about her experience. This part of the exercise must begin with the word 'I'. Allow 15 minutes.

4 Now you have a picture of your character from the outside (third person narration) and from the inside (first person narration). How did the two writing experiences differ? Which did you enjoy most? Jot down anything you noticed.

5 *Writing in the third person: character into plot.* Now imagine your character getting ready to leave the café. She gets up from the table and goes to the door. Using the third person mode of narration, write a description of where she goes. Be careful to follow her – don't decide in advance. Pay attention to her walk: is she eager, slow, decisive or unsure? Allow 20 minutes for this part of the exercise . . . but if it is getting interesting . . . carry on!

Note

Sometimes I start writing in the third person and this doesn't feel right: I need to begin again in the first person or vice versa. There are advantages and disadvantages to both. If I have decided to write in the first person I have committed myself to seeing the world through one person's eyes – it is then more difficult to describe what is taking place beyond their field of vision. For example, if I want to inform my reader of what is happening in the next room, I have to let my character get up and walk through the door to see it. Whereas if I am writing in the third person I can say 'She didn't know that on the table in the next room was the letter that X had left for her'. On the other hand, the great advantage of writing in the first person is the degree of natural intimacy that this mode provides: 'I' simply feels and thinks and the reader learns this directly, whereas with 'she' the reader has to rely on what 'she' says or does or what the narrator tells us she is thinking or feeling.

What I have found useful about this exercise is the notion of surprise. It is necessary to believe in my characters – to be prepared to let them show me who they are and what they want to do if I am expecting a reader to believe in them. This said, I must add that I have also found that I cannot simply follow them around! What happens when I want my character to go shopping and she insists upon writing a letter or making a long telephone call which is quite irrelevant to the plot? Often I struggle with my characters. In the end a compromise is reached; we work it out together. However infuriating this struggle is, it has a vitalising effect upon the work.

Exercise 3: Taking Off from Other Writing
Moira Monteith

Aim

To encourage ease in writing, perhaps using material you know well, and from this evolve your own writing.

Many writers have begun with parodies of other writers or forms of writing (for example, Jane Austen with *Northanger Abbey*, and Ernest Hemingway with *Torrents of Spring*). In parody the form has already been established, though the tone will not be the same as the original since there will inevitably be some irony, and maybe 'insider' jokes depending on knowledge of the original text. Straight sequels or endings to unfinished novels written by another author seldom read well, even when built on notes left by the first writer, so it does seem necessary to change direction in some way. For example, Emma Tennant's *Queen of Stones* is another and different book from *Lord of the Flies* which in itself is a development from *Coral Island*; and Jean Rhys' *The Wide Sargasso Sea* concentrates on what many readers in the last century and this may have considered of little interest – the background of the mad wife in *Jane Eyre*.

The original writing must *rasp* at you in some way. Either you consider it inauthentic, or (as with the West Indian background to the mad wife) you are aware it is almost totally ignored and neglected, or it makes you so annoyed you want to articulate some comeback. Or again you may be so moved by the original that it stimulates you into redefining your own past.

Method

If you are working in a group.
1 Select a text for discussion. This discussion could involve

critical interpretation if you wish but perhaps more usefully will concern reactions and responses to the original. The text must be comparatively short if intended for a group reading, perhaps one short story or a section of a novel or a poem or a scene from a play. Usually there is no problem generating discussion. If the text is interesting it will evoke numerous and argumentative responses and developments.

If you are working by yourself.

2 The original text can be longer, and you can parody it or write a sequel to it, or unwrap the story of one of the minor characters whose situation can be further developed from the one which interests you. Consider, for instance, Sue Roe's comment in conversation with Emma Tennant on her novel *Estella: Her Expectations*:

> I think, in *Estella*, I didn't realise at all, until it was long written, to what extent I was responding in thinking of it in the first place to a sort of stereotyped, female imagery. Because at the centre of *Estella* for me now is the very, very potent image of Miss Havisham and Estella and the notion of time, locking and standing still, and the image of two women both arrested somehow, and hidden from history. (M. Monteith (ed.), *Women's Writing: A Challenge to Theory*, p.119)

Writing which is in some way sympathetic to the original, perhaps an autobiographical response to it. An interesting feature I noted when a group of women wrote after discussing 'No name woman' from Maxine Hong Kingston's *The Woman Warrior* was the number of us who did not have an entirely respectable stereotype family of mother/father/ two or three children. Everyone had gaps or 'problem' members of the family who were disapproved of in some way. What we discovered as a group was the vast variety of *secrets* that virtually all of us concealed to some extent.

The writing was often very powerful. This meant that the writers were not always willing to share their work (at least not immediately) with other members of the group. The exercise certainly encouraged several women to write other pieces developed from this initial stimulus.

The discussion brought out the careful way Maxine Hong Kingston organises her material. First she tells the basic story very vividly and then she goes over the account several times, each time attempting to give a rational explanation as to why her aunt died. This reflective quality was commented on in discussion and was a notable feature of the first written drafts. Two women however did not like the passage and, although they wrote, did not consider their pieces of much significance. I am sure this would hold true of any stimulus: it won't work for everyone.

Writing which is antagonistic to the original. There are many blantant masculine fantasies revealed in literature, so that it is often useful to unpack them by discussion and subsequently write a new version. I have noticed that a disturbingly large number of male students (often young but sometimes middle-aged and older) write rape or soft porn fantasies. So far I have not been notably successful in discussing these fantasies in mixed writing groups. Attitudes are generally polarised along gender lines, with the male writers maintaining the acceptability of this kind of writing and deploring the notion of any kind of censorship. More successful have been *writing* sessions when we have taken head on some published male fantasy. One example is the murder of the protagonist's wife in Norman Mailer's *An American Dream*. The account legitimises the dream that any redblooded American male may move from log cabin to White House but may also enjoy murdering his woman. The writing is extreme. For example, after the murder: 'I was weary with a most honourable fatigue, and my flesh seemed new. I had not felt so nice since I was twelve.'

After a discussion which included comments on the effectiveness of Mailer's writing, and why it exercised such a power over us, our own writing did, I think, liberate us – at least briefly – from the pervasive and pernicious effects of such values within society. Most people freed the wife. She was allowed to fight back and win, or at least escape. Two people punished the protagonist (he goes scot free in the novel), but no one, I think, brought him to repentance.

Several of the group said it had made them think much more about how they were writing and what subtexts might be involved. They felt quite positive about their written responses to the original stimulus.

Writing which is a new development from previous writing. Liz Cashdan, a teacher and a writer, was greatly struck when she came across the 'language' devised by Sara Coleridge, and which she called her 'Lingo Grande'. Sara wrote letters in this but no poems, so Liz gave her a voice using the words of 'Lingo Grande', and wrote about her husband, the poet Samuel Taylor Coleridge, who neglected and eventually left her. It is almost as if the Sara Coleridge who devised the original lingo (her own 'woman's language' which helped establish her as a person in her own right) has left the 'language' ready for another woman – in this case Liz Cashdan to create a voice with.

Oh, Esteesi, he's my thumper, my undoer
my cutter-up, full of the detesty of opium.
It has snatcherumped our love
turned Sara into Asra
whom he thinks he loverates.
A dreadful falling-abroad in his body,
upgatherum I cannot.
I am left, all empti-cum-nothingness.

There was a tendrum time he rolled my
    name around his mouth –
miraaculous lollipop – Mrs Coleridge
Coler – Idgecole – Ridge.
Oh, how we lovibummed and laughicummed!

But when the milk of paradise turns sour
the mind is cruddled with the bowel.

(An extract from Liz Cashdan's poem, 'The
    Mariner's Tale.')

Openings

Exercise 1: First Sentence
Joan Downar

Aim

To emphasise the importance of opening sentences to gain a reader's attention. This is a group exercise.

Method

1 Read a selection of opening sentences from short stories and discuss in your group what information is conveyed, in terms of character, situation, place, time and mood.
2 Ask each member of the group to write an opening sentence on a piece of paper, then collect them in and fold them.
3 Redistribute the papers at random.
4 Each person will then have to use the given sentence to begin a story.

Note

Sometimes I use this purely as an exercise for beginnings. We discuss only the first few paragraphs and don't continue with the rest of the story.

The Haunting
Sue Roe

I can't tell you how to begin your novel any more than I can tell you how to fall in love or choose a dress or a house or develop a taste for this year's Beaujolais Nouveau. You've got to feel it. I can't give you an exercise, because beginning a novel is more like brushing up against someone or something and feeling an unexpected frisson than like reading the book of instructions that tells you how to work your ansaphone. Get in touch with the world: that's what you have to do first. Practise at the bar. Do some scales. Mix a few colours, try a few new brushes. Now I have hit on what's odd about writing: it doesn't feel as if it's anything to do with technique. It is, of course, but it's a technique you can only develop by doing it. There aren't any rudiments. Get drunk, and see what's uppermost in your mind. Go for a walk on the beach: it'll feel boring, but see if anything seems different when you come back into the house. What do you want to say?

That's the crux of it, of course. What do you want to say? Nothing in particular: you just want to write? Then you are probably not a writer. You're not sure, but if you thought about it you'd probably find there's something that keeps cropping up, every time you see a film, meet a new person, read a book, that feels like your subject? That's more like it. It's a feeling of possessiveness: hey, that's mine. My . . . you're talking about. And what's more, I know more about it than you do. I could say it better; recount it better; paint it better; film it better; write it better; or at least differently, with a different emphasis.

Sometimes things haunt you. I was haunted by the baby kidnapped recently from a London hospital by someone posing as a health visitor: a childless woman, who had been reduced to stealing a baby. First I was haunted by the baby, then – when the baby had been found – by that woman who had looked after it so well, until they tracked her down. She had pushed its pram, kept it clean, and even bought a pethedine injection and put the wrapper in the rubbish bin outside the house as proof of motherhood. She really was its mother, in her mind's eye. One day I want to tell her story. Not *hers*, of course: some story that she and I could share.

Then there was that woman estate agent who took a man to view a house and then just disappeared. They never found her: just her car. Late at night, for ages, I kept expecting her to come knocking at my door. She and I share a story. I don't know what it is. I have never been abducted, just as I have never stolen a baby, but something in both of these stories relates to something in a narrative of my own. It's probably *because* I can't make the connections that the story feels as if it might turn out to be quite powerful. Only after I have written it will the links begin to emerge.

It is imperative that while I am writing, the impetus will come from the tension of my having had to keep these things under cover. If the story works, it is only in the process of telling it that the connections will unfold. To the reader, the connections between these stories and any story of mine will of course be immaterial. What will be important will be the force with which I tell it. All I am saying is this: pick something that moves you. Choose something that absolutely haunts you. And then forget about yourself. Submit to it. Let it get you by the throat. You will have to be prepared to be its victim, its accomplice.

Now start.

She backed into the narrow hall, pulling the heavy pram towards her. Mercifully, the baby still slept. As she tugged it over the threshold the wheels seemed to jam: the feeling of panic which had just begun to abate caught her by the throat again: calm down, she told herself. You've done it. The worst is over. No one's going to find you. You're alone here. No one's going to come . . .

You see: because I have given you the genesis of this beginning you can trace it back to its origins in my mind, but it is important not to think it can work the other way round: don't think you can begin by setting out the origins of an idea, and then expect to be able to trace the story directly forward. I had to go away and do something else for three hours before I wrote those first few sentences of something that might turn out to be the beginning of a story. I wrote something else altogether (a long overdue letter); made a few phone calls; hung out the washing; fiddled about with some chicken breasts. I put lemon juice on them, and then some Pernod, and then something stopped me from putting them in the oven. I sat down and listened to some Michael Nyman music and then suddenly in my mind's eye I saw a woman dragging a pram backwards across a threshold into a hall. The music still on, the oven still on, the chicken breasts abandoned in their Pernod, I just came in here and got it down.

Beginning Fiction
Ursula Holden

For me, the urge to write another book must be intense in order to overcome the dread of that blank page one. I'm starting something that may take me two or more years and something that I cannot plan.

I'm a subconscious writer and I often start my books with a remark, a situation or a scene that I find riveting and which serves to project me into unknown mists. I like throwing my characters into trouble and seeing how they will fare.

Sometimes I don't know the characters' names or even their sex until many more drafts are done. The first few days may result only in a page or two of groping and fumbling at sentences, just fragmented thoughts.

Four is a lucky number for me, I tend to work in units of four, redoing each page four times before proceeding. When I have a chapter that I can bear to read over, I redo it four more times. This first chapter is probably the hardest of the book. I liken it to a launching pad for a space rocket, or a sculptor's armature on which the piece depends – the base must be firm and true. If I can get the characters right they will tell their own story, so the more sure I am about them the more confident I become. At the beginning I try and concentrate on mood, the atmosphere engendered by two or more people, and I try to keep going until my brain feels like a dry orange before resting.

I like dreaming about my people; the subconscious never rests. After about four chapters and umpteen drafts I begin to feel more courage.

I need to be physically fit before starting, as well as having my equipment in good order. I need a large thesaurus, many dictionaries and reference books, reams of copy paper. My five old manual typewriters need to be in good nick and my work table tidy. I work in my bedsitting-room which leads on to a yard where I can be in hot weather. There is a shed for when it rains. I like flowers but a minimum of clutter. During working hours the telephone is my enemy unless it's my agent, with good news.

Isolation and silence are vital. Sometimes I work at the British Library where I can hire a locker for one of my dear portables.

Writing is tiring; I like to look as well as feel good before I start, carrying on for as long as possible every day, including weekends. A midday sleep is good, also lovely food. I freeze dishes so that I needn't stop to cook.

At night I like contrast. I go to keep fit classes and movies as well as see friends. Music and sleep are favourite relaxations. I practise yoga seriously.

Opening Scenes
Jill Hyem

Opening scenes are critical to the success of any play, whether it is written for the screen or for radio. It is that which will make the potential buyer read on, and which will hook the audience when it is ultimately transmitted.

I would suggest, as an exercise, that you watch and listen to some opening scenes and analyse why they succeed or fail in holding your interest.

In television and film there are various devices one can use to create immediate interest.

1 *An exciting action sequence.* A post office is held up. As the criminals escape a woman goes to stop them. She is bundled into the getaway car.

2 *An intriguing incident.* We see a young man walking along the street. He goes down a subway and comes up on the other side dressed as a woman.

3 *An involving piece of human drama.* A woman is driving along, her mind elsewhere. She hits a cyclist. Seeing that he is

dead, she panics and drives on.

4 *A character with whom the audience will at once identify.* An old woman sits on a suitcase in the hall of her empty house. Her bossy daughter chivvies her out to a waiting car. She is to be driven to an old people's home.

When writing for film or television one should never try to give too much *verbal* information in the opening scenes. Use them to convey atmosphere, suspense, intrigue or impact.

The beginning of the popular series *Howard's Way* provides a good example. I rewrote it several times before I arrived at the best opening.

We came straight in on the end of an exciting sailing race in which two boats are battling it out. One of them is captained by Tom Howard (our hero) and crewed by his son and daughter. We quickly establish their relationship as they shout urgent instructions to each other. We cut to a spectator boat where Jan, Tom's wife, is watching the race with a friend. A couple of lines tell us that she does not share her family's enthusiasm for sailing. Two male spectators cheer Tom on. One says, 'I hope Tom wins. He could do with a morale booster. If the rumour's true.' And back to the race.

In less than a minute we have established the setting for the series (the prosperous sailing world) together with the four central characters and their attitudes to sailing. We have also, with the minimum of dialogue, given the audience two reasons for watching on. Will Tom Howard win the race? What is the rumour that may adversely affect him?

The opening scene of a radio play presents more problems as you have to rely entirely on what can be *heard*. It is therefore essential that the dialogue is economical, that not a line is used that does not carry the story forward or tell us more about the characters. Always avoid what I call 'hello/goodbye' dialogue. Avoid too a plot that requires imparting too much information to the audience before the story starts.

One can often use sounds, rather than speech, to create immediate tension or atmosphere. A police siren approaching, footsteps echoing down an empty street, the monotonous ticking of a clock. Think in terms of sound and you will discover all sorts of possibilities. Andrew Sachs once wrote a half-hour radio play about a prisoner on the run without using any dialogue at all.

In my play *Look at Mr Punch* (a psychological drama about a man who had killed his little sister as a child) I opened with the sound of a Punch and Judy show on a beach. In this way before the action even started – a mother looking urgently for her lost child – I had established the location (gulls, waves), the children (laughter, clapping) and the Punch and Judy show itself with its underlying violence.

In some of my suspense plays I have used the 'teaser' device to hook the audience. The following is an example from my play *Origami* in which a young Japanese businessman moves into a flat previously occupied by an old lady whose husband was killed in a Japanese POW camp.

FADE IN:

YOUNG WOMAN'S VOICE: (CLOSE ON MIKE, WITH DEEP INTEN-SITY. SHE IS READING FROM HER DIARY) Today they came and told me he was dead. They didn't need to tell me. How could he live after all they did to him? (PAUSE) I feel nothing. Nothing but hatred. Hatred for every one of them. But most of all for the man responsible. I shall never stop hating him. Never.

(ECHO CARRIES ON 'NEVER – NEVER – NEVER')

(EDGE IN SINISTER SOUNDS OF A JAPANESE INSTRUMENT. THEN FADE)

In the scene which follows our Japanese man arrives to enquire about the flat. What would have been a fairly routine scene now contains a sense of underlying menace.

And so the audience listens on . . .

Continuings

Deciding Which Genre to Write In

Writing for Radio (1)
Sheila Yeger

Radio is a very liberating medium for the writer, allowing her to paint on a huge canvas with big, bold strokes, ranging back and forth in time and space, a luxurious freedom for the imagination.

But, at the same time, radio is a very intimate medium. Your characters speak direct to the audience, sometimes employing an 'inner voice' to add a further dimension of intimacy. Thus thoughts, dreams, imaginings acquire their own powerful reality, alongside more mundane matters. This makes radio a particularly good medium for women writers, a golden opportunity to give expression to our inner lives, and to make contact with the inner lives of other women, our 'listeners', who always respond readily and with grateful recognition.

Radio is a very visual medium, because you have to create a scene and characters in the listener's mind, without the aid of costume, props or scenery. Doing this with words, music, sound and silence calls on all your skills as a writer, as well as demanding an active response from the listener. This makes me see radio drama as a particularly harmonious collaboration between the writer and her audience.

Another exciting aspect of radio is the fact that you can pose yourself ridiculous problems and find a way of solving them. In my play *These Animals are Dangerous*, the central character is a gorilla. I decided, after some deliberation, *not* to let him speak, but to evoke his speech and thoughts through the medium of the other main protagonist, his keeper, Flack. Gorilla and man thus merge, till, at the end, when a single shot is fired, we do not know, (nor is it actually important), whether it is the man or the gorilla who dies. The gorilla was played by a gifted and dedicated actor who spent three days in a studio grunting, lolloping and barking to such good effect that many listeners (including the keeper of the Ape House at Bristol Zoo) seriously considered the possibility that there was a real gorilla in the studio!

Radio is also rewarding for practical reasons. When your work is produced, you can take a very active role in the process, which is quick, fascinating and extraordinarily efficient. You will be consulted on every point and see your work come to life through the combined skills of writer, actors, director and technicians. It's a very endorsing experience for a writer and always makes me want to go home and start another radio play immediately!

Writing for Radio (2)
Valerie Windsor

Radio was my first love, and remains the one medium where, as a playwright, I feel completely free. In radio, virtually nothing comes between the writer and the listener, so that a radio play is an intensely subjective experience, a direct communication between two minds. Ideas, images, characters, explode straight into the listener's head without any of the distancing hardware of television or film, whose very nature requires the audience to be objective outsiders. Even in the theatre, where the audience is invited to enter a group conspiracy, it's still necessary to sit outside the action and observe. A radio play, on the other hand, like the novel which it so closely resembles in everything except structure, has a subjective directness which I find very rewarding and which seems to me to be a seriously under-used and undervalued power.

So what is this power? Well, first of all, on radio, the whole responsibility for the piece lies with the writer. This, of course, is a double-edged sword. On the plus side it means that what you have written will not get taken away by a massive team of producers, producers' assistants, directors, art directors, designers, wardrobe mistresses, make-up artists, lighting and camera technicians, and turned into something you hardly recognise and certainly never meant. On the other hand, there's nothing to hide behind: the inadequacies of your work, the failures of characterisation, the weakness of structure are all brutally exposed. Subtle direction, some good action sequences, clever camera angles can turn a weak television script into something that looks very good indeed, but on radio there's nothing to distract the audience from the word, and the word has to create all those things which, in other media, an army of creative talents will do for you. It's for this reason that radio is such a good training ground for writers. Of course, the logical deduction of all this is that what you write for radio should in some way be beyond the massed creative talents of the art directors and designers to interpret. If your play would, as written, work equally as well on television, then perhaps you're not fully using the power of the medium; perhaps the piece lacks that extraordinary edge which radio can offer.

The first and most obvious technique at your disposal – also one of the most exciting – is the voice in the head. In radio you can go right inside the mind of your character. You could, for example, write a play in which no one communicates with anybody else except on the most mundane level; yet all the time, in their heads, they're weaving the most wonderful fantasies about one other. I once wrote a play in which the central character refused to speak at all, and her troubled and disjointed thoughts, her inability to endure the pain of life, her determination to kill herself are heard as a kind of desperate whisper in her head, while all around her the life of the hospital ward goes inexorably on.

An extension of this is to use the voice in the head as a narrator of the past, so that the character remembers seminal events in his or her youth and is then able to comment on the action with all the irony of hindsight. Alternatively, the voice in the head can be very much in the present tense, the observer of the action, the hoverer at the edge of the lighted circle, the alienated outsider. Or it can be a voice that always tells the truth while the action is a web of lies. Or the narrator can be omniscient guide to the action like Captain Cat in *Under Milk Wood*. The possibilities are endless.

One quite extraordinary strength of radio is its ability to cope with the non-realistic or mythical approach. In *Jump* by Ken

Whitmore, a very clever play about international relations and disarmament, the mole population want to save the world by making some essential underground readjustments. However, this will require every human being on earth to jump at precisely the same time, a piece of international co-operation which does not come easily. A cartoon version of this might work well enough, but it seems to me that any kind of external visualisation of such a brilliant idea would weaken its impact. It works exactly as it is: a funny and powerful piece of pure radio.

Radio is also good at getting right to the heart of primeval human emotions. What, for example, is the root of fear? If you try to give fear a shape, even if you hint at that shape, you immediately begin to tame it, and although film can be brilliant at exploring the darker reaches of the human mind, what radio can do is to put the listener in touch with the root of their own fear instead of offering someone else's interpretation of it.

So where do you start? You start of course with a good story. Without that, all the other essential elements of drama are meaningless. Then the characters you choose to tell this story must be real, must live independently of their creator. We must believe in them; we must care about what happens to them and how the events and conflicts of the story change them. Even the most distanced, the most stylised characters, must have their own absolute logic. Finally, the piece must, if possible, have resonances beyond itself. I don't necessarily mean a social or political message, or a great universal theme, but some kind of resonance which makes the play larger than the sum of its parts. If afterwards the listener says: 'Yes, very nice, but so what?', you've missed the whole point of your story. But if you're lucky – and very clever – a mood, an image, an idea from the play will haunt that listener's mind for years to come.

After that, the problems are all technical ones: the introduction of conflict, skilful dialogue, the careful and economical introduction of essential information, keeping your listener alert and interested by carefully pacing how much you reveal to them and when, structuring, focusing – these are the problems that apply to any kind of dramatic writing. How do you learn them? I don't know: I'm still learning most of them myself. All I can suggest is that you listen to as much radio drama as you can. You read everything you can lay your hands on. You make yourself as open as possible to all kinds of writing. Whenever you come across a problem in your own work you immediately turn to the work of a writer you admire and try to find out how he or she solved a similar difficulty. Whenever you read something that moves or impresses you, you try to analyse how on earth the writer did it. You spend the first years of your apprenticeship copying all the things you admire in other people's work until, out of this curious jumble, your own voice, your own style starts to emerge. And you never stop learning, you never stop trying to do it better, you never stop listening to criticism.

In order to make a living I now write for all the media, but radio remains the one medium in which I feel free to experiment and to fail, to take the kind of risks no one can afford to let you take in television, to go to the edge of experience and look over. This is where the real adventures lie.

Writing Fiction
Rosalind Brackenbury

Writing fiction is very much like living: you don't really know how you do it while you're in the middle of it, and I doubt whether there is ever a time when you say to yourself – yes, that's it.

But to be asked to think about how I do it and to try to give some practical suggestions to others – well, that's a useful and fruitful request.

I think that out of all the novels and stories that you could probably write, it's important to find the one that *will be written*. There is a story that will embody your strong and real desire to write. I am not saying that the desire to write can exist without the story; rather that it predates the story. When I was young, I think I was all desire to write and no story. Many people speak to me of being in this predicament. Young people in school very often have the desire and get provided, artificially, with a story. They are 'set' something. This can have the effect of making you lose your own story, the one you really need and want to write.

The other extreme is a capable story and no real desire. You can spot these books; many of them are published. Most writers can turn them out, if they try. But they break no new ground and they are a product rather than a process. It is very easy for a writer to get side-tracked into them out of a longing to get published, be recognised, sell. But, ironically and rightly, it is so often the weird one-off idiosyncratic books that get recognised; because there is, in spite of all the commercial pressures, an inextinguishable desire in all of us to be told something new.

Fiction has to be alive. That means it has to speak. That means that not only is dialogue important but that there has to be a tone to it, a certain liveliness that is recognisable. And you have to show this right from the beginning: look, this story is alive. So plunge in. Don't have pages and pages of introduction or explanation. Take a risk with the reader. Ask the reader, in there with you, to do some of the work. Fiction is not a one-sided exposition, but an invitation to complicity.

A story has to develop. It is an orchestration of different sounds, rich and complex, but not confusing. So after you have plunged in you have (metaphorically) to swim. And the reader has to swim with you (sometimes underwater, but trusting all the time that you know where you are going and will come up for breath before you reach the opposite bank). So you need to know how to pace yourself; as for any long-distance endeavour, you need to be sure that you are going to be able to get there. Not that the movement is necessarily always smooth and regular. There may be spurts foward and then periods of slow, relaxed progression. Tone matters, rhythm matters; and you will get a feel for all this. Sustaining the momentum of a long piece of prose is sometimes a matter of pausing to get your breath, sometimes of putting on the pressure. But you will learn this by doing it.

A story has to begin and end, whereas real life tends to meander on. Creating its span is like putting a frame around something. Painters who paint from landscape often put a rough frame around what they paint. You cannot put in everything. Increasingly I think that writing fiction is choosing how much you can dare to leave out.

Fiction is about people. I remember hearing an Australian writer say: I never write about landscape unless there is someone in it. The novel is for people and relationships. The complexity of human life is what lives in fiction, nothing less.

Your fiction will be, to some extent, about you. Your thumb, as D. H. Lawrence once pointed out, will be in the scales. But what you write will also be the playground and theatre of the people you have conjured up. As soon as you start to write about someone, you begin to create them, even if you thought this was to be a close-to-life description of somebody you know well. There are many many different ways of writing about people, of inhabiting and manipulating and being led by your characters, and you will have a good time experimenting with this. But once you have found your characters let *them* speak and act. Work through them. Unless of course you decide to let yourself be a character in your story in which case you will join them, and discover things about yourself you never knew before.

I think that fiction should ask questions rather than provide answers. I think stories are as gadflies to society rather than textbooks. The novelist asks questions of the reader, which the reader will try to answer from his or her own life. But a novel is a quest, not a route-map; it asks far more than it settles. I have learned certain things from novels I have read – how to put in a diaphragm, how to make raspberry jam – but, in the end, you have to go back to your own life.

Thinking about writing fiction, I realise how very idio-syncratic it all is. You find your own way of working, in the end; you tunnel, or swim, your own way through. But I would say: keep going with that momentum, however you feel it, and do not stop till you have reached the end. You can read bits to friends, but some strong part of you needs not to take any notice of what they say. Some tough, determined part of you needs to develop imperviousness – at least until you have got there. Then you can afford to stop and think about other people's opinions. But another good habit is to put the novel away for a while once you have finished it. Then, better and more accurately than any critic, you will see its flaws. After a few weeks or even months you will see what is right and what needs to be changed. I think that to subject it to other people before you have done this can be confusing, because other people, however sincerely they are trying to think about what you have done, will be partly thinking about themselves and how they would have done it; and it is your novel, not theirs.

Write the things you care passionately about; but write them in a controlled way. The desire will fuel itself; but the form requires control. Walk about until you have got the burning molten stuff of it under control. Then you can begin.

What you will sometimes discover when you have finished a first long draft is that you have before you a thing which contains a novel but which is not yet quite the novel itself. There will be parts which seem to be doing all the work and parts which sag or slow down the action. There is usually a pruning job to do here; be as ruthless as you can be with what evidently needs to be pruned. There will also be new bits to be written, to make good the connections. Rewriting is I think the secret; not poring over every sentence or radically changing the plot, but paring away some parts, building up others. The finished construction will be made up of masses of material juxtaposed. And it has to be solid. You can write the beginning at the very end, just as you can start with the ending. For a while, nothing need be fixed. But in the end, you do have to decide what goes where. And your own decision is final. At some point, you have to trust yourself enough to know that you do know what you are doing. There is an order in all this and here it is.

In fiction you can do anything. You can, these days, borrow from film, music, tell a story backwards, in fugue, or not at all. The novel is the freest of forms. But because it can be so many things, I think it is important for the beginning novelist to learn to refuse temptation, too. Some of the best and most powerful writing consists of saying something as simply as possible. Check every step of the way that you really mean what you are saying, that it is not some other writer speaking, that it is not just there for the effect. Check the structure – does it hold together? When one word will do, use it. Is this exactly what you want to convey? Is it how you imagined it? Or has some fashionable idea or superfluous word crept in between you and what you have written? Do not leave in anything which you are even faintly ashamed of or doubtful about; when the novel is in print it will look ten times worse. This is different from censoring yourself. The censor tends to operate at the beginning, when you are starting to write; it is what gets between you and the page in the first place. The slight faults and inconsistencies of things you have not quite noticed accurately will be far worse to live with in the future than the massive risk you have taken in writing the thing in the first place.

The hardest part, in my experience, is in these final preparations. There are very many people who have a talent for writing, but comparatively few who are prepared to do the work. What we all long for is to be easily and quickly acclaimed as geniuses and have our manuscripts swept off to earn thousands of pounds and instant fame for us. Luckily, for most people this does not happen. We are left with the work and the reality, the pleasure and the slog. When you have written the first draft of your novel, you have probably done about a quarter of the work, but you feel as if you want an immediate reward. Have a holiday, do something else, but come back to it with enough energy and determination to do all the rest. You have to be a perfectionist with it because nobody else is going to be. And finally, when you send off the typescript to an agent or editor, have it looking as good as possible; do not undermine your own chances by a last act of negligence. Don't send the copy that the cat sat on and half your friends read. Give your writing a chance.

Writing Science Fiction/Fantasy
Lisa Tuttle

Great ideas

To the reader, *ideas* are the great attraction of science fiction, and there are plenty of stories which have overcome the handicap of poor writing to sell and even attain the status of classics purely on the strength of a great idea. But, as a writer, never assume that you are the first person to whom your great idea has occurred. Chances are that it has been done before, and if you write a story, the sole purpose of which is to reveal, at the end, your great idea (surprise!), a well-read editor, unsurprised, will send it straight back. If, on the other hand, you take your great idea and explore what it might mean in human terms, how it might affect a particular character – if, in short, you write a good story, then you will have written a good book, even if H. G. Wells, Ursula LeGuin and Gwyneth Jones all explored 'your' idea first. And if in addition to this, by some chance, no one has ever had your idea before, and it really is great – then you'll be a star.

Background

The setting – whether the future, the distant past, another planet, or Faeryland – has a particular importance in this genre; because the interaction with it often determines the plot, the setting can almost be considered another character. For some writers, world building is one of their chief delights; others simply want to banish the tedium of offices and supermarkets and put their heroine on the back of a horse (or dragon). Whichever you are, remember you do have to create the world on paper before it exists. No matter how clear it is in your mind, your reader can't see it until you write it; you can't rely on the common knowledge of the 'real world' as mainstream writers do. But this does not mean you have to write pages describing the local flora and fauna in detail; much better to get on with the story, providing a few hints as to how 'there' is different from 'here', a little local colour, and concise descriptions of the most vital bits of the landscape, integrated with the action. SF readers tend to be quite sophisticated in their ability to imagine a whole world from a few, well-chosen pieces. It's not necessary to describe the corridors of your spaceship in detail on page one any more than it is necessary to give a detailed history and physical description of every character as soon as they appear.

Facts

If you are writing anything to do with the known world (that includes the past and the near future) do your homework; get it right. You needn't be bound by the facts we know – you can write about a flat earth or a world where magic works – but there is a great difference between a story in which time travellers rescue dinosaurs from extinction by bringing them *forward* in time, and one in which an early patriarchal civilisation is responsible for the death of the dinosaurs . . . Change the facts, but do know them first. There should be method in your madness. Remember to be consistent, and to think things through: even tiny changes can have a ripple effect throughout society. Extrapolate. Ask yourself questions. And remember that even wild magic has rules.

Exercise 1: A Detective Story
Caroline Natzler

Aim

To think about motivation and detection and to map out themes for a detective story.

Method

1 Think of all the possible meanings a particular action may have, e.g. 'the poisoning to death of a pet cat'. This could be euthanasia, vengeance against or a warning to the cat owner, experimentation with poison (whether for scientific or more nefarious purposes), commercial greed (the fur trade?), hatred of cats, an existential gesture . . .
    Make up an event and go through its possible meanings and motivations.
2 Invent a character, and a rough story line, to go with each motivation.
3 Take several of your characters and try to put them into one (rough) story, so that you have a culprit and other people it is reasonable to suspect.
4 If you doubt the plausibility of your characters and their action write briefly (notes or continuous prose) about a time when you, as an adult, committed a crime, or thought of doing so.
5 Write several short pieces about being puzzled by something that has happened; draw from your own life and use fictional material. Think about why you/your characters wanted to solve the puzzle, and how you/they set about it. Think about how it felt wanting to know the answer, and to be getting, or not getting there.

Note

You may find this rather cerebral if mapping out does not suit you as a writer; but it may help if you are stuck or if you have just one scenario and do not know how to flesh it into a story.

Writing for the Theatre
Sally Worboyes

Is there a play inside you waiting to burst out? Are you ready to write but not sure how to start? If so, maybe the following tips which I've picked up along the way will help get you going.

There are some questions that seem to arise time and time again:

Q: How should a writer go about thinking and working on an idea and story in terms of the actual physical nature of the stage?
A: Be realistic. There isn't normally much floor space, so keep the number of characters down. Actors like to move with freedom and unless you've written it into the script they won't want to smack each other in the face. And don't ignore one player while concentrating on another; if they don't need to be in a scene, see them off.

Q: How does a playwright create characters that reveal themselves in a convincing way through their dialogue and actions?
A: Create real people before you begin. Get to know them; the way they feel, think and react to one another. Give them lines which will drive the action of the play forward as well as showing the type of person they are.

Q: What's the best way to go about writing dialogue?
A: Eavesdrop.

Q: Is it best for a new writer to try to get her play published before sending it to a theatre?
A: No. A publisher is unlikely to be interested until it's been tried and tested.

Q: How can a writer tell if she has talent?
A: She can't, but others can. Keep writing and sending the work out. If the reaction is constantly demoralising then the writer, and *only* the writer must decide whether to go on or not.

Then again, if she enjoys her work in spite of rejections – why stop? After all, people who love to play tennis don't give up the sport because they can't make the centre court at Wimbledon, nor does an angler stop fishing because he or she hasn't had a bite.

Q: Should one give up a job in order to write that first play?

A: No. Wait until an income from writing is probable first. The argument of course is how to find the time to write when in full-time employment. If the play *has* developed and grown and refuses to go away, the writer will find the time. It might mean burning midnight electricity but at least that's cheaper than the daytime rate.

Q: How much does a playwright earn?
A: About 10 pence an hour – before tax.

The first play I wrote was for a local children's drama group which I founded when my brood of three were young. Their involvement helped dissolve the 'guilt' suffered for spending time enjoying life outside the kitchen – they were having fun too. I told myself I could always write my 'West End Production' once they were all at full-time school.

That was 13 years back and although I have enjoyed brief spells in the sun hearing my plays on the radio and seeing my first drama on television, the desire to write for the stage has never left me.

I enjoyed those early years working with the local children, but my big mistake was to be a one-woman band: casting officer, producer/director, special effects, lighting and general dogsbody. I imagined that if I saw the play through from beginning to end it would make life easier. Wrong. The problem wasn't getting the production through to the first night; it *was* the first night.

I remember peeping out to see the village hall packed full with mums, dads, aunts and uncles, not to mention the proud grandparents, some of whom had spent hours sewing a fine seam on costumes. It wasn't just my voice that momentarily left me when it was time for lights down, but also my nerve. What if it didn't work? What if they forgot their lines? What if my sudden attack of paralysis didn't wear off in time for me to press light switches and music control? What if the playing audience didn't think our little comedy was very funny? What if I just legged it out the back door and escaped across the sugar-beet field?

With just a few hiccups which the friendly audience told us they hadn't noticed, we apparently managed to pull it off to rapturous applause which I missed while outside throwing up in a ditch.

Subsequent plays were more organised – I had learnt to delegate. The group continued for a few years until most members reached their teens and wouldn't be seen dead on the village hall stage, which was just as well because my children were by then catching the school bus at 8.30 and not returning until 4 p.m. At last I had time to write my epic!

Before I set out on this new venture I decided to take myself away for five days on a play-writing course at the Arvon Foundation in Devon where I had a wonderful time with 15 other struggling writers and two established playwrights who were our tutors. I learned a lot in that short time, the most valuable lesson being that I had much more to learn; I settled for writing a thirty-minute play instead of a two-hour production.

It was through a contact made at Arvon that I discovered the Riverside Studios Writers' Group in Hammersmith, London. I attended a play reading which was given by professional actors and was so impressed that I joined immediately by submitting a play in progress. That was seven years ago and I'm still a persistent member, having now had several plays read there at workshop readings.

An excellent way to see if a play comes off the page is to organise a reading. Try approaching your local amateur dramatic group. Having worked on a script for months it's often difficult for the author to see it fresh, but once the actor gets a hand on it and the speech pattern can be heard, a transformation takes place. It will help a great deal if you can persuade those taking part in the reading to discuss the play afterwards. This can be useful providing you are receptive to criticism. If you can then manage to get the same people to give a further reading after a rewrite, great. In fact, at this beginning stage this kind of help can be invaluable.

It's all very well talking about a play coming off the page but how does it get there in the first place? For me, it starts with a happening – something I've seen during the day. I don't know at the time that it's the beginning of months of hard labour, but when I wake in the morning and it's still there, I begin to get suspicious.

Once I've decided that I am going to elaborate on an incident, I begin to wonder about the character involved. Where she might live. Does she have a family? Debts? Problems? Problems; of course she'll have her fair share of those and it's for me to choose which ones to give her. Once that's been decided, I begin to create characters to go round my heroine. Their part is to hinder or help. What they musn't do is hang around being a sounding board.

Next step, a setting. I usually go for a building and place I know – it saves time. By now I should be ready to work on a plot, to make up a story and tell it as best I can not giving too much away at the beginning and making sure attitudes have changed by the end. Most of my tales are worked through while I'm soaking in the bath after a day of pulling strands of the story together while cleaning windows, shopping, cooking, ironing . . .

All of this can take weeks. Finally I'm ready to sit down and see what it looks like on the page, see what these characters in my head have to say for themselves as they push the action forward. That's the exciting bit; if not *the* most exciting of all.

Writing Poetry
Sue Stewart

Writing this chapter is a bit like frollicking through a minefield: spontaneity is the order of the day, but one false step and a dozen certainties will blow up in your face. Setting oneself up as a know-all is madness, so I have decided to sidestep the whole issue by saying that, for someone just beginning to write, no advice can substitute abundant reading, extensive writing, and the freeing of the imagination and spirit in whatever way seems fruitful, barring total anarchy. Some people need their life to be reasonably secure before a poem will come; others can write their way out of misery. Some write to a timetable; others wait for some moment of crystallisation, a brainwave or slow dawning. All are right, providing they are following their own tune, not echoing some prescriptive score. And it's this finding of the tune which is important, hearing the still small voice inside yourself which is like no one else's, and feeding it, and watering it, and letting it out for air from time to time; one day it'll be old enough to take care of itself.

Along with the growing pains comes a need for conciseness. Not that a poem need be short or stripped of all ornament; just that it be as accurate and succinct as possible, according to its subject. For instance, adjectives dilute the power of the noun they describe, so must be handled with care. Some examples of 'wasted' adjectives would be: red poppy, cold winter, dark night, hard table. They're all self-evident: poppies are usually red, winters cold, nights dark, tables hard. More telling would be broken poppy, early poppy, Californian poppy, war poppy, faded poppy . . .

Adverbs are tricky too, as they're often thrown away: slept soundly, ran quickly, smiled winningly . . . sleep is usually sound, except to insomniacs, running quick and smiles winning. You could use more surprising adverbs or, better still, cut them altogether. As qualifying words, they're much less use than adjectives, and the odd one will always sneak in whatever you do, so it pays to be ruthless.

I tried to have no fripperies at all in my early poems, and this was a useful stage to go through, though the cutting and snipping led, in the end, to a frayed and desolate rag. I then worked on putting the texture back, letting the natural voice come through unhindered. This, despite the difficulty, was the right way round for me: control before freedom. Most people when they begin to write are not short on material: they have plenty of words, too many; what they need is a net to gather them in with, a blade to cut them down with, hot water to shrink them with. This is where the practice of formal technique comes in, lending order to chaos, so what I'd like to do is give a few examples of poetic forms that perhaps you might like to try working on, then move on to free verse, and some examples from contemporary women poets.

It might be invigorating first to take a ramble round contemporary poetry, look it square in the face and not turn to stone. What's the nature of the beast? A favourite definition of mine is from another century, Coleridge's 'the best possible words in the best possible order'. But 'best' is a slippery snake to catch, shedding skins. There are some absolutes: the strength of nouns and verbs, the qualifying power of adjectives and adverbs. But what to do with them, there's the itch. Poets today give expression to confusion as well as celebration, and for many, free verse more accurately expresses their needs, desires, preoccupations. The freedom is relative: it can be a subtle harmony or a teetering-on-the-brink-of-formlessness. The oral tradition is enjoying a renaissance, mainly thanks to the rich influence of our multi-racial society.

Poetry magazines are the first place to look to see what's cooking: also, to submit work to (details at the back of the book). Populists dislike the literary bastions such as *Poetry Review*, *The Times Literary Supplement* and *PN Review* for their scholasticism, the favouring of the abstruse, the esoteric, the 'difficult', yet recent issues have featured the work, or reviews of the work, of performance, bawdy, witty, gutsy or lambasting poets. Other smaller journals publish according to stated editorial criteria of 'celebratory', 'unconventional' or 'green'. Poetry presses don't run on parallel tracks either, and it's worth exploring their lists to find poets you particularly respond to. Faber, Secker, OUP and Chatto publish more poetry than others in the big league, but the smaller, exclusively poetry presses easily rival the giants in the quality of their list and production. Bloodaxe, particularly, brings out several new poets each year: others to watch are Anvil, Carcanet and Peterloo. Smaller still, often struggling, with grants or without, are Enitharmon, Giant Steps, Hippopotamus, Mandeville and Phoenix.

A poet needs to find her or his individual voice, and this can take a long time. Some poets are tangential, allusory, rich with metaphor and syntax. Others are abrupt, plain speaking. Certain poets are instantly recognisable, and this difference is what any writing is all about: how to say something, even something said many times before, in a fresh way, avoiding any hint of cliché, imitation or sloppiness. The voice can change over the years, sometimes through a dramatic change of direction or a new discovery, sometimes through a gradual fermentation. Some poets, though, hardly change key all their writing lives: they develop a particular style and remain loyal to it, or it to them.

This is a musical resolution as much as linguistic one, but before this voice can be found, tuned and let loose, an apprenticeship needs to be worked through. A useful metaphor might be that of learning the scales before you play the piano: studying, too, the old masters before improvising. But contemporary poetry is more immediately teachable and nourishing if you can be both open to its good influence and wary of imitation. The best effect it can have is a lateral one; it frees you, often from a kind of inner logic that was previously sustaining. It breaks habit; it is, in its psychological effect, liberating. A good start, particularly if you feel the need to discover a lost heritage of women poets, is *The Penguin Book of Women Poets* and *The World Split Open* (see Bibliography).

On to some poetic forms. I've taken three – the haiku, the villanelle and the sestina – to show the different effects that can be achieved.

The haiku is a very simple and attractive form. It has three lines, the first having five syllables, the second seven and the third five. (There are variations but this is the most popular.) In the Japanese tradition haikus are rather wistful poems, reflecting on the brevity of human life as compared with the permanence of nature. This sounds glum, but the poems are celebratory as well as pensive, drawing on the changing seasons, or the details of a particular flower, tree or landscape. But of course, you can do anything you like with it:

> Tea-leaf in my cup:
> did you read your own future,
> growing in China?

Here's one where I broke the form slightly, for the sake of brevity:

> Elderberries hang
> like a bunch of purple keys
> unlocking wine.

Haikus can be addictive, and another form that gets under your skin and is easier than it seems at first is the villanelle. Dylan Thomas's 'Do Not Go Gentle Into That Good Night' is a villanelle, but the form can be used equally well for comedy, with its repeating lines and insistent rhymes. The language has to be pared to the bare minimum, as the repetition of two lines throughout the poem magnifies any carelessness. It has three-line stanzas (tercets) rhyming a-b-a until the last stanza. The first tercet brings in the two lines (A1 and A2), repeated alternately thereafter in the third line of each tercet. They are used together at the end of the last stanza of four lines (a quatrain): a-b-A1-A2. The poem usually has five tercets and a closing quatrain, but can be varied as long as the tercets remain an uneven number. This ensures that each refrain is repeated equally. This might sound like double Dutch, but it's quite simple when you see it on the page:

Lucinda's Act

Releasing the faithful trapeze,	*A1*
rehearsed excuses in her head,	*b*
Lucinda Love is ill at ease.	*A2*

Her sequined partner's hard to please.	*a*
Was it something her stand-in said,	*b*
releasing the faithful trapeze?	*A1*

She hopes to God he doesn't freeze;	*a*
one slip from him, she's good as dead.	*b*
Lucinda Love is ill at ease.	*A2*

She keeps her gaze above his knees.	*a*
Depression weighs her down like lead,	*b*
releasing the faithful trapeze.	*A1*

What he thought real was just a tease;	*a*
their balanced poise he took as read.	*b*
Lucinda Love is ill at ease.	*A2*

He's caught a 'cuckold' on the breeze,	*a*
remembered last week's unmade bed.	*b*
Releasing the faithful trapeze,	*A1*
Lucinda Love is ill at ease.	*A2*

Another versatile form is the sestina, which has a rather
complex system of repeating words and can lend itself easily to
comedy or, if not tragedy, a type of haunting melancholia. It's
an unrhymed form of six stanzas, with six lines each, finishing
with a three-line stanza (or envoi). The end word of each line is
repeated throughout, in changing order, like this:

1st stanza: 1-2-3-4-5-6
2nd stanza: 6-1-5-2-4-3
3rd stanza: 3-6-4-1-2-5
4th stanza: 5-3-2-6-1-4
5th stanza: 4-5-1-3-6-2
6th stanza: 2-4-6-5-3-1

The envoi uses all six words: the first line has word two in the
middle and five at the end. The second line has word four in the
middle and three at the end. The last line has word six in the
middle and one at the end.

Here's an example from Marion Lomax who, interestingly,
has changed the usual pattern of the envoi:

The Father's Story: a Pre-Raphaelite Dream

The lamps were flat white lilies in my sorrow.
The window, tree, and curtain made a
        painting.
Inside her cot she waited for an angel:
A polished tile – the pool of light was empty.
Mary, your name could not have graced our
        daughter:
Her place was usurped by a ghostly sister.

Christina. Stand-in, like Rossetti's sister.
A silent child whose face meant only sorrow,
Who never heard or knew the name of
        daughter,
Who lay so still and lifeless like a painting
Draining my heart until it was quite empty
And I the victim of an evil angel.

Rossetti knew there should have been an
        angel.
Just like the one appearing to his sister.

A girl to make the void no longer empty.
A single tree for Paradise and Sorrow:
Eden. Golgotha. In a window painting.
A fragile thing of glass and blood, my
       daughter.
Only a splintered dream, this icon daughter
Who should have grown to be a living angel,
A painted heroine who left her painting
To run and play with those calling her sister:
Now locked unborn inside their mother's
       sorrow
To curse her damaged womb, forever empty.

At last I journeyed where the fields were
       empty
To paint a red bird swooping to my daughter.
The light had to be right to catch the sorrow.
Circling the skies a predatory angel.
The river took her down to meet her sister:
I buried them together in my painting.

Her small life floats there still within this
       painting,
Spread out with grass and flowers, her face
       empty.
I carry it for all of them – each sister
They feared might be a changeling like my
       daughter.
The whole tribe can feel safe because an angel
Has exorcised their fears and killed his sorrow.

Goat-like in sorrow, my dead eyes are empty.
A sea of painting swallows up my daughter.
A lonely angel on a beach calls 'Sister'.

There are many more forms you can try, and for an introduction
to them Frances Stillman's *The Poet's Manual and Rhyming
Dictionary* (Thames & Hudson), despite its offputting title, is
excellent. Stillman also discusses rhyme and half-rhyme,
rhythm, metre and free verse. It's worth saying, I think, that

forms aren't cast in tablets of stone: they were invented by poets, and can be modified as you choose. Better still, experiment: try inventing your own form.

Free verse remains popular, and can be more difficult to get right than a formal poem, which has its structure clearly defined. Often there is a type of syncopation going on, counterpoint to the main theme: a catch to the voice. There are also many devices on hand, from assonance and onomatopoeia to the use of metaphor and simile. With the former, it's better to leave this to your natural ear – or train the ear into it by reading and listening to poetry. Ideally, you're conscious of the effect without striving for it. Of the latter, metaphor, particularly, I like, as it seems to spring from a need to unify: a type of alchemy comes into play, one object being so like another that it actually becomes it. For instance:

the step is a chair
a page is a cliff
buds are claws

You then then rearrange or 'hide' the metaphor to avoid its obvious use:

the steps are table and chair
the cliff of your chalky page
salmon claws of the early beech

Here are a few lines from some contemporary poets, to give an idea of the musicality of free verse, and of individual voice:

from **Portland**

By the valerian, which is itself
hundreds of tiny poised butterflies
pricked into flowers, by its pink heads
the humming-bird hawk moth hangs
blurring its grey and tawny wings
in eager speed, its two inch tongue
proving each flower. Grey and sleek
it rested on rock, contented stone
down in the weares, by the rabbit runs
and the convict rocks, where my daughter
once

met with the adder and does not forget
its old gold and brown rearing up at her
    feet . . .

Alison Brackenbury

from **Mansize**

Now you aren't here I find
myself ironing linen squares,
three by three, the way
my mother's always done,
the steel tip steaming over your
blue initial. I, who resent
the very thought of this back-breaking
ritual, preferring radiator-dried
cottons, stiff as boards, any amount
of crease and crumple to this
soothing, time-snatching, chore . . .

Maura Dooley

Boy

I liked being small. When I'm on my own
I'm small. I put my pyjamas on
and hum to myself. I like doing that.
What I don't like is being large, you know,
grown-up. Just like that. Whoosh. Hairy.
I think of myself as a boy. Safe slippers.

The world is terror. Small you can go *As I
lay down my head to sleep, I pray* . . . I
    remember
my three wishes sucked up a chimney of
    flame.

I can do it though. There was an older woman
who gave me a bath. She was joking, of
    course,
but I wasn't. I said *Mummy* to her. Off-guard.

Now it's a question of getting the wording
    right
for the Lonely Hearts verse. There must be
    someone
out there who's kind to boys. Even if they
    grew.

Carol Ann Duffy

Bulb Seller

Hot pollen at the door, a sting
of buds among the clattering hail.
I shift to yellow, your bag releases
them with a sly squeak of plastic.
Keep them cool, you say; I burning
in a small house, spreading deserts
on the page to plant flowers out.
Paws on the kitchen floor, if I'd
reached Egypt; my god's a tool
to dig with, cast out noisy stones.
Thank you, I say, I will; the price
of Eden rattles in his yellow hand.

Nicki Jackowska

from The Rose-Pirate

The rose-pirate is a bad sport –
He steals my old gold hybrid teas,
My hand-painted, my dwarf and cushion
    roses.
The oil on their leaves smells of cinnamon
    and apricots,
They win for me golden brooches,
Rose-water in the cut-glass rose-bowl.

I dream about them at night,
Under their private nicknames,

My long rows of maiden plants that will sell
Under the ugly names of towns,
The daughters of park superintendents,
Blowsy and deeply veined . . .

Medbh McGuckian

from Silver

Silver is a She,
a listener riven from earth,
shaken and washed
in the long shuddering boxes of the
    winnowing shed.

Silver is scalded into many shapes,
a ring of hopes,
a prize-day cup, a silver bird
with second sight, a child's spoon
shining and fasting in the morning sun.

Silver changes from lost to found.
Silver has power
to be born as many originals;
one day a chain of innocence around my
    neck,
next morning a profane noose . . .

Penelope Shuttle

If you have the opportunity, do go to readings, or listen to poets
read their work on radio or television. You can be comforted or
enlivened by old favourites, or surprised by them: simply the
tone or pitch of a voice, or an unexpected emphasis, may lead
you to a new reading of the work, a different interpretation.
You can also hear new poets, and if you like their work follow it
up. There are frequent readings at the Poetry Society and at the
South Bank, as well as at venues throughout the country. The
South Bank Poetry Library has a comprehensive international
selection of poetry books, magazines, reference books, cassettes

and videos which you can consult or borrow.

Finally, I think it's important to keep a sense of perspective when you begin to study in earnest. It's easy to feel like a pipsqueak in the wake of tradition and the contemporary establishment. But tradition's a movable feast, and it needs continual replenishment: who's to say your poems won't be on the menu next week?

Writing Songs
Maria Tolly

I have always enjoyed writing. I also enjoy music, and it seems amazing to me now that it took me as long as it did to realise that I could join my two loves together by writing songs.

On average a song lasts about three minutes, and during that short space of time it will, one hopes, capture the imagination of the audience. It may comfort, or disturb, prompt questions, move to laughter or to tears. It is a very direct and immediate form of sharing.

To explain this passion of mine, it will be easier if I first say something about the various stages in my method. I will follow this with some concrete examples.

Subject matter

A song begins when I want to express something, perhaps a personal experience, or the experience of someone I've met. It may be inspired by a piece of information which delights or appalls me, causing me to feel the need to pass it on. Every minute of the day provides inspiration of some kind. A conversation or an event may arouse feelings and thoughts that I want to share.

If the theme is a personal one, then I spend a good deal of time thinking it through, jotting down thoughts at random. If, on the other hand, the theme is about something or someone outside myself, then I spend weeks, perhaps months, doing research, interviewing people and reading, until I feel I have enough background knowledge on which the song can rest.

Form

Having decided what I want to say, I must then choose the
vehicle, so before beginning to write, I look at the theme from
every possible angle to see how best it can be presented. For
instance, should it be a narrative tale in the first or the third
person? Should it be ironical? Allegorical? A series of images? I
must also start puzzling about the best kind of music to carry
the theme. For instance what kind of rhythm should it be?
Would it be useful to have a chorus? What kind of pace will it
need? Is it going to be a blues? A folk song? A ballad?

Lyrics

As I begin to write it is crucial that I make decisions as to the
structure of the song: i.e. length of line, length of verse, rhyming
pattern and so on, though I may change my mind countless
times once the words begin to come.

Whatever kind of language or whatever kind of rhyming
scheme I use, I must work consciously and consistently. I must
avoid clichés or any form of jargon, making every effort to find
fresh ways of communicating what I want to say.

There must be space in what I write for the singer to breathe,
and for the listener too to take a breather. As I write, I say the
words out loud to make sure they flow easily. It is often by doing
this that the tune comes into being.

Music

I begin to write the music as soon as the lyrics have reached their
first draft. The rhythm is already in the words.

Now, with the help of dischord and harmony, together with
the rise and fall of the notes, I can emphasise particular words,
give a phrase added meaning, create the atmosphere I want.

At this stage I may well discover that the lyrics need to be
tightened, or that the rhythm of some words must be changed.

Performance

All of these stages intertwine and overlap each other. As I speak
the words out loud to make sure of rhythm, accent, and flow,

and as I later sing the phrases to see how they sit with the music, so I begin to have ideas about how the song might be performed.

(In case you're thinking that I have a rather rigid attitude towards the creation of a song, I should now admit that I don't always manage to follow my own advice, and often rush along on a wave of enthusiasm which may well land me in a cul-de-sac. I may have to begin again, and again, each time restructuring the form, each time getting nearer to the essence of the song.)

Humour in songs

'Message from the Government' (Recorded on 'Gonna Get Up')

The following song was inspired by a deadly serious newspaper article which amazed me to such an extent that I found it laughable. I wanted to share the information as well as my amusement.

Because the article reflected Mrs Thatcher's attitude, and because I wanted people to laugh at it, I decided on a Victorian, music-hall style. The alliteration, the use of 'perfect rhymes' and as many 'internal rhymes' as I could muster, help to make the content amusing, as opposed to merely appalling. The rhythm of the words also enables the performer to keep the audience waiting for the 'punch line', thereby hopefully raising a laugh, or at least a smile.

Here is the intro followed by a chorus in 4/4 time. The rhythm is marked out with an accent above the appropriate syllable.

> Cóme to the Fálkland Íslands gírls,
> you'll have éverything ón a pláte;
> with márvellous, mácho, military mén,
> from whóm to chóose a máte.
>
> And you'll fly the Brítish flág gírls,
> high in the Sóuth Atlántic ský,
> and while you're hólding the fórt gírls
> the Émpire will not díe, will not díe,
> so cóme to the Fálkland Íslands, gírls,
>   cóme, cóme, cóme.
> For there's nó work hére,

but thére, there are lóts of jóbs
just wáiting for yóu.
For whére there are lóts of mén,
there's lóts of wáshing and íroning tóo.
Cléaning, cóoking, máking, ménding,
enóugh to máke you wéep
with jóy, for lífe brings its ówn rewárd
for yóu, as it dóes for the shéep.

Writing to a brief

Example 1, 'Right of Way' (recorded on 'Voices')

This is an example of a song which did not come out of my
imagination, or out of personal experience. A group of disabled
people wanted a song for their annual conference which was to
be on the subject of disability and unemployment. They felt that
a song would be a more engaging way of saying what they
thought about their lack of access to 'an ordinary life'. We had
many meetings together, and I recorded all that they told me on
countless cassettes.

As I went through each stage of the song I was constantly on
the phone, making sure that I was getting it right, for though it
was my pen doing the writing, I wanted the song to be theirs.

I decided to use a narrative form and tell a story. In this way I
could give a great deal of information without sounding like a
pamphlet! Also, a story is an easy way to keep people's interest.
I wanted, as an able-bodied person, to be able to sing the song
myself to an able-bodied audience, so it had to be in the third
person.

I knew from the beginning that the music would need to be
lively, reflecting the energy of those who were the song's
inspiration. I also decided, at an early stage, to use direct speech
and plenty of colloquialisms, using the phrases that disabled
people so often hear.

Because disabled people so often do not have access to the
things able-bodied people take for granted, I wanted to bring
this segregation home to the listener, and so I explored the
meaning of the words 'access' and 'need' in the chorus. The song
is packed with information and I was well aware that able-

bodied people are far from used to listening to a song about disability, so I formed a very tight structure, similar in each verse and with a chorus to give a break from the story, thereby setting a convention that would ensure easy listening.

The rhythm and structure of the verses are far more important in this song than the rhyme scheme. The music is simple and I 'speak' (as opposed to sing) the words in quotes.

Here are two of the four verses, plus a chorus. The timing is 2/4.

When Súsie was a kíd, she was tóld by her Má,
'You néed an educátion or you wón't go fár',
So they wént to the schóol and they knócked on the dóor,
But the téacher said, 'Whát on earth are yóu here fór?
I'm sórry, my déar, but it's agáinst the rúle;
You've gót special néeds and you néed a special schóol;
If we ónly had the móney it would bé ÓK.
It ísn't up to mé to find a wáy.'

5, 4, 3, 2, 1,
Ríng up the cúrtain, the tíme has cóme
For ús to make an éntrance, we've sómething to sáy.
Oúr only néed is the ríght of wáy,
A way ín, a way úp, a way dówn, a way thróugh,
The ónly way to gét it is for ús to tell yóu
They've got to stóp spending móney
The wáy that they dó,
So we can spénd it on thís instéad.

When shé was in her téens she was góing insáne,
She cóuldn't compéte with no tráining to her náme.
So she wróte to the Póly, and they ásked her alóng,
But when she wént to board the bús they wóuldn't let her ón.
He sáid, 'I'm really sórry, it bréaks my héart,
You've gót special néeds, and you néed a special cár;
If we ónly had the móney, it would bé ÓK.
It ísn't up to mé to find a way.'

Example 2, 'Wonderful Women' (recorded on 'Up To Here')

I was asked by a theatre group if I would write a song about

women in the mining communities. I started off by trying to talk
to the women I knew in the communities on the phone so as to
set up some meetings, and these phone calls became the subject
of the song. While I would have liked to have put every phone
call into the song this would have made it far too long, so finally
I had to grit my teeth and throw away many a good story,
retaining just enough for each verse to deal with one phone call.

I chose 3/4 timing, because it swings along at a good pace.
When not quoting directly I used as much alliteration and
internal rhyming as I could, so that the words would flow as fast
as the conversations which had inspired the song.

The music helps express the words. Each verse begins in a
major key, giving the words a positive air, followed by another
four lines in the tonic minor which echo my failure to talk to the
woman in question. These changes in tempo and key also
maintain the interest of the audience. Here are the second and
third verses, in 3/4 time.

'Is that dóuble eight double síx four? I'd liKe to speak to
    Lýn.'
'So would Í,' he repliéd, 'she's at yet ánother effíng meeting,
Toníght, she's with the CŃD, but wait a mo' it's so
    confusíng.
She míght have gone with the wóman next door, Dóreen,
    who's complaíning
At the Lábour Party méeting how the cóuncil's always uśing
All the rates we pay for their banqueting and boózing.'
Í should have knówn it . . . no chance of finding her ín,
She hadn't changed a bít, always out campaígning,
So I lóoked up another náme, and óff I went agaín.

'Sórry to distúrb you but cán I speak to Jó?'
'I'm sórry too,' he saíd, 'she up and left me mońths ago,
I júst can't understand it, it wasn't me that was to blame,
Éver since the strike, the wife neVer seemed the sáme;
Would you beliéve it, she's got a bedsit, does a course at the
    polytechníc?
At hér age . . . learning Karl Marx and Leńin?'
I saíd, 'Yes, I beliéve it,' what moré could I saý?
In my mińd I raised my gláss to the one that got awáy,
Then I tóok another lóok in my télephone boók.

Personal songs

In some ways, these are easier to write, simply because the only expectations are your own. Instead of interviews, discussion and reading, the research is done by wrestling with your own thoughts and feelings. I'm not saying that this is easy, but at least I've only myself to answer to, and I will be the only one who is disappointed if I don't succeed.

Usually, I find that if I want to write about myself, it is because I need to work something out. As a result, the very act of writing the song is bound to be fruitful, even though it may be difficult.

Example 1, 'Woman and the Rock' (recorded on 'Up To Here')

In this song I am exploring an emotion through the use of images. I found it a satisfying way of expressing myself without feeling as if I had 'taken my clothes off in front of strangers'. Because it is so personal, I suspected I was being rather obscure, and I was prepared not to be understood.

As with any bluesy song, it is slow moving and repetitive. Repetition in a song, when used consciously, gives the listener time to absorb the lyrics and feel the emotion that is being expressed. The sense of sharing is a very comforting feeling.

Here is the second verse and the 'middle eight', in 4/4 time. I have not marked the accents, as the lyrics move freely over the beats.

'How do you manage, oh so alone?'
said the woman to the rock by the sea,
'So solid, so sound, like nothing gets you down, the way a
　　　rock ought to be,
So solid and so sound, like nothing gets you down,
but when there's a hush, can't you hear deep inside
that echo where the waves are sucking you hollow?
As you stand against the tide.
As you stand against the tide.'

'Just look at that rock,' the people cry,
'imagine the view from up there of the sunrise.
Wish I were like that,' you'll hear them sigh,
as they pass on by.'

Example 2, 'Into the Music'

This song also came very much from inside myself, written at a time when the world seemed a dark place to be.

In most of my songs, the lyrics are the most important aspect, while the music is more or less a tool to aid communication. But in this song, I allow myself to indulge in sound and rhythm for their own sake. Notice how many 's' sounds there are. Consonants have their own characteristics. 'S' is soothing, and alliteration, when consciously done, is very effective. The repetition helps create a lulling effect for the chorus, while the verses, being in lines of five, help the song to flow.

Here are the first two verses with the chorus. The timing is very syncopated with two bars of 3/4 followed by one of 2/4, so I haven't marked the rhythm, as I feel it might confuse the reader.

Casting around in the dark,
Searching the shadows for inspiration,
Let the music start,
Soothe away the desperation,
Looking, looking for new ways out,

And if I'm getting into the music, getting into the music, oh,
If I'm getting into the music, getting into the music
It's my way of hanging on in there, hanging on in.

Rhythm soft as rain
Easing the tension with its weeping,
Melody dulling the pain,
Rocking the senses till they're sleeping,
Waiting for morning to come again.

Sometimes, people give me poems they have written, hoping I will set them to music. But poets can, if they choose, use the kind of vocabulary which does not translate into song. The constraints imposed on my lyrics by rhythm and melody call for words which literally fall off the tongue. Also, it is essential that the natural accent of the words should match the accent of the music, otherwise the listener can easily lose the meaning.

More and more, I delight in finding new structures, which

while they tie me down (and almost always tie me in knots) often reveal fresh aspects of the subject matter, and in the final draft aid easy communication.

Writing for Children
Elizabeth Hawkins

It seems quite wrong to begin this article, designed to encourage women to write for children, by pointing out why one should not write for children. But that is what I intend to do.

Why do you want to write for children?

For a start, it is not a back door entry to the adult fiction lists. Publishers have separate editorial teams for their children's lists with specialist children's book editors. In some ways writing for children is harder work than writing for adults. In writing for adults you are free to wander where your novel takes you and in any manner you choose. With children you need to bear in mind the age group you are writing for, their interest level and the vocabulary they can cope with. Few children, for example, will put up with long passages of evocative descriptive writing.

An occasional offering in the classes I teach on writing for children is that of a sentimental story 'for children', very often accompanied by references to a 'dear little doll's house', or a 'naughty little boy'. When questioned the writer has no idea whether the story is suitable for a four-year-old or an eight-year-old, and yet there is a greater developmental gap between a four-year-old and eight-year-old than there is between a twenty-year-old and a forty-year-old. The story usually wanders around various age ranges, but reveals itself primarily as an adult's story about children. To a child a doll's house may seem a large toy, whilst a 'naughty little boy' might appear a galumphing great bully.

Here is the crux . . . are you writing through the eyes of a child or an adult?

Many successful children's writers have written for particular children, or have had close contact with children professionally or through raising their own. This may help but it is not essential. Dr Seuss, whose hilarious books such as *The Cat in The Hat* are loved by most children, told me when I interviewed him years ago that he had no children, and did not particularly like children, but . . . and here we have it . . . he wrote for the child in himself.

Many children's writers talk of clear and intense memories of what it is like to be a child: the joys, the fears, the excitements and the disappointments, the vulnerability of the child at the mercy of an adult world; these they can empathise with. They write for the child within.

I hope I have not discouraged you unduly. On a more encouraging note good writers for children will probably not find it too difficult to get published. Children's publishing has doubled in volume over the last ten years and is profitable to the extent that in some publishing houses the children's list helps subsidise the adult fiction list.

Let's begin by looking at books.

1 Picture books for young children

How is a picture book different from any other sort of story? First and foremost it is a story that is conceived in visual terms. The writer needs to be aware that the child cannot read the words but she can read pictures. Pictures portraying one setting or little variety will be tedious, so that a story that takes place entirely in one classroom would not allow much scope for a picture book. Similarly scenes that are static in composition are much less appealing for a young child than action pictures, where something is going on. The story should be imagined in visual images. Often words can then be left out of the text if the picture can better 'say' it.

A word of caution here about asking your artistic partner/ friend to illustrate the story. If you are not an illustrator most publishers prefer to receive the story and then look around for a suitable illustrator. There are obvious exceptions, such as the talented Janet and Allan Ahlberg of *Cops and Robbers* fame, but for the most part it can lead to embarrassment if your story is liked but not the illustrations, or heaven forbid, the other way round.

With picture books for young children, say two-to four-year-olds, the skill is not only in your original idea, but in creating a satisfying whole. This is more difficult than it first appears.

Picture books for young children tend to work best with a

series of incidents held together by a theme, rather than a conventional plot structure. In *Noisy Nora* by Rosemary Wells, a classic story of the middle child who feels neglected, the story is held together by the series of attention-seeking devices Nora indulges in. Alfie, in Shirley Hughes' *Alfie Gets in First*, finds himself locked inside the house after the door slams, with his mother and baby sister outside on the step. The story relates the attempts of various helpers, neighbours, milkman and window cleaner to break into the house, before Alfie opens the door himself.

A major problem is to make these incidents cohere into a satisfying whole. One device is to make the story return to the point at which it started, such as in *The Wild Things*, by Maurice Sendak, when Max returns home to his bedroom after being king of the Wild Things, and finds his supper waiting on the table, 'and it was still hot.'

Another device is to supply a common ingredient to each incident. In *Noisy Nora* everyone is preoccupied and has no time for Nora. In each incident in *The Elephant and the Bad Baby*, by Raymond Briggs, the elephant takes an apple or a bun for the Bad Baby, without asking.

The Elephant and the Bad Baby illustrates another crucial aspect of the picture book – it must sound well. The book will be read aloud, so that every word must have its place. Like a poem the text must flow and, like many poems, rhythm, repetition and rhyme contribute to this. A good example is *On The Way Home*, by Jill Murphy, and *Winnie the Witch* by Korky Paul and Valerie Thomas.

A word of warning about stories set completely in rhyme – they are difficult to sell. All publishers these days have an eye to foreign sales, and rhyme is impossible to translate. Occasionally a wonderful book in rhyme is published, such as *The Giant Jam Sandwich*, by John Vernon Lord and Janet Burroway, but this is rare. Secondly, writers often have to do contortionists' tricks with words to fit the meaning to the rhyme, so that the rhyme ends up containing stilted and unnatural words.

Picture books for older children, five-to-seven-year-olds, can take a more conventional plot treatment. For instance there can be a concrete aim for the story, such as when Little Tim has lost his parents in *Tim All Alone*, one of Ardizzone's classic Little

Tim stories. The story chronicles his adventures and difficulties as he sets out alone to find his parents.

Finally with picture books, even if you are no artist, you need to be aware of the problems of layout. Picture books are printed in page spreads in multiples of eight. A simple book for very young children, such as Dick Burningham's series of *The Rabbit*, *The Dog*, *The Cupboard*, is set over 24 pages. Most picture books are spread over 32 pages, with a few longer books, mostly for older children, spread over 40 pages. However of these 24, 32, or 40 pages, only 16 to 18, 24 to 26 and 32 to 34, respectively, may be used to tell the story. The rest are used for sticking to the card cover, or title pages. Check in picture books to see how many pages are used.

In addition to presenting a publisher with the text of the picture book in which page divisions are clearly indicated, it is helpful to include a dummy of how the book will look. I usually sew together the required number of pages into a primitive book, write my text into the dummy where I want it to go on the page, and give instructions for artwork where necessary on each page. A writer-artist with an imaginative use of layout is Shirley Hughes. I am no artist, but if you can sketch out your ideas, however badly, it is an advantage. Presenting a simple dummy also shows the publisher that you have thought out how your story will look.

First story books

By the age of six many children can enjoy stories which are not so exclusively visual in appeal. I have never known a child of this age not love Roald Dahl's *Fantastic Mr Fox*, and following that, his *Charlie and the Chocolate Factory*.

Particularly popular with this younger age range are books in which each chapter contains a complete mini-adventure or story in itself. Examples of this are *Pooh Bear* by A.A. Milne, *My Naughty Little Sister* by Dorothy Edwards, or *Clever Polly and the Stupid Wolf* by Catherine Storr. Interestingly enough many of these books were written some time ago and there is something of a dearth of good, contemporary stories of this nature. The young child gets to know the main character and enjoys meeting him or her in a new adventure each storytime.

The skill in writing these stories depends as much on memorable characterisation as on a suitable story-line. Initially writers can err in making their characters too complex, or alternatively, too wishy-washy for the young child. I like to draw out one characteristic to the full, expressing this characteristic in dialogue and action. Look at the charm of *Pooh Bear*: Pooh is a lovable bear of little brain, Eyeore is a misery and pessimist, Kanga is warm hearted and motherly, while Tigger is bouncy and obstreperous.

One of Roald Dahl's great skills has been to understand the need for full-blooded, simple characters. Look at the opening of *Charlie and the Chocolate Factory*. Dahl tells us that Violet Beauregarde is a girl 'spoilt by her parents', Mike Teavee is 'a boy who does nothing but watch television', while Augustus Gloop is 'a greedy boy'. Young children love these strongly drawn, clear-cut characters.

Books for young readers

As children begin to read there is a need for books that are simply written but with subject matter appropriate to their interest level. The trend away from exclusive reliance on reading schemes to 'real books' has encouraged publishers to assemble stories in series identified by their length and reading difficulty. Many excellent contemporary writers, such as Dick King Smith, write for these series.

The writer is not bound by the constraints of a reading scheme, and indeed, need have no knowledge of the reading process, but she will find it best to check books in the series in the young readers' section of her local children's library to see the interest level and the formats of the various series. They can be identified by the logo on the spines which reflect the series titles.

Examples of these series are: Hamish Hamilton's Cartwheels and Hodder and Stoughton's Hedgehogs of not more than a 1000 words, followed by Hamish Hamilton's Gazelles, Hodder and Stoughton's Roosters, Anderson's Tigers all at under the 3000 word mark. Other series to investigate: Heinemann's Banana and Superchamp series, André Deutsch's Toppers, Nelson/Walker's Blackbirds and Redwings and A. & C. Black's

Jets, Crackers and Comets. Books for older readers, at about 7500 words include Hamish Hamilton's Antelopes and Hodder and Stoughton's Cheetahs. This is not an exhaustive list, so check your library, and write to publishers for guidelines and copies of their catalogues.

Writing for eight- to twelve-year-olds

These are the years when children, given the opportunity and access to attractive books, can become voracious readers. However they are not so easily won unless we consider what attracts them to a book and keeps them reading.

What do they read?

Enid Blyton would still come pretty near the top of most lists, with many boys adding the American *Hardy Boys* adventure series by Franklin W. Dixon. Before we start groaning about quality of writing we had better look at why children still love the adventures of the *Famous Five* or the *Secret Seven*, because wouldn't we all love children to find our writing so irresistible?

All the series mentioned in the paragraph above are fast-moving adventure stories, with children acting as the heroes to resolve the initial mystery. It's the sort of reading that keeps you going with a torch under the bedclothes when your light is meant to be out, rather than the '60 pages read, eight more chapters to go', schoolbook plod. This urge to keep reading, to find out, depends on that old-fashioned writing skill – plotting.

Plot tension

Plotting is, I believe, one of the most important writing skills in writing for children. It's rather unfashionable to talk of plotting in literary circles these days. It's too often associated with down market, 500-page blockbusters, which it is true, are often examples of skilled plotting. How else would you last through 500 pages? Ask any child and they will admit to skipping the 'boring bits', that wonderfully evocative description, the clever flashback, or that marvellous fleshing out of character. They want things to happen and the story to move.

Plotting is too big a subject to treat adequately here, but the key to holding it together is to have a point or theme to the plot.

Themes such as how Jane and Emily come to terms with who they are rather than who they want to be, I tend to regard as phooey. Getting down to a concrete theme or purpose is better, such as the search by Jane and Emily for their missing mother. They may well come to terms with who they are in the course of this search, but that I regard as character development.

Having got your theme clear in your mind, I then think of plotting rather as I would a Mills and Boon romance. The usual romantic story goes: will she get her man? She does of course get him, but only after missed assignations, he falls briefly for her best friend, his family dissuade him because of her humble origins, etc. In other words there are a number of difficulties or hiccups on the way to the solution of the plot. One hiccup or difficulty leads inevitably to a new development. If the plot is tight, you won't be able to take out any link in the chain without the plot collapsing.

This all boils down to plot tension. Plot tension is what keeps the child turning the pages, not being able to stop at a convenient chapter ending but feeling compelled to read on. This is what children want from their reading.

Several years ago a survey of 650 children in Rochdale schools was conducted by Her Majesty's Inspectorate. They were looking at library provision. When asked what they wanted out of books, most pupils wished they were 'more exciting, interesting and adventurous'. Enter Enid Blyton, 'because', according to the Rochdale children, 'there's always something going on'.

There are a good number of better writers than Enid Blyton, writing adventure style stories with more original themes and characterisation. Nina Bawden springs to mind with *The White Horse Gang* and *A Handful of Thieves*. Unlike Enid Blyton's super-competent characters, in Nina Bawden's adventures her characters face reality: drainpipes to be shinned come away; villains being trailed appear just after the children have given up spying. Michelle Margorian's remarkable first novel, *Goodnight Mister Tom*, is a long book but one with superb plot tension; it keeps the child reading avidly the whole 304 pages, as does Jill Paton Walsh's *Gaffer Samson's Luck*.

Humour

After plot tension, humour rates high at every age for children's books but particularly so at this age. Roald Dahl once said: 'It is an absolutely vital ingredient. I only know one thoroughly successful children's book with no humour in it at all, *The Secret Garden* by Frances Hodgson Burnett.'

Humour can be woven into characterisation or into situation. A good example of the former is the characterisation in Ann Pilling's *Henry's Leg*. Henry's mother is quite scatty, in contrast to his friend Graham Snell's prim mother who 'hoovers everything in sight'. Noreen, the lodger, is a friendly punk art student while Henry himself is full of foibles.

Humour can be effectively introduced by way of the minor characters. New writers are often afraid of overwriting their characters, of 'going over the top'. I have never yet suggested that someone should tone down a character, but I have frequently ploughed my way through dull, unmemorable characters.

Humour in situation is wonderful when it works, as in Diana White's delightful picture book *Bother with Boris*, but it is more difficult to write. The good books that have hilarious stories are memorable because there are so few of them. My favourites for younger children are *The Boy Who Sprouted Antlers* by John Yeoman, and Gene Kemp's *The Terrible Term of Tyke Tiler* for older children.

Fantasy

By the age of 10 children develop a deeper sense of time, past and future as well as present. The notion of moving into other worlds becomes intriguing, an interest catered for by fantasy.

This makes it all the more unfortunate that historical fiction has been out of vogue in recent years and it is not now easy to interest a publisher. I hope interest will return, particularly with the new developments in GCSE history emphasising empathy with other ages, and that once more we shall see writers of the calibre of Rosemary Sutcliff with her Romano-British novels such as *The Eagle of the Ninth* and Henry Treece with his fast-paced viking trilogy *Viking's Dawn*.

Fantasy can look both forward as well as backward. Imaginary scenarios of the future can be as enthralling as the worlds of the past. John Christopher's trilogy *The Prince in Waiting* creates an England of the future devastated by earthquakes and volcanoes, a violent land of separate principalities united only by their hatred of machines.

Fantasy novels can move between the real world and an imaginary world, a technique that heightens credulity. In *Tom's Midnight Garden* by Philippa Pearce, a dream world of the past is revealed when the grandfather clock strikes 13 times, while C. S. Lewis' world of Narnia, entered through the wardrobe, still remains one of the most popular fantasies for children. A more recent writer in the field is Jenny Nimmo with her Welsh trilogy *The Snow Spider*, centred round Gwyn's discovery of his magical powers, a trilogy that improves with each book.

Some of the most outstanding fantasy novels for older children draw on ancient mythologies. Most obviously Tolkien's *Lord of the Rings* draws on Norse mythology, while Susan Cooper in her *Dark is Rising* series draws on Welsh Arthurian mythology. There is no reason why the writer could not draw on quite different mythologies such as those of the Aborigine or Eskimo.

However, the writer of fantasy is free to create an entire world of the imagination, as Mary Norton did for young children in her world of the little people who live beneath the floorboards, *The Borrowers*. For older children Ursula LeGuin's *Earthsea* books reveal an invented fantasy world, much as, though very differently, Richard Adams created a world of rabbits in *Watership Down*.

While not strictly fantasy, an area of children's publishing which is increasing in popularity is that of the thriller and tales of mystery. If one remembers how much previous generations enjoyed the tales of Conan Doyle and John Buchan, it seems surprising that this area needed to be rediscovered. Several publishers have brought out collections of ghost stories, while publishers such as Blackie have produced a series called *Thriller Firsts*. As in all series it is wise to check with the publisher as to approximate length.

Skills

Writing skills such as composing dialogue, handling viewpoint, characterisation, setting and time are similar to those of adult fiction and are discussed later in 'Continuings'. The major difference is that your viewpoint character will usually be a child. Dialogue needs to be appropriate to the age of the child speaking, and narration seen through the viewpoint of the child should not revert to a narrator with an adult voice. The following example of narration from *The Runaways* by Ruth Thomas convincingly conveys the 11-year-old child's viewpoint:

> Being the weekend, of course the weather had turned blustery and squally. Julia felt silly with her school anorak over the sixteen-year-old outfit. The big clothing shops were closed, but she managed to get a smartish mac in one of the little places on the seafront and shivered in that. The sea was grey-green today and choppy. A few hardy souls were bathing, but Julia didn't fancy it.

Writing for teenagers

This is very much an expanding field. Finding good writers for 'young adults' is now a concern of many publishing houses. The development of specialist teenage lists such as André Deutsch's Adlib series, Livewire Books for Teenagers from The Women's Press, Upstarts from Virago and the Plus list from Penguin has all been within the last 10 years.

What happened to teenage reading before?

Bookish, intelligent teenagers probably went straight on to adult fiction at puberty, as many still do, but an awful lot of children, and especially boys, gave up on fiction. Even for the intelligent teenager, a novel with characters drawn from their own age group still holds great appeal.

The trend to write specifically for teenagers began in the US, and for a while all the best writers were American. For some reason American writers were less hung up by 'good writing', and were more able to write gripping social dramas with teenage characters. The appeal of these writers was enormous. I knew one boy who got through three copies of

S. E. Hinton's *The Outsiders* through re-reading it and passing it round his friends.

What is immediately apparent with these American writers is that they are able to identify with the whole business of adolescence; with the concerns of puberty – who am I? what do I want out of life?; with the inevitable disillusionment with parents which precedes the adolescent's acceptance of her parents as ordinary mortals rather than infallible authority figures; with concerns about appearance and physical development; popularity with both sexes; falling in love and general feelings of alienation as the adolescent struggles to mould her own world.

Recently excellent writers whose work appeals to the adolescent reader have emerged in this country, writers such as Sue Townsend, with her Adrian Mole diaries, Anne Fine, Jan Mark and Ian Strachan to mention but a few.

From the writer's point of view, writing for teenagers allows greater freedom of style than writing for younger children. For instance a first-person viewpoint can work well in telling a story for young people. It can reflect the musings and the stream of consciousness style that appeals to this introspective age group. The 'I' narrator is more difficult to use with younger age groups.

Similarly, the fast-packed plot is no longer so crucial. The plot still needs to move but it does not need to be so firmly bedded in the concrete. Emotional developments, such as a relationship with parents or boy friend, could well constitute a movement of the plot in a way which would never work with younger children. Also the need for a happy or successful outcome to the plot is no longer so essential. The plot could resolve itself in an alternative way.

Humour too can be more sophisticated and satirical. One has only to read Adrian Mole to see this.

As for style . . . this can be tricky. If you try to write your dialogue complete with the current jargon it will most probably be out of date by the time the book runs off the presses. There is also something false about adults trying to write teenage jargon. A straightforward language style works best. A teenage idiom only works well in the hands of those naturally skilled at it. If you can't do it, don't try.

Finally, some thoughts on subject matter. Not every teenager is struggling to come to terms with her parents' divorce, her mother's alcoholism or her feelings of sexual inadequacy. Adolescence is the great age of idealism as well as of introspection. Why should we as adult writers feel that we need to ram home the tough lessons of life, the disappointments and the compromises?

Some interesting and popular books for teenagers are about young characters who are not always in agonised, soul searching situations. Janni Howker's *Isaac Campion* tells, in a spellbinding first-person narrative, the story of the teenage son of a horsedealer who is taken out of school in 1901 to work with his harsh father; or there is Russell Evan's *Survival*, the story of a political detainee on the run from a Siberian prison camp.

Looking to the future for children's writing, one hopes for a balance between encouraging authors of sympathetic outlook, such as fiction which is anti-racist or which portrays sex roles on an equal footing, with the demands of the good story. With the massive expansion of children's publishing the market has been too easily dominated by fashionable 'isms'. At the time of writing 'green' themes are understandably to the fore, and publishing houses are producing a flood of books with green themes, some well written but many mere expressions of our current fashionable preoccupation.

No book will work for children because of its theme alone. Nothing can replace the skills of the good writer who can write the tale that keeps a child reading. To write well, the author must choose a theme which engrosses her whole imagination, rather than one dictated by fashion, and employ all the writing skills of which she is mistress. Then, I believe, children will get the books they deserve.

Writing Drama for Film and Video
Eugenia Liroudia

Writing for film and video may sound a demanding and distant task. It is not a case simply of writing a story or describing a situation, you also have to create the 'image' which will enable the viewer to 'see' the characters, 'hear' the situations, 'learn' the secrets. In other words it is about writing images. In a sense you have to master two languages at the same time: the literary language of the script and the visual language of film or video.

Film and video both have the capacity to deliver a vast spectrum of information by collapsing a large amount of time into the 'objective' time of the film (approximately two hours) or episode (in the case of a television series). Film and video have the ability to overcome their 'real' time and space limitations and to narrate events that took place in say a week in just a few cinematic or televisual minutes. Much of the hypnotic effect of the moving image is based on this ability, and if one adds in the case of cinema the presence of a group of people taking part in a common experience inside a darkened room, one realises why films are so often associated with dreams.

The film and video industry has, on the whole, kept its secrets well hidden and this has created a gap between the vast audience that receives the 'image', and the 'secret' society that creates it. The reasons for this are both commercial and political. The infamous star system could never have survived if there had been no distance between the making of the product and its consumers; also the politics of media influence has required that film, video and television keep their processes well hidden from the ordinary viewer.

The first requirement in learning to write for film and video is to learn to read film in its own language, for only then will the writer be able to identify the way films and videos are made and follow the network of choices that have led to the final product. It is a process that grows easier with practice, and the best methods are to see a lot of films and videos and to see some of them several times. It is amazing how by watching the same film more than once you begin to discover different elements, such as how the text is separate from the image, how the dialogue is separated from the action, and how silence conveys so much on the screen. A script must therefore include a certain amount of information about the visual form of the film.

From an idea to an image

The choice of the main idea for the story – the theme – of a film is something that has always caused me a great deal of debate and trouble. It is true that most handbooks on writing for film and video provide a list of popular themes which convert easily into images. The problem with this approach is that it tends to narrow our imagination and condemn us to thinking in a stereotyped way about the marketing of our ideas; we try to conform rather than to create.

Any idea has the potential to develop into an image as long as it is properly worked on and contains a coherent structure. It is through observation of our ordinary lives that we will find the subject matter for a film. The images are all there, even if we are dealing with the most extravagant, science-fiction type plot. Reading the images of our ordinary lives will provide the seeds of our fantasy; the choice of subject will then come naturally.

The subject matter can vary. It can be personal or impersonal, social or philosophical. It does not have to be clear from the beginning; it will form during the unfolding of the story. Whatever the subject is, it will almost certainly contain some kind of conflict. The conflict might be between a person and the environment she lives in, between two people with different values, or between nations. One thing that is certain is that every situation that is put on screen will demand a 'solution'. Once an idea is presented to an audience, the writer then has the task of developing it, placing it in some kind of context, putting it in conflict or doubt, and finally in some way 'resolving' the conflict.

An important task during the early stages of writing for film and video is writing what is called 'the concept'. This is the main idea and plot of the film expressed in a few sentences. It is important to be clear about what we want to express and the writing of 'the concept' provides the writer with a coherent form through which to clarify her ideas for the story. She must make choices from among the many possible facts and ideas in order that the story does not drown in an ocean of events, destroying all coherence. Remember, you have only so much time and the audience knows nothing about you or your characters. You need space to introduce and develop what you have to say. Expressing your story in a few sentences helps to achieve this coherence.

Many writers also undertake market research about the type of audience their story will appeal to. Although it is useful to have an idea about the audience you are writing for, writing a specific recipe for a particular type of audience is not a good way to begin for two reasons: first because it is more difficult than it sounds, and second because it is not very good for your integrity as a writer. Everyone's mind has different capabilities: let's explore these possibilities rather than try to classify them.

Once the idea has been formed you are ready to begin putting the words down on paper. This is rather like embarking on a long treasure hunt. Your tools: constant awareness and observation of your environment; a knowledge of cinema vocabulary; the discipline of writing a certain amount within a deadline. Creativity needs a certain amount of organisation in order to become stimulated and remain alive. Millions of people have ideas for films or videos, most of which are never started on or if started are never completed.

Once you have developed your ideas, the discipline of writing must become almost rigid in order to allow all this material the space to expand and to prevent it from evaporating. A definite time of the day and a deadline schedule will help the creative process now. This discipline will enable you to write with fluency and to have control over your material.

If you have some relaxation time during the day devote it to thinking about your idea. Take your idea into your own life, experience the moments your story and characters will.

Writing down 'the concept' will have helped test whether you really have a story. This brief synopsis will have identified the time and place, the characters' functions, the climax and solutions. Now you can start thinking about more complicated story-lines, events which will enhance your story, and the introduction of other characters. In films each presence has to have a reason and the traditional dramatic structure of 'beginning–middle–end' must take account of all the elements in the story. The audience lives the film in expectation of a conflict, a peak, and a resolution. You cannot afford to throw in events or images which bear no relation to this structure. Their presence might destroy the whole film.

Once you have this basic story you can move on to the details of the events and the narrative. One thing to bear constantly in mind is that your characters must have credibility. No matter how surreal your material, it has to convince on screen. Every detail of the setting, every mannerism or phrase has to form a part of this whole, so that even incredible things become believable.

Writing images

I have already stressed the importance of knowing the medium you are writing for. Film and video have developed a number of techniques and it is essential for the writer to know these.

The visual information given by the writer must be written in the format used in the making of films. Although this article does not have the space to offer a full film vocabulary, here are some of the main elements of film language. Writing for film and video embodies three different kinds of information:

1 Information related to the story which defines the space, time and action, e.g. 'An interior scene, daytime – a London pub. Two characters are arguing about work.'
2 Information related to the way the image is presented by the camera: how the people and objects are seen. The writer does not have to describe every shot, but she may want to define an angle on her characters, e.g. 'Focus on Jane including her sister'. If the writer wants to be more specific she can describe the way the shot will be filmed. The terms used to describe the different shots take as their example the human body:

   CU: close-up, as for the shoulders and above.

   ECU: extreme close-up, to describe a detail of the face.

   MS: medium shot, as from the waist up.

   MCU: medium close-up, a tighter MS.

   LS: long shot, as showing a full person. (Sometimes called 'full' shot.)

   MLS: medium long shot, taken from closer in than the above.

   VLS: very long shot, as for crowds or introductory shots of landscape.

   OS: over the shoulder, as in a shot of someone taken over someone else's shoulder. Often used in conversations.

   POV: point of view shot, we see something as a character sees it.

   INSERT: an inserted close-up shot, e.g. 'INSERT – the stained shirt.'

INCLUDE: to include in the shot someone who was not previously there.

3 Information related to the movements and position of the camera:

PAN: left or right movement from a stationary camera.

TILT: up and down movement from a stationary camera.

ZOOM IN, ZOOM OUT: in or out movement of the camera's lens.

TRAVELLING: indicating that the camera is moving.

TRUCK: right or left movement of the camera.

CRANE SHOT: the camera moves upwards to give a general view.

Besides these three categories there are a number of other terms indicating shots or movements.

FREEZE FRAME: a frame is frozen as a still picture.

O.S: off screen. Describing an action or sound not shown on screen.

V.O: voice over, to narrate over an image.

SPLIT SCREEN: dividing the screen into two halves with a different action taking place in each.

Once the story is developed the writer can begin to transfer the narrative to the screen-play format. The screen-play is both the literary and visual presentation of the story. It contains all the action, dialogue, and other sound elements and is divided into 'scenes' which present the story sequentially.

A scene, or a series of scenes, is the narration of events unified by a common time, space or theme. This can range from a single shot to a whole series. A group of scenes containing related events forms a sequence which may or may not occur in continuous time.

As for the events and characters, the scenes should exist only if they function to keep the story moving. There is nothing more boring – or more obvious – than a scene which has no purpose.

A very important element is the continuity of each scene, the way in which events contribute to the film's overall effect. The scene has to have a story-line, which may consist of furious action or incorporate long silences. It is the flow of the scenes that will form the rhythm of the film and the relation between them is crucial.

The first step in writing down the scenes is to compose a scene outline or list of scenes in chronological order with details of their beginnings, endings and transactions. Once the outline is written it is important to check it thoroughly, highlighting any weak points and trying to 'see' the images. It is at this stage that all the visual elements have to be considered, such as the settings, camera angles, sound effects, clothes and props. The thinking at this point must be in terms of images. It is the images that are now the main instrument of the film.

The next step is the actual writing of the screen-play. Every scene needs to be written with detailed information as to the location, time and action – in the order of sequence. Here is an example of a scene written up with details:

MORNING. INTERIOR. CATHERINE'S BEDROOM.
Catherine is sitting on her bed writing a letter. The door opens and her mother enters, interrupting her. The mother announces that she has to go to an important meeting. She leaves in a hurry.

MORNING, EXTERIOR. OUTSIDE CATHERINE'S HOUSE.
Catherine's mother comes out of the house and gets into the back of a waiting car. The car disappears down the road.

The final version of this will be the complete written film, including all the narrative and visual elements, the dialogue and any specific points the writer wishes to emphasise. The more complete and detailed the screen-play, the more control the writer has over the final product.

Once the screen-play is finished you may find you want the opinion of someone you trust. You need honesty now, not a stream of vain flattery. But it is useful to see whether or not a reader has grasped the points you wanted to express – whether or not the story seems coherent – the reader is, after all, part of your audience. If your reader makes suggestions, take your time before you decide on any changes. Once you are on the production path some alteration will be inevitable.

Finally, remember to present your screen-play as tidily as

possible. Choose the title bearing your story in mind and not just as a verbal device, and always give a contact address to whoever you sent it to.

A note, not for the end, but for the beginning.

An idea is conceived, a story is written, a screen-play is developed. Choosing to write for film and video is choosing to write for a medium which is largely collective. Making a film involves a vast number of collaborators, and there is nothing more constructive than having a team of people around you with whom you can work and trust. For many projects, the team that writes, produces and directs already exists. In a male-dominated industry, getting together with other women and producing projects together is a step which can help our work flourish. There is no need for a huge budget to produce work of quality. The use of video, which costs much less than film and allows far more control during the shooting, is a good medium for producing work for television. There are plenty of workshops and courses on writing and producing, and it is a good way of meeting other women and developing ideas and skills. The seemingly distant world of film and video will, gradually, become simpler and more accessible. The problems of obtaining equipment, finance, hiring different facilities vary enormously, but you will find an answer to all these questions, and working with a group will help. The world is changing every day. New ideas are created every minute. Now is the time for these stories to be seen.

Writing Television Drama
Julia Jones

Requirements for television plays have changed over the past few years, the principal change being that the slot of the single play has virtually ceased to exist and new writers must cut their teeth in series, such as *EastEnders*, *Coronation Street* and *The Bill*. So, as an aspiring TV writer, it is a good idea to study series and decide which of them suits you best as a writer, then find a good story to fit their format. The next step is to write your play and send it to the producer of the series.

A good story is the first consideration of a writer, and before thinking of the technical requirements of TV it is a good idea to develop your story and get it on to paper either in prose or as a formal 'treatment' (see 'Endings').

At this stage it is vital to decide whether or not the story will make a visual piece. Can it be told in pictures, using dialogue to develop characters and their thoughts? A TV or film writer must be able to think visually – to see pictures of the people moving in their world with the mind's eye. Told in this way the camera can short-cut narrative by going into a scene half way through, without laboriously moving the character from A to B. A fluid quality is necessary for television – don't keep characters seated at a table for three or four pages. Move them to other backgrounds – backgrounds which contribute to the story.

Now for the actual structure of the play. Conflict is necessary. There is no drama without conflict. Conflict between characters, or between characters and their environment. The rise and fall of the conflict and tension of the story will contribute to the shape of the play. Build each scene so that it finishes at a point which leaves the audience expectant and looking forward to the next development. Always remember that the camera can move in on faces to capture thoughts and emotions and so at times eliminate dialogue.

Having once got the story moving in the mind, get it down on paper. The best way to learn to write is to write.

Bear in mind that all stories have small beginnings and are not written overnight. A scrap of conversation overheard, the turn of a head on a bus, can trigger an idea, which then needs much attention and patient work before it becomes a play.

Dialogue should help to reveal a character by accent and use of words. Victorian speech had different rhythms from modern speech. Train the ear to listen. Writers are both watchers and listeners.

Presentation is important. The easier a piece is on the eye the more likely it is to be read. Use double spacing and place the names of the characters centrally above the speech:

        JAMES
    I love you.
        MARY
    I love you too.

Directions should also be placed centrally. Likewise scene headings, which should be underlined:

1. EXT. A SMALL PARK. EARLY MORNING
2. INT. A PARLOUR. DAY. SOME WEEKS LATER
('EXT.' = exterior, 'INT.' = interior).

Describe the settings briefly but clearly:
2. INT. PARLOUR. DAY. SOME WEEKS LATER.
A small room with modern furniture, a table, four dining chairs and an armchair set before the fire.

Describe the characters loosely unless it is essential to the play that they are fat, thin, fair or dark. This is to allow scope for casting.

Finally bear in mind that plays for TV have definitive lengths and can't be changed owing to programme requirements. Most series are 53-minutes in length, and a fair guide as to how much to write is to allow one page of A4 per minute.

Writing Feature Articles
Sue Teddern

Why features?

Of course you want to write . . . or you wouldn't be reading this book. Perhaps you've already looked at the sections on fiction, poetry and drama, and are now trying to decide which medium is 'you'. Or perhaps you've always wanted to write features and came to this section first.

Whatever the case, it's important to take some time to decide: why features? Remember, a poet, playwright or novelist can be far more individualistic and expressive than a feature writer. Will you be happy with this less personal form of expression?

The bottom line is this: what you want to write is not as important as what the editor wants to publish and, ultimately, what the reader wants to read. That's not to say you'll be forced to make your living writing 'Elvis Ate My Fiancé' stories for the

Sunday Sport. With any luck you'll find subjects that interest you *and* your readers.

A few years ago I made myself a promise: never to write what I wouldn't want to read. That may sound restricting but it isn't. The thing is, if you saddle yourself with a subject that bores you, writing will become a real chore, and that'll show in every sentence.

Who are your readers?

If you want to see your articles in print, it's important to understand the variety of titles in the newsagents. It goes without saying that an article on child-care in the nineties wouldn't appeal to *Punch* or *Autocar*. But would *Woman* publish it? Would *Elle*? Would *Spare Rib*? Would *Prima*?

This is where research is vital. Take a good analytical look at all the different magazines on the news stand to see who they're aimed at, what they write about and how they angle their features. Going back to the child-care idea, check whether *Elle* ever writes about children. And in what ways would *Spare Rib*'s article differ from *Prima*'s?

Exercise 1

Beg, borrow or buy the four or five publications you would most like to write for and study them carefully. Then write a short description of who you think the typical reader is. We'll assume she's a 'she'.

Ask yourself how old she is. Where does she live? If not alone, who with (flatmates, parents, lover, friends, husband, children, etc.)? Does she have a job? If so, what? How does she vote? How does she relax? What's her favourite TV programme, her newspaper of choice, etc? Does she read this magazine to be entertained, informed, enlightened, inspired?

The clues are all in the magazine. Look at its design. Is it slick and sophisticated or bland and basic? Are the ads for Bendix or Benetton? And who's being profiled: Michelle Shocked or Michelle from *EastEnders*? Are recipes more prominent than careers advice? Are the features long and in-depth or bitty and lightweight for interrupted reading? How aspirational is the magazine? How witty?

You might think this is a cold, slightly cynical way of analysing the different publications in the market-place. But the long-term plan is for you to be able to match your ideas to the right magazine and know instinctively how its readers would want subjects covered.

Ideas

It's no good saying 'I want to write a feature about Portugal, herpes, poverty, noise, friends . . .' You have to know *how* you would write it, and then choose an angle, rather than opting for some vague, all-encompassing overview which proves impossible to write.

Besides, features editors don't want articles on Portugal, herpes, etc. They want a specific angle, an original approach. Your study of the market may have convinced you that *nothing* you've read is original, and you may have a point. But try putting yourself in the features editor's shoes and imagine how she would fill her pages. She may not always know what she *does* want, but she invariably knows what she doesn't.

Once you're established, features editors will come to *you* and say 'can you do me 1000 words on Portugal's breakthrough in the treatment of herpes?' Until then, coming up with good ideas is the only way you can prove to her that you're on the magazine's wavelength

So it's up to you to keep your eyes and ears open. Cut interesting items out of newspapers and make a note of people/places/topics you hear about on the radio. Start an ideas file and fill it with all your jottings and cuttings. If a friend tells you about an experience she had with her estate agent, ask yourself if this might make a good article. You're not exploiting her, just using her story as the catalyst for what could turn out to be an altogether different feature.

Are you an expert, through work or study, in an area that doesn't get enough objective coverage in general magazines? Or could you write about it for a specialist or trade publication? Once again, it's important to assess the knowledge and interests of your potential readers. An article about the training of social workers would be treated differently in *Society Guardian*, *Time Out* and *She*.

If you feel your brain is totally devoid of any feature ideas, don't panic! There are ways of finding inspiration.

Exercise 2

Think of a word: something simple and everyday like house, book, green, coffee. Now use it as the inspiration for a list of feature ideas, matching each one to a suitable magazine. Imagine how the article would look, how long it would be, who you would interview, etc. Here are three rough ideas on 'coffee':

1 A feature on some of London's most famous and distinctive cafés. From Hampstead's patisseries to Soho's espresso bars and the Turkish coffee houses of north London. Who's in charge? Who are the regular customers? This would be an atmospheric, fly-on-the-wall piece with lots of grainy black and white photos. Might suit the magazine of the *Sunday Times* or *Evening Standard*.

2 An in-depth look at the world's major producers, the political complexities of harvesting in countries like Kenya and Nicaragua, and how inequitably the profits are shared between poor farmer and rich City broker. Suitable for *New Internationalist* or *Observer* magazine.

3 Coffee and health. Are we dicing with death every time we brew up a cuppa? Is decaff the answer? What about this new cholesterol scare? Interviews with producers, scientists, addicts, ad people. Very busy, informative article across a double-page spread, for *Woman* or *Me*.

You get the idea? Maybe you don't want to write articles like this but it's a great way of cranking your brain into activity, and will show you that you're capable of coming up with lots of good ideas.

The approach

So . . . do you send in your completed feature 'on spec' or do you approach the magazine with a list of ideas? The simple answer is: it depends. Big-name magazines tend not to have the time to read through stacks of unsolicited articles – they may even warn you of this on their contents page. Smaller magazines, however, often publish features that have been submitted on spec.

You could phone first to find out if they take freelance material. What's their lead-in time? (In other words, how far ahead do they work? It's no good ringing in May to suggest a piece on Wimbledon when they're planning their November issue.) If they haven't said 'thanks but no thanks', the response you'll probably get is: 'Can you put it in writing?' At least now you know who to send your ideas to.

What you write in your letter is up to you, but I reckon the following (adapted accordingly) isn't a bad start:

Dear Kate Brown
Following on from our phone conversation yesterday, I'm writing to you with some feature ideas for *Human Resources* magazine and also to tell you a little more about myself.

As a senior social worker with nine years' experience at the 'sharp end', I feel well qualified to write about this subject, but I do appreciate that you may not be able to commission a writer who is new to your magazine. I'm happy to submit my first feature to you 'on spec' because I'm a regular reader of *Human Resources* and am very keen to write for it.
1 First idea
2 Second idea
3 Third idea.

I can come in to your office to meet you and discuss any of the ideas in more detail. In the meantime, I'll leave you to think about them – perhaps I'll phone in a couple of weeks to see what you've decided.
Yours sincerely

It's a good idea to find your feet by choosing topics you have better credentials to write about than one of her staffers. Outline each idea in a couple of sentences, explaining how you'd cover the subject, who you'd interview, what your angle would be. Don't lie about your experience (or lack of it) in journalism, but enclose one or two relevant cuttings, if you have them.

Every established writer was new once, and a good features editor may be more inclined to consider an article by you if she doesn't feel under any commitment to use it. The advantage of this approach is that your first feature for her will be one she has already approved of as an idea, which is much better than sending her something she didn't expect, doesn't want and perhaps won't even read.

And the reason for telling her you'll phone in a couple of weeks is that: (a) now you *have* to! and (b) she's less likely to 'sit on' your letter. The important thing is to sound confident, show her you understand the magazine and have something to offer it.

If she says 'yes' to one of your ideas, you'll probably talk about it in more depth with her before getting started. Take thorough notes of your conversation with her so you know exactly what's required. Establish length, format, deadline, and the magazine's rate of pay. This can range from £40 to £300 per 1000 words.

Interviewing

Interviewing can be scary, occasionally disastrous, but it's better to quote food additives expert Dr Jane Smith direct than to lift huge chunks on the subject from some dusty tome in the library.

If you take shorthand, great. If not, teach yourself to write clear, concise notes that you can understand afterwards. The advantage of note-taking is that you need only write down what's relevant. The disadvantage is that you can fill your pad with total gibberish which makes no sense the next day. So read through your notes as soon as possible and fill in any gaps while the interview's still fresh in your mind.

Tape recorders are a good idea if you're interviewing more than one person. They also provide an accurate record of the interview if you're covering a particularly controversial subject. But I've had a few disasters with tape recorders: when I forgot to replace batteries or interviewed someone next to a very noisy cappuccino machine. Also when you're transcribing, it's hard to judge what's important, and you may have to wade through hours of tape in order to use just one quote.

When you set up your interview, be sure to say how long it will take and give your subject a rough idea of the format of the article and their part in it. If you're interviewing someone face to face, try to choose a location which is not too noisy, too full of distractions or hangers-on; your subject may feel unable to answer personal questions if she's surrounded by friends or colleagues.

Have a list of prepared questions in front of you but be flexible if the interview dictates it. Be in control. If your subject strays too far from the topic, bring her back. Don't ask someone who's very busy and important for information you could easily have checked in *Who's Who* – it just wastes time and implies that you haven't done your research. Don't wind up the interview until you're sure you've got what you came for and ask if you can perhaps give your subject a ring should you think of some vital questions you forgot to ask.

Writing

There's no hard-and-fast formula for feature writing. Some articles work, some don't. But what you *can* do is cut out a magazine article you've read and enjoyed and try to analyse *why* it worked. Did it have a good opening paragraph? How was it paced? How were facts, anecdotes and information woven into it? How did it conclude? Then do the same with an article you didn't like.

I do have one observation about writing in general which I'm happy to pass on: procrastination is part of the process. So instead of beating yourself with twigs for postponing the moment you put pen to paper, just acknowledge it and accept it. Clean the kitchen, walk the dog, paint the bathroom, whatever . . . *then* write your feature!

Every journalist has their own system of writing and you'll probably evolve your own. This is mine:

1 Go through all the information you've collated and throw away anything that's not relevant. Highlight all the important bits of your interviews, bumf, cuttings, etc. and notate them in the margins so that you can find them easily later.
2 Make a list of all the points you must cover, either in the right order, or in any order – you can number them afterwards.
3 Write. Get it all down. You can rewrite/cut and paste later.
4 To avoid writing far too much, estimate how many pages your feature will fill. For example, I can fit 300 words on to a page. So a 1500-word feature will fill five pages. Page one will be my

introduction, page five will be my conclusion, and pages two, three and four will (I hope!) accommodate everything else.

5 Put the completed feature away and come back to it the next day. You'd be surprised how much you can prune 12 hours later.

Remember . . .

Are you aiming to entertain, inform, inspire, provoke? And what does your reader want to know? Answer her questions.

Choose your words carefully to link and lubricate, to give rhythm and pace, to add wit and style. Use short and long sentences and alliteration for light and shade.

Don't paraphrase people – use their own words to bring the feature to life, and if relevant describe the way they speak. For instance, 'I will survive' has different interpretations depending on whether it was said nervously, defensively, aggressively, cynically, flippantly . . .

The quality of what you write will depend on the quality of the information you've collected.

Presentation

When Spencer Tracy was asked how actors become successful, he replied: 'Learn your lines, be on time and don't fall over the furniture.' The same goes for journalism. A brilliant feature may be rejected if it was too late, too long and looked a mess. Before you hand it in, ask yourself the following questions:

1 Did I do what I was asked to do?

2 Is it the right length? If they asked for 800 words, they don't want 1200. Besides, someone else might cut your favourite bits out.

3 Is it checked thoroughly for good punctuation, correct spellings, consistency of tense?

4 Is it easy to read? One or two corrections, in neat handwriting, are allowed, but don't cover your copy with notes, asterisks and Tipp-Ex. Double space your work and leave good margins.

5 Are the pages clearly numbered? Write 'm/f' (more follows) at the foot of each page and 'ends' at the end.

6 Should I buy a new typewriter ribbon or better quality paper?

And finally . . .

After all that, your feature may be sat on for months, lost, rejected, accepted but totally rewritten. You might never discover why it didn't fit the bill because a busy features editor won't have time to tell you. Perhaps the person who liked your idea has left and her successor is doing a 'new broom' act. Perhaps the magazine is going through subtle changes that haven't yet shown up in published issues. Perhaps they've nicked your idea and have asked a staff writer to do it. (New writers are always convinced that their ideas will be hijacked, but this doesn't happen often, honest!)

So put your feature away and look at it again in a month or so. Maybe then you'll see why it was rejected. Or you'll suddenly think of some new way it can be written for a totally different market. But don't keep sending the same grubby article to seven magazines in a row because (a) it will give off an air of rejection, and (b) every magazine has different readers and different requirements.

But there again, it might have been accepted! If so, don't waste time. Send in more ideas. Capitalise on your new contact, show you're keen and use this cutting as a way of getting a foot in the door with other publications.

Keeping the Momentum Going

Staying on Course
Sue Roe

Continuing, once you've got it started, will feel like the dodgy bit. The trouble is, you will begin to see what you are doing. Once you can see what you are doing you will be absolutely desperate to get to the end. Be careful. Try to slow down. Remember: speed kills. But if you absolutely can't, try something else: try going with the feeling of desperation. Don't put it off. Write at full pelt. Now is the time to cancel your holiday, offend your friends, risk your relationship, decide not to have children, take your phone off the hook, let the mail pile up in the hall. Now is the time to let the world fall into ruins around you.

What? You can't possibly? Well, this can mean one of two things. Either the project is not as important – or not working quite as well – as you thought, or you are simply nowhere near getting to the end. What? You have written a hundred pages and suddenly you have hit on the absolute centre or core of the book, and it might not be going quite as well as you thought? In that case the whole lot might be worthless, a complete waste of time. Perhaps this idea of yours is lousy. Perhaps you just can't write. But hang on: why have you got stuck? Why has this sudden blast of euphoria suddenly been removed and replaced with a kind of seeping doubt? Probably *because* you are on to the next lap. It's starting to feel a bit difficult. Once you finally, eventually, agonisingly got it started, it suddenly started to flow. You reached a kind of climax. And then it just sort of fizzled out. Yes, it does sound as if you are in the middle. Now what?

Look hard at what you have got stuck with. You want to describe someone, something – a place, a character, and you were just about to plunge hell for leather into a description when you suddenly realised you don't really know what you are talking about. There is this character called Bruce. But you have never been to Australia, your own grandfather was not a convict. It is the middle of winter; you have forgotten what it feels like to walk about without a coat in December. You can't really do an Australian accent. You are not a man. You are not forty-two years old. You have never been windsurfing. Whatever were you doing inventing such a character in the first place?

You force yourself out of the house. You hang about furtively outside the travel agent's, trying to catch sight of an illuminating poster about Australia without anyone noticing you and seeing immediately that you have absolutely no intention of booking a flight, you are just some failed writer looking for a bit of subject matter. You go miserably in and ask for some brochures. When you get home, you ring up the local bookshop and see if there's anything on convicts. Or windsurfing. It is your grandmother's birthday, you explain. She has rather catholic tastes, you tell the assistant. You force a laugh, you try to set up a feeling of conspiracy with the bookseller (perhaps she can help you: surely someone can help you . . .).

But whatever are you doing? You are going completely off course. None of this has anything to do with this Bruce character who has suddenly interrupted the flow of your narrative but who was suddenly beginning to feel rather crucial. Why?

Who is he, anyway, this windsurfing, family-history-researching stranger who has suddenly plunged destructively into your narrative midst?

At some level, you know the answer to this; you know Bruce and who he is all right, or he would never have got on to the page. You have two courses of action now. You either need to tell yourself you know about windsurfing too, and convicts – at least the aspect of these things which you are going to need to continue with your story – and you are going to have to trust to the authority of your imagination to see Bruce through. Or – and this is equally possible – Bruce is not an Australian at all; his grandfather is not a convict; he hasn't the faintest idea how to windsurf.

Walk about with him for a few days. Have a drink with him. Try talking to him about your job: no, that's not it. Why not try going to bed with him? No? Well if none of this works, forget about him. Then go back to the bit of the text where things were going pretty smoothly until Bruce came in.

Your character was sitting in a bar minding her own business when suddenly this bloke called Bruce settled himself at her side and started talking. There is definitely a current between them. Something is about to turn the narrative, you can feel a new momentum; something he is getting ready to tell her is about to link up with that idea you brought in two-thirds of the way through section one, and if you can take it in a certain direction, the event you have planned for section three will . . . but wait a minute. She is asking him something again. Your heroine is asking him to repeat something. What was that? She didn't quite catch his name? What?

Hugh?

From where?

East Anglia?

Keep going. Don't panic. The only way out is through. Continuing is full of hurdles like this, full of tangents. With hindsight you will see that these are actually lines of escape which you will deviously have tried to set up for yourself when the going began to get rough, without even realising what you were doing. Once you've got started it will feel like quite a responsibility, you see. It will feel like quite a burden to have elected to carry around for the next few months, possibly even the next few years. You will find that you will be quite amazed at what the writing mind will do to try to distract you at this stage. You will keep trying to get out. The temptation will be to try to find a way of proving to yourself that it isn't working, so that you can feel justified in getting rid of it. It's a bit like trying to manoeuvre your way through a busy airport. You will begin to wish you had never suggested this trip in the first place; you will start wishing you could just go home.

You have already checked in your baggage though; the flight is already booked. It is too late to turn back now. You will just have to fight your way through the crowds. That person who just thumped you across the ankle with his suitcase: swipe him back. Pull a few punches. Keep fighting.

Continuing Fiction
Ursula Holden

I'm over the first hurdle, the fight is on. My characters should be getting clearer – should be dictating to me soon. It's important for me to stay in charge though and not vice versa, they mustn't get out of hand. I must stay faithful to my subconcious, which means examining the wildest thought before dismissing it, believing that the book exists in perfect form inside me. My task is to get it on to the page.

I work on in units of four, often ending a chapter on a note of enquiry or expectancy, to keep myself, and the reader I hope, keen to continue.

There comes a point when it all seems impossible. How do you eat an elephant? I think of Carl Gustav Jung who believed that it was essential for the artist to feel that any creative endeavour was totally beyond his/her capacity. I remember T. S. Eliot's lines 'And so each venture is a new beginning, a raid on the inarticulate with shabby equipment always deteriorating ... For us, there is only the trying. The rest is not our business.' And I imagine the large white hands of Ford Maddox Ford, poised over his typewriter, waiting ... waiting ... These are some of my mentors.

I love writing dialogue, it drives the narrative on as well as revealing character. Constant statement makes for dull reading I try to show rather than state.

The writing blocks will come whatever I do. I feel exhausted, I feel ill, I feel depressed. I believe that the mark of a professional writer is the routing of these blocks and I deal with them in various ways. I vary the position of my table, I do some yoga, I go and work in the British Library. Saying anything that comes to mind into a tape recorder can help. I try to bring my moods, the differing weather conditions into the text, wasting nothing. However diverse my characters are, they must be part of me; I must write through them as well as about them, so no feeling need be wasted.

It is better not to read my favourite authors when I'm stuck. For instance Jean Rhys, Edna O'Brien, or Beth Henley the extraordinary American playwright, all write with a distinctive tone which could affect my own style, and without realising I can become imitative. In fact there are times when I read no fiction at all.

It is lovely when I become aware of the rhythm of my sentences but I feel this should not be obvious to the reader. I'm writing a novel, not a prose poem.

Finding the discipline gets no easier, but now I do have time. I started writing when I had young children and outside jobs. That first book didn't get published but through it I was learning the craft. I tried not to let a day pass without at least a sentence, which meant rising very early. I tried to regard myself as a professional during these long years, though I had little encouragement and it was a long time before I became one.

I like to distance myself from the real heartbreaks of life, not to write about them until time has elapsed. Keeping a diary is valuable and necessary. I feel that what did happen is of less importance than what I can make happen on the page. It's fiction I'm writing, after all.

Just Another Book ('How's it Going?')
Jeannie Brehaut

Last week I bumped into an old friend with a new job who was about to get married. These are the busy years for both of us and I wanted to sit down and talk to my friend properly, but we didn't have time.

She said, 'Are you still "waitressing"?'

'Yeah.'

'How's the writing?'

'OK. It's going.'

My friend did deserve a better answer than that, I know, but I'm so cautious about saying anything before my work's done. Until my book is finished I don't know how I'm going to use what I'm currently writing. If I tell my friend about something I'm doing now then my work might become too fixed, or, by saying it out loud, I could ruin it and decide not to use it. Instead, I ask my friend about her life.

The whole time we've been away from each other my friend has been making things. You can see what she's been doing. When we used to run around together she wore plain black, white socks, red lipstick. She liked dollar-sign earrings. Now she has a cartoon eagle over her heart, hand-knitted, devil dogs in sierra red grinning out at us, one on each hip-bone. I know she dreamed up her sweater, the way I do my novel, cycling home late one night.

We're on the platform at Earl's Court station and everybody is looking at us. I would like to show the book I'm writing to passers-by as well as to my friend, but only when it's finished. If I don't finish my book nobody will ever know what I've been doing. What if I'm writing 'just another book'? I'm afraid I might be and so I don't want to say how it's going. I kiss my friend goodbye for one more year or so and get on the train.

I'm a waitress again tonight. Tomorrow morning I'll be a writer. I've done both activities next to each other often enough to know how. So my problem isn't with finding balance anymore so much as maintaining inspiration. My rent and my telephone bills keep me 'waitressing'. I do (mostly) love the act of writing. Keeping the energy going in one project for a long enough time though is tough.

The novel I began working on five years ago is different from the one I'm writing now. Five years ago I was taking notes on some very based-on-me characters. We've all grown up since then and I've got some good distance between me and them but I'm afraid if I keep working for too much longer I'm going to lose the book I started. It may be that the book I started isn't meant to come to fruition, but I'm too involved in my work to know that. I am writing 'just another book', but with all its limitations and preoccupations I believe it's important. Even when I don't believe it – for weeks I'm writing without inspiration – I sort of trust that my feeling for the work will come back.

When people ask me how my work is going I can't really answer their question. I want friendly interest in what I'm doing, but without anything to show and tell them, I feel a fraud. Perhaps I'll find my old friend and get her to design me something that will answer people's questions. My friends could look and say 'I can see you've been working'. Then we could move on to speak of other things, and one day – when they all least expect it – I'll finish my book, get on the phone to all the people I like, and tell them about it.

Exercise 1: Self-Censorship
Janet Beck and Cheryl Robson

Aim

To identify and overcome a writer's personal blocks with/
without a specific piece of work in a group context.

Method

1 A volunteer takes a chair in the centre of the circle. The leader
  asks her to choose members of the group to 'act out' her blocks.
  For example if the woman in the hotseat feels that a particular
  teacher at school, or a parent, sibling, favourite writer is getting
  in the way of her writing – is acting as a censor – she chooses
  another member of the group to represent each person she has
  mentioned.
2 Women playing the censors then stand around her and place
  their hands lightly on her shoulders, and the volunteer explains
  to them the inhibiting attitudes of the people they represent.
3 The volunteer then begins to talk about her current project, or
  her writing in general, or her feelings about being a writer. Each
  time she says anything that might offend/alienate/upset one of
  the censors, they press on her shoulder and she must ask them
  what she has said to offend them, and then argue against their
  censorship, convincing them to remove their hand. When a
  censor feels convinced, they remove their hand and sit
  down.
4 The process continues until each censor has been confronted
  and has removed their pressure.

Note

A volunteer may choose censors for a variety of reasons. The
censor may be: a friend/relative/colleague who specifically
disparages her writing; a favourite writer who is so good the
volunteer feels that there is no point in competing (this is also a
good exercise for establishing a personal voice); a family
member whose attitudes are important to the woman, and who
is discouraging, or who specifically/implicitly censors a certain

subject area, e.g. a parent may not like a daughter writing about her sexual experiences.

(This exercise is adapted from a workshop given originally by Jules Wright.)

Exercise 2: Getting Past Page 40
Rosalind Brackenbury

Aim

To write the whole thing, not stop out of panic.

Method

1 When writing a novel or longer piece of fiction, there will inevitably be a point at which you decide you do not like what you have written, that you would be much better writing something else. In my experience, it happens around page 40.
2 This is akin to the experience of looking in the mirror before you go out and deciding you hate the way you look. You do not need to take notice of this feeling most of the time. Just notice it and get on.

Note

I think this is a last-ditch attempt by some old habit of self-denigration to take hold of us. Almost inevitably, in the course of any piece of work, this feeling appears. You may panic and think 'I can't possibly go on writing like myself, I had much better write like X or Y. I can't write my story, quick, quick, I must start writing someone else's.'

You may dislike your nose or eyebrows, but you can't stay indoors forever. No more can you afford to get stopped by disliking, momentarily, your own writing.

Exercise 3: Fear of Failure
Janet Beck and Cheryl Robson

Aim

To explore in a group the fears we have about success and failure and to look at the ways in which we try to sabotage ourselves and our work.

Method

1 (a) In pairs, A tells B a problem about work/writing. B demonstrates through *body language* (non-verbally) that she is not interested. Swap over.
  (b) Same pairs. This time, each partner expresses a great deal of enthusiasm and encouragement in acknowledging the other's problem.
2 Discuss these responses and the ways in which people communicated their attitudes. What strategies were used? How do we feel about a negative/positive response? Do we often get a negative response which blocks us? Do we continue to seek encouragement in the wrong places? How do we ensure we get the right response?
3 In groups of three, C tries to interrupt, destroy, distract from the conversation A and B are having. When C has succeeded in steering the conversation in her own direction, stop and swap round.
4 Discuss the strategies that were used to sabotage the interraction between A and B. How did it feel being excluded? How easy was it for each person to sabotage the others?
5 In a circle, the whole group does a round of:
  (a) I could sabotage this group by . . .
  (b) I could help this group by . . .
  (c) I sabotage my work by . . .
  (d) I could help my work by . . .
6 In the whole group, ask for a volunteer to 'mould' or 'sculpt' members of the group into a *frozen picture* of a memory of an incident involving sabotage, either self-sabotage or by another person. The rest of the group walk around, and look at the picture and comment on what they see in it, then give the picture a title.

Note

The tableau or frozen picture is a way of crystallising emotions in one remembered or symbolic image. Members of the group are positioned by the 'sculptor', and the rest of the group discuss the final image whilst they hold their positions silently. Members can swap in and out of the picture in order for everyone to see it.

Exercise 4: Writers' Block?
Angela Brown

Aim

To keep the novel in production.

Method

1 List some of the episodes and experiences that you want to write about in the course of your novel. Do some of them obsess you? (This can be useful. *The French Lieutenant's Woman* came from John Fowles' abiding image of the storm-battered woman on the Cobb harbour wall.)
2 Examine the point at which you are stuck. How far do you need to move on to restart? Leave what space you think you need and just resume where you know you *can* go on writing. Write with enthusiasm.
3 The solution may eventually suggest itself as the subconscious knits the pieces together for you.
4 You may even find that you did not need that unwritten part at all. Anything necessary may be implied in the passage you *do* write.

Exercise 5: Technical Exercises for Word Processor Users
Helen Flint

Displacement activities

There will be times when you *must* write (you have a clear hour, there is no excuse not to) but you can't get your mind in gear. You have, as it were, your thumb out and no car will stop. Displacement activities are not necessarily a waste of time. It's simple – switch on the machine, and *play* – check all the spelling so far, mindless, but it sweeps you through what you have already done and concentrates the mind despite you. Or 'repaginate', or make a fancy typeface for fun. Or change all the names of your characters, then copy the whole document into another document (so as not to destroy potentially useful material) and do a really silly thing with your story like turning it into a play or a poem – this often gives you a strange idea which may turn out to be useful. Lists are also good – open a new document and write a shopping list for each character. One of them will want to buy a packet of condoms or an African machete. Why?

If in your rewriting you come across a sentence or phrase which is pedestrian, you ought to cross it out. It has no business being there. But suppose it's a whole passage which has within it some point or points you very much want to make, which does bear on your overall plan of the book? You don't have to delete it completely. With the word processor you can send the whole passage somewhere for a holiday, either with a return or a one-way ticket. I find this very useful, and in fact when a book is finished I usually discover these 'villains', who are all well tanned and completely drunk with their prolonged holiday, and I wonder how I could ever have fancied them! And yet I'm sure in the past I would have erred on the side of caution and left them there. In a way you are being your own editor and flushing out dubious chunks which, in the normal course of things, your publishing editor would only object to later.

Exercise 6: Listening to Music
Christian McEwen

Aim

To help build on what you have already written.

Method

1 Read over the piece you are working on, and consider what kind of music would be helpful to you. Perhaps Beethoven would help you work your way into the character of the old grandfather in your story. Perhaps you need some Irish folksongs for the cheerful aunt.
2 Get copies of what you need. (Many public libraries have records and cassettes you can borrow.)
3 Look over your particular piece again, and listen to the music. It might be helpful to listen *as if you were* the grandfather or the aunt. But in any case, allow your mind to wander. You are not listening to the music itself, you are listening for the images, the feelings, the connections that it brings to you.
4 Take notes while all these things are still fresh in your mind.

Note

Writing is not necessarily such hard work as it is often thought to be. There are more ways of building a piece than sitting at a desk and frowning. Give yourself the chance to explore the enjoyable ways too.

Exercise 7: Alberta's Trunk
Gerrie Fellows

This business with the little scraps of paper in the night-watches was another sore spot on Alberta's conscience. The following day she would be dazed and incapacitated. And the pile of loose sheets in her trunk had been lying there for a long time, filling it up and making it untidy. They fluttered about in it indiscriminately. One day she would have to come to some decision about them. She could not be for ever opening it, slipping more into it, and shutting it again.
(Cora Sandel, *Alberta and Freedom*)

Aim

In a long poem or poem-sequence, to fit the parts together; to find a coherent structure for the scraps of paper in the trunk.

Method

At a point where you begin to feel overwhelmed by the mass of material:

1 *Visible strategies*
Begin by laying out the papers on the floor
in a line or semi-circle or tree.
Now you can move pages around,
Cut them up and move the pieces separately.
Use blanks to denote a connecting idea, not yet written.

2 *Perspectives*
Think back to your original inspirations.
Have your intentions changed?
How have you travelled from there to here?

What were your first ideas about form?
Do they correspond to what you have now:
Narrative – one story or many stories?
Description?
Interior speech?
One poem/linked poems/collage?
What does the material say to you now about its form?

3 What are the *forces at work* in the material?
V ere are they taking it?
Is this where you want it to go?

Are there questions to be answered or clarified?
Are there changes in perspective through the poem?
Is there one voice or many voices?

4 *Texture*
Take a look at the form of the text;
its sound, its visual appearance, its 'feel'.
Why is this piece of text thin, long on the page?
This one broad, easy going, conversational?

Is a superficial difficulty with the text
actually caused by an underlying problem in content?
Are there contradictions between the 'feel' of the text

and the meaning it carries?
Do these work against the meaning?
Do you want ambiguity?

5 *If a word is a key – ascertain its history.*
Is the title a key to the poem's meaning?
Think about the words;
Break them down into their constituent parts,
Look them up in the dictionaries,
Examine their etymology.

Do the same for any recurrent word-concept.

6 How does the poem conclude itself?
Is its ending hidden in its centre?
Is its ending not a closed final statement,
but *a question posed at the heart of the material?*

7 *Echoes*
Cross check for repetitions.
This is interesting – it shows up concerns and obsessions.
Decide what you want to keep,
where you can make substitutions.
Do you want a literal echo?
Or an echo of substance using different terms?
Or is an event repeated to no purpose?

8 *Cutting*
Deleting a repetition may mean
you cut a link
and have to search for another.
Use this – it may bring out hidden aspects of the material.
Or it may expose a weakness you kept glossing over as you read.

9 *Glossing*
To create a complex poem,
you have to work with temporary constructions,
imagining and re-imagining the whole.
Gloss – assume your material is complete
except where you are taking a close-up view.

Examine everything
but don't pull away all the poem's supports at once.

10 Look at the cross links, the *connections*.
If a piece of text is not in the right position
they will be your pointers to the other possible placings.

11 Keep changing *focus*.
Don't work so close you forget to notice the overall balance.
Examine the particular then look at it in the light of the whole.

12 *Guessing towards the hidden*.
Having clarified the structure,
you can begin now to write the blanks, the missing links.

Note

This exercise is an attempt to formalise certain processes and decisions which I am aware of going through during the writing of long, multi-faceted poems. In my experience there comes a point where the accumulated material has to be examined in the light of original motivations and of new slants which have developed.

This decision-making process may happen many times over during the writing, with different aspects taking precedence at different stages. Some of the functions are most simply achieved by computer (word searches, cutting and moving text) but the computer, though it scrolls the material, gives you only a small window of text at any one time. The value of actually spreading sheets of paper out on the floor is that your eye (and your mind's eye) *can hold different parts of the work simultaneously*, and is not restricted to linearity.

The various steps of the exercise are designed to work interrelatedly as a process, but can also be used singly, individual steps being repeated over time.

Writing Skills

The Rubik Cube
Christine Crow

At last our narrative structure. There it stands four-square on its ocean rock. Is there any reason to stick with it simply by virtue of having first thought of it that way? Working on the trusting principle that to be able to lose or disrupt a certain order is to be able to find it again enriched elsewhere (nothing ventured, nothing gained), why not take that particularly smug or lifeless sequence down a peg or two by twisting it round and hoping to deepen the meaning in turn?

1 Tell your story from beginning to end, progressing smoothly line by line.
2 Now ruthlessly alter its sequence, perhaps thinking through the changed consequences in a diagram to avoid lengthy premature commitment (though remembering that some of the most interesting discoveries come from the process of writing itself, the 'substance' of language allowed to interact with its theme).
3 Equally radical in some ways, rewrite your opening in a different voice or set of tenses or from a different point of view, perhaps even fictionalising the different personae involved in a single consciousness with its impulse towards and away from the finitude of words.

Note

The Lighthouse, my second novel, born from the wish to write turned reflexively upon itself (a useful way to bootstrap oneself into the world of literary form), eventually consisted of three parts: A, B and C, of which the middle section, B – Minerva Peacock's 'writer's journal' describing just such a twist from 'nothing' to 'something' – was originally the first, followed by Ralph Raymond Corbet's first-person account of his adventures as lighthouse keeper (and would-be novelist) in the Bell or Inchcape Rock Lighthouse, just off the north east coast of Scotland where I live. A thinly disguised 'writer's journal' followed by the fiction to which it apparently gave rise? Nothing exactly to set the house on fire there. Twisting my cube a little, I decided to explore what would happen if I split Corbet's narrative in two (A and C) and placed the originally initial journal (now B) in the middle. Result: a challenging two-way structure or even 'Möbius strip'[1] effect in which the 'character', Corbet, was now free to comment critically on the fictional novelist, his wife and proud inventor, by reading the journal of his own conception, finally plagiarising it for his own auto-biographical lighthouse adventure novel, and where – most unexpected topological return of all – the real writer found herself caught up in an intricate, fictionally embodied decon-struction of her own writing and the cultural 'male/female' oppositions at work in language . . . a continuous spiral if not lighthouse stair, and, with it, a host of unprogrammed, multi-faceted (cubist?) ideas obsessively to polish in turn, turn, turn.

Notes

[1] A band twisted in such a way that one can pass from the top to the bottom surface without crossing an edge.

Exercise 1: Unexpected Consequences
Julia Casterton

Aim

This is a game in which a group of writers can play with characters and events, shifting them around in ways that can be startling and very funny. It's a good game to try when you're thinking about different possible structures for a story.

Method

1 Meet together with some writer friends, each with a sheet of paper. The game is like 'Consequences'. You all agree on where the incident will take place. The rest is up to the individual writers.

2 The format of the game goes like this:

    (a) Someone
        meets
    (b) someone
        in
    (c) a particular room/part of the garden/area in the city where you've decided this incident is going to happen.
    (d) One character tells the other about the event.
    (e) They act on it.
    (f) There is a consequence to their actions.

3 It's a good idea if you use the names of people in the room, or people you all know, to keep the stories roughly related.

4 At the end of each stage you fold down your sheet of paper and pass it on. The narrative is therefore an amalgam of all the players' ideas, and you get a full sense of the possibilities that can emerge from two characters meeting together.

5 When you've completed your narrative you pass it on to your neighbour. Then take it in turns to read out what you have on your sheet. The different parts will connect up together, but in the most bizarre ways.

Note

This game shows how much you can get out of playing with unexpected configurations of character and incident. It's good for revealing the humour/absurdity/strangeness that can come out of not quite knowing what's going on in your narrative. It can also develop into 'cut-up' writing, where narrative unity is completely disrupted by splicing two or more stories together.

Exercise 2: The Perfect Plot
Helen Flint

Aim

To rescue the plot from the mundane.

Method

1 Find your perfect plot: when I first read 'Sir Gawain and the Green Knight' I felt strange all over; it was as if I had finally come across the story I had been waiting to hear all my life. Quite apart from the fact that it has *everything* – sex, violence, a moral, sociology, psychology, a chase, betrayal, loyalty, paradox, suspense, drama . . . it has a perfect symmetry which is divinely satisfying.

2 Aim for this symmetry – even make diagrams of stories or books you have enjoyed and see what I mean. Martin Amis' *London Fields* is a good one – it is cruciform – the pub is called the 'Black Cross'.

3 Design the plot with love – it has to be a thing of beauty in itself, not just a necessary evil.

4 Never never never panic at the end and let it all be a dream!

5 Ending at the beginning is a bit dreary (oh gosh it was cyclical after all, what a surprise!).

6 Nor should you trail off into dots, leaving the reader puzzled or furious or . . .

7 Ideally the *end* of the story/book/poem/play should be both integral with the plot and advance it or provide, in the case of a poem, perhaps an epigrammatic 'summary' of the outcome (in a deeper sense than simply 'what happened'). Beware of sudden reinterpretations of the entire goings-on of the story – the reader might feel cheated and alienated by this (what a fool I've been), unless the story is a murder mystery and it only makes sense in the light of this revelation.

Note

Sir Gawain of course has the ideal ending – an explanation which lifts the surreal events of the plot into myth.

Exercise 3: Fast Forward/Freeze
Joanna Scott

Aim

The purpose of this exercise is to explore the potential of any given moment of narrative. Suspense pushes both the writer and the reader forward, sometimes pushes too forcefully, so that we don't have a chance to appreciate the meat of a narrative. It's as though when we're reading we're worried that the end won't wait for us, especially as that end becomes more defined. And when we're writing, we're aware that the end – open or closed – gives the fiction its form; we want to know that end, seize it, use it to justify all the preceding words. But digressions, pauses, hesitations, disruptions are as necessary to a fiction as suspense – indeed, they serve to intensify suspense. So *Fast Forward/Freeze* aims at delaying the end and binding the writer to the middle of the narrative.

Method

There are two basic parts to this exercise.
1 In three pages, tell the 'story' of an accident that a character has narrowly avoided. You may focus on a single character, you may use a first person narrator to describe the accident herself, or you may keep your narrator detached. Give as much or as little background material as you want.
2 Choose a moment from this three-page narrative and without moving forward in time, extend it over three pages. Describe an image in detail, describe a digressive thought, describe the character's panic or calm, describe sounds and sensations. Fill the pages with words without using these words to carry the plot forward.

Note

Nathalie Sarraute's *Tropisms* are helpful models for this exercise. Each of Sarraute's succinct fictions is richly detailed and resists the conventional forward movement of narrative without sacrificing suspense. In my own work, I've tried to translate this 'exercise' into a process, so that as often as I'm writing toward the end, I'm dawdling, examining, and even wandering far, far away.

Exercise 4: The Description of Objects in Context
Frankie Finn

Aim

To explore different ways of describing the same object. Choosing a descriptive angle.

Method

This is an exercise which can be done fairly quickly; it is concerned with the reasons for choosing a particular descriptive perspective rather than with descriptive precision.

1 Imagine a chair. Jot down a few details about it, e.g. armchair: old, saggy; or office chair: swivels, squeaks.

2 Write down five names at random. Quickly sketch a character for each name. Try to make them very different from each other.

3 Imagine your characters each taking a turn to sit down in the chair. Write down a few details about how each person does this: do they throw themselves into it, or position themselves neatly on the edge of the seat? Is this a chair they feel comfortable in?

   Now jot down a few points about the *chair* which echo or strongly contrast with aspects of each of your characters. For example, for character A the bright buttons on the back of the chair might echo her eyes, for character B stumpy chair-legs may contrast with thin legs, etc.

4 Choose one of your characters. Imagine this character is sitting in the chair. Write a monologue beginning: 'Sitting in this chair reminds me of . . .' Make it about a memory. Come back to the chair every now and again. (Allow five minutes.)

5 Imagine the empty chair in some unlikely place. What does it look like now? Write a quick description concentrating on the theme of the object being out of place. (Allow five minutes.)

6 You are sitting in the chair. The chair develops wings. How does it fly? Where does it go? (Allow five minutes.)

7 The chair is back in a room which contains a lot of furniture. Something is hidden under a cushion on the chair. Decide what it is. Your intention is to mention the chair, interestingly, but not too obviously; you don't want to disclose the whereabouts of the missing object yet. How would you do this? You could, for instance, let a cat walk in and rub against it; or follow a ray of sunlight around the room; does the chair have a certain patterned cover which is echoed by the wallpaper? Has its leg made a mark on the floor? Decide on a strategy and jot it down.

Note

As I write, I become increasingly aware of the function of my description of objects in relation to the work as a whole. What do I want to convey through descriptions? Am I primarily concerned with setting a scene, creating an atmosphere, or using the object to give the reader an insight into a character? Is the object's importance largely linked to plot, or do I wish to use it to echo an image or theme?

If my object seems unconnected to the work, then perhaps I should discard it. I have to *choose* which objects I want to highlight and which particular descriptive slant to take. Too much detailed description will clutter my intention.

Exercise 5: Why Here, Why Now, Why These People?
Sheila Yeger

Aim

To move away from generalisation to the particular when writing for the theatre.

Method

Ask yourself these questions and demand an answer.

1 *Why here?*
Where shall I locate my play? Don't choose the setting at random. It informs what you have to say. A play set in a launderette, for instance, will evoke images of hygiene, cleanliness etc. Your setting should liberate your ideas, not constrain them. Think wide, think open, explore, test out, experiment.

2 *Why now?*
What is the best point of entry into your story? Is it necessary to tell the story from the beginning? Do we always need to know all the facts? What has just happened, or is about to happen which sparks off the events in the play? What is special about *this* moment; what makes it different from other moments? Is it a high point, a low point, a crisis, a crux?

3 *Why these people?*
Why are *these* the characters in your play rather than any others? What is the particular interaction between them which sparks off conflict, leads to crisis? Can you give each character an authentic voice? Do you know them well enough? Can you let them speak without interrupting them?

Notes

Why here?
Adrienne Rich remarked that women live their lives in one room. So you may find it liberating to set your play in one all-purpose setting which encompasses and informs what you want to write about, rather than depict a naturalistic setting which constrains you.

Marie, one of my workshop students, wrote a play about two women accused of attempting to defraud a supermarket. It was about the individual against the might of the establishment, about buying and selling and big business. At first she used a series of naturalistic settings but then started to see that it might be more effective to set the whole piece in a supermarket, using the objects to be found there in a non-naturalistic way to tell her story. So the three-piece suite on sale in the corner of the store could be deployed as the 'living room set' she needed, and the Tannoy system could be used to relay the songs she wanted to point up the action.

In the same way, a play about an artist might be set in an art gallery or a studio, where all the paraphernalia of the artist's life would come naturally to hand. There is no need to be *literal* about setting in the theatre. Objects can serve a variety of functions. Spaces can be differentiated, pinpointed, subtly changed by lighting. Theatre is magic and you are the magician. The audience is only too willing to enter into the fantasy world you create.

Why now?

Experiment with different approaches to timescale. You could start at the end and work back to the beginning. Past and present can co-exist on the stage, the one informing and illuminating the other.

Ask yourself what sequence of events will be most *dramatic*, will most excite the audience, make them want to know 'what next?'

Sometimes the question is not *what* happens, but *why* it happens. Iris, another workshop student, set her play on the day in which two elderly people are found dead by their son, having carried out a suicide pact. The events of their lives are then shown in a series of flashbacks, while the son awaits the arrival of the police.

Exercise 6: Image-Making
Caeia March

Aim

This exercise is in two parts which may be used together or independently. The aims are (a) to explore familiar images in new ways and (b) to create new images. A further aim/extension could be to use the images as a basis for characterisation/ atmosphere/or mood. As a group exercise, the exchanges of images and ideas can be very interesting, leading to poetry, autobiography and fiction. In a group each part takes a minimum of two hours, if ten women are sharing their work.

Part 1: Landscape

Method

For this part a large selection of pictures and photographs of landscapes is required – national and international, urban and rural, taken during night or day and in all forms of climate/weather. A group might make such a collection, lending and borrowing personal photos, pictures from old calendars and adverts. An individual might borrow a selection supplemented by library books – sections on different continents, meteorology, and geology.

1 From the many and varied pictures on display choose one or two which feel right for you at this moment.
2 Now sit with the pictures in front of you and talk to yourself as if you are the landscape in the pictures. Start with 'I am a . . .' then name the place: 'I am a river bank . . .', 'I am the ocean . . .', 'I am the sky . . .'. Then, talking to yourself, begin to say what you are like as this landscape: 'My colours are . . .', 'My outline is . . .', 'My surface is . . .', 'Inside I am . . .', 'Overhead/above me are . . .', 'My feelings are . . .', and name everything else that comes to mind: how you are, what you are, how you feel, how you look. Then think about the landscape in the past and in the future. Talk to the landscape, using 'In the past I was . . .', 'In the future I shall be . . .'. Think of colours, textures, shapes and moods. Think of any living things that have a positive connection to this landscape. (Leave this out if it doesn't feel right.)
3 Now, with the picture beside you, write down what you have spoken to yourself. Do this in any order that comes to you. It doesn't have to be the same order as when you were talking to yourself. Other things may come as you write – they can be included if you want them to be.

Note

Some landscapes/seascapes/skyscapes will work for you and some will not. Some will work sometimes and others at other times. Some aspects/parts of landscapes may be more significant than others. The meanings may shift while you are doing this exercise. What you think you will do when you begin may not be what comes up once you have started. Go with whichever sequence emerges.

Part 2: Trees

Method

In addition to writing materials, you will need plain paper for drawing and coloured pens/crayons/pastels for this part. Some women like to repeat this part from time to time, as the variety of response is extraordinary, both for an individual over a period of time, and within a group, where it's fun.

1 Think of a tree, any tree in any context.
2 Draw the tree, in any way, with any combination of materials. (If you use pastels, spray them with fixative to avoid smudging.)
3 Talk as the tree 'I am a . . . tree.'
  Then describe yourself as the tree:
  My branches are . . .
  My trunk is . . .
  My leaves are . . ./I have no leaves because . . .
  My roots are . . .
  Around me is/are . . .
  Above me is/are . . .
  Below me is/are . . .
  In the past I was . . .
  I came here from . . .
  In the future I shall be . . .
  My feelings about all this are . . .
4 When you have talked about yourself as the tree, thinking of everything you want to include, write what you have said, in any order, as it comes to you, adding anything you feel like.

In a group you can then show the group the image you have created, and read or speak about the words that accompany the image.

You can use this part of the exercise as a mental springboard to create other images, which may not arrive so freely as the tree did, but which may be enlightening, exciting and interesting for autobiography and fiction.

Suggestions to try are: any other plant; a form of climate/

weather; a vehicle, e.g. train/ship/plane/car/carriage/pram/set of skis/roller skates; an animal; a vase; a piece of furniture (this is a classic!); a building or boundary; an amount of time; a geological event/movement (e.g. a glacier).

5 This work on image can then take you into further writing, using imagery to create character, mood and atmosphere. The possibilities are infinite.

Note

In a group it is important to set up such exercises in an emotionally safe context. Since part of the aim here is to *blur* the boundary between autobiography and fiction, both parts of the exercise involve risk taking, both at a conscious and an unconscious level. If two images or more come to mind in a group situation, I suggest a woman writer has the right not to reveal the more risky image(s), to take care of herself. Having said this, there has been so much laughter, love and recognition in these image-creation assignments that it would be a shame not to try them.

Editing As You Go
Joan Riley

There is no denying that one of the chief stumbling blocks for new writers is editing. A great deal of exciting and innovative work falls down because the construction – although fresh and imaginative – is hidden deep in a clutter of excess words and stilted phraseology. There is no point, for example, telling someone that the temperature on a particular day is unseasonably hot or below zero in the hope that they might feel some form of involvement. Your writing has to demonstrate that sense of heat or cold.

Suppose I want to give a sense of heat. I could, of course, just say it was hot. Equally I could tell you the temperature. The trouble is neither of these statements would give you the *feel* of heat. By contrast, if I talk about the physical manifestations of the heat, I am inviting you, the reader, to participate in the experience. I can do this by talking about parched ground or baked earth or by using such picture-evoking phrases as 'the heat shimmered just above the pavement', 'the heat was a tangible thing wrapping around her like recently ironed clothes', or 'it was airless outside after the goose-pimpling chill of the air-conditioned shop'.

Equally problematic is the text that insists on describing every step and every individual movement each character makes. In my experience I find that unncessary inclusions slow the pace of the story and become tedious for the reader. How many times have you found yourself skipping pages and paragraphs in an otherwise gripping book because somewhere along the line either the thread of the story started to unravel, or a particular scene or incident drags on beyond the point where it can hold your interest?

What is important is to get a sense of balance, to follow the instinct that says this is enough and not to push along a description or scene just to have another page of writing to add to the pile. The discipline of writing is to be able to go back and delete or rework, however painful this process may be.

Sometimes the weak points are where we simply used words for convenience. For instance in the middle of a flow of words we might substitute a word or a phrase when just the right expression eludes us. This is a useful and valuable method of working. To stop and look for the correct phraseology might mean that the original creative thoughts that followed would be lost forever. And yet once the flow of ideas is down it is quite easy to see the structure as complete and to allow these substitutions to be forgotten.

The same scenario can be turned on its head. There are also times when the flow dries up and somehow there is a gap in our thought process which makes it difficult to move the story on. The temptation is to push the story along, tell the tale when what you probably should be doing is putting the distance of time and space between you and the work, thus allowing yourself to return to it fresh. Remember it is better to have spent time getting your writing right rather than to have a requisite number of words on the paper that have nothing of originality or creativity in them. Discipline is all well and good but if the story is not working it is better to settle for less in word terms than to write yourself into a corner and a possible block.

Eureka
Christine Crow

'Vouloir, vouloir, et, *même*, ne pas excessivement vouloir'
'To wish, to wish, and *even* not to wish excessively' (Paul
Valéry)

No wonder Archimedes found inspiration in the bath. Not only
can writing damage your health (you can pass out at your word
processor through not remembering to breathe), but insufficient
distance can damage the health of your writing as well. Ideas
become dry and airless, lacking the quality of 'voice'. (We
are on the other side of the fence now, you notice: unable to
break off from writing, there where, before, we were unable to
begin.)

A bath, a walk, yoga, music, the fertile interruption of a
night's sleep and perchance, as every mathematician also
knows, the solution of the problem in a dream (reflected or
invented dreams can usefully find their way *into* the work as
well): all such acts of conscious deflection demand a paradoxical
form of effort and will-power based on trust in the waters on
which we must remember to cast our bread. A faint source of
light seen more clearly from the corner of an eye? Freer
movement of unconscious or semi-conscious associations to
combine in different, unexpected ways? Whatever the case, the
power to let in the x-factor of experience is obviously of vital
importance in such things.

1 If your situation allows it, experiment with writing for different
  lengths of time and at different times of day. While a certain
  degree of fatigue may help loosen a certain type of imagination
  (meticulous editing can come later), too much can be detri-
  mental – again that precious judgment which treats the self as a
  living organism with different levels of response all equally to be
  catered for in some form.

2 If you are a bath addict, notice how this particularly relaxing
  form of interruption seems to allow previously trapped 'ideas'
  to bubble, flow, well up or breathe again almost immediately
  (no wonder terms to do with water or breath are so often found
  in the context of creative invention), particularly those to do
  with the form or structure of the work as a whole . . . a shift of

focus doubtless permitting you to jump from your bath – Eureka! – and run for your text if not through the town.

3 Only slightly different from the cultivated creative lacuna is a form of redirected concentration as in meditation (L. *medieri*, 'to cure'?), where, once emptied of the immediate problems of narrative structure and so on, your mind can let itself be filled instead with the presence of some simple thought or object: a tree, a cloud, a nearby piece of furniture . . . Such mental exercises (L. *ex-arcere*, 'to drive out of enclosure') seem not only to enhance the yield of perception, but, however indirectly, the 'grain' of the voice as well. Form and emotion go hand in hand and the inception of many a successfully living poem may even depend on something as simple but neglected as remembering to deepen and slow down the breath.

However eagerly awaited our ideas for writing, their intrusion in the heart of that carefully achieved passivity can be irritating and inconvenient (constant grabs for a notebook in the middle of the night or when dripping from the bath). Always hoping for the point where individual ideas repeat themselves and become redundant by fitting into an already established structure, I myself frequently make use of a kind of mnemonic – four or five favoured objects stored in pre-arranged sequence (a goat, a clock, a lighthouse, say) – with which quickly and easily to associate even the most abstract concepts or words: visually wrapping a red chiffon scarf for Mary Wolfe round the horns of my goat should I want to remember a way to allude to Little Red Riding Hood, for instance, or making the hands of the clock emit the smoke of 'Auld Reekie' if the word 'Eureka' is needed for the present piece. The mind is a natural computer rearing to be programmed and activated with the twinkle of an eye.

On the other hand isn't the whole point of 'Eureka' a trust that the idea will come back by itself if it's worth its bath salts? A comforting thought for people with only restricted times available for writing is that full-time writers often generate strange problems of their own. In such important matters lightness is all, though one may need long apprenticeship to appreciate the fact.

Exercise 7: Point of View
Christian McEwen

Aim

To rescue a piece of writing which has got stuck.

Method

1 Most people tell a story from the point of view of their regular selves: that is, in the past tense, and using the first-person singular. Look at the piece of writing you have in front of you, and consider whether some other angle might not better serve your purpose: present tense for example, and the dominant voice not yours, but your little brother's.
2 Make these changes for a scene that is important to you.
3 Allow the new information that the changes bring to infuse your sense of the whole piece.
4 If it works for you, keep going.

Note

There is a kind of leeway, a generosity of perspective, that comes when you tell a story in a voice that is not your own. It can free the imagination, make you more forgiving, both of other people and of yourself. If you have a lot of pieces which never quite got off the ground, it is a good way to salvage them.

Exercise 8: Tongues of Babel
Joanna Scott

Aim

Literary critic Henry Louis Gates has described the linguistic changes in the contemporary world as 'the reemerging presence of the tongues of Babel'. He's referring, specifically, to the breakdown of the 'Eurocentric notion of a hierarchical "canon" of texts.' While some critics complain about the gentrification of language, Gates sees a diversification as oppressed groups acquire unique voices. The challenge for these groups, according to Gates, is to 'reshape the critical canon with our own voices in our own images'. It's a challenge that every woman writing today should take on. This exercise focuses on the development of a voice that is supposed to be silent.

Method

In five pages, your 'narrator' will confide in her reader. The basic elements of the situation are this: an object has been broken. No one but your narrator cared about this object; no one but your narrator thinks twice about its loss. Your narrator describes the object to the reader and indirectly – slyly, timidly, inadvertently, purposefully or satirically – reveals herself.

Note

With this exercise I've tried to design conditions that make Gates' challenge to black critics ('our own voices in our own images') the main challenge to the writer. The narrator cannot speak directly about herself – no one wants to listen. But with innuendo and metaphor, in a voice that is distinctly hers, she tells what she needs to tell. The *Soweto Stories* by the South African writer Miriam Tlali are a particularly rich source of inspiration, filled as they are with private, public, and tribal languages and narrated by women who are supposed to do nothing but listen.

Exercise 9: The Murderer Wore Pink Socks
Nicky Edwards

Aim

To add substance to your characters, however slight their role.

Method

1 Pick a minor character from a story you have written or are in the process of writing.

2   What information about this character are you going to provide
    to the reader? (e.g. 'A grizzled man, in his forties, leant against
    the Belisha beacon, nonchalantly picking his teeth with a
    flick-knife.')
3   List all the details about the character you are not going to
    supply to the reader. What is his/her name, age, occupation,
    place of abode, height, etc? What did s/he have for tea? Does
    s/he read a newspaper? If so, which one?
4   When you feel you know everything there is to know about this
    character, down to the colour of their socks, go back to the
    story. What purpose does the character serve? Does s/he do
    anything. (e.g. 'With a cry of inarticulate rage, the man flung
    himself at the Secretary of State for Transport, knife in hand.
    "Build a motorway through my grandad's allotment, would
    you?" he demanded, poised for the fatal blow.')
5   Go back to the list of details. In the light of what you now know,
    is his/her speech and behaviour in character? If their role in the
    story is to remain unchanged, is it plausible that s/he is wearing
    pink socks?

Note

Consider how much more you need to know about your
characters than it is necessary to reveal in the story. If you can't
believe in the people you have created, how will the reader be
able to?

Exercise 10: Character Stereotypes
Rahila Gupta

Aim

To make the writer aware of the dangers of stereotyping and to
move in the direction of building a rounded, three-dimensional
character.

Method

1   First, it is worth spending time thinking about stereotypes. If

you are working in a group, start by listing characters from TV dramas, novels and short stories. When you have reached a consensus about one or two characters, the discussion should be steered in the direction of why these characters are stereotypes and what could be done to round off the character. Part of the discussion should take into account the role the character has in the drama or fiction and, if it is a subsidiary role, how much space could or should be given to developing it further. If you are doing this exercise as an individual you could list stereotypes and write down why you consider them to be stereotypes and then note how you would develop them further.

2 (a) Imagine that you have picked up the phone to ring a friend and instead of getting a dialling tone you have picked up a crossed line. There is a particularly dramatic conversation going on. You tune in to it for five minutes. Write down a dialogue which has no beginning or end, and which has very few clues as to the context. There is only one clue and that is that the two agree to meet in some public place to carry on this discussion.

(b) From the dialogue and other clues such as the tone or inflection of voice, accent, silences, who interrupts whom, etc., write a character sketch for both characters which should include what you think their occupations are, how they might dress, whether they are cruel, kind, intelligent, jealous, etc.

(c) The next stage is when you turn up at the imaginary meeting place. You are well placed to hear the conversation and you now get many more clues about the characters' lives. What you hear and see now will probably overturn many of your first assumptions. Write a fuller character sketch for each character in turn, detailing these changes and any additional information you have gleaned.

(d) Spend a short time thinking about or discussing each stage of the exercise. What changes occurred in your writing? Why? Your thinking discussion should focus on any hidden assumptions you may have made in writing the first character sketch. Each group member could be asked to comment on what assumptions they might have made from eavesdropping on that conversation.

172   *Continuings*

Note

The exercise could be developed with a character sketch of the third person who has adopted the role of curious listener, and how the character of this person affected her perceptions of the other two. This would then lead to the question of character interaction. With groups, I have usually stopped at (d) when doing this exercise. The results have been great, sometimes arbitrary though usually hilarious or unpredictable. We have discussed how stereotyping is often the result of a partial perspective, and how sometimes, in popular television drama for example, stereotyping is often deliberate, since the moment you introduce another perspective and the character no longer conforms to the audience's popular prejudices about 'foreigners' or 'women', the drama or fiction loses its 'popularity' and becomes a 'serious' work.

Exercise 11: You and Your Character
Caroline Natzler

Aim

To give you insight into the character you are writing.

Method

Write 100 words about yourself from the point of view of a character you are working on.

Note

This is a challenging exercise, but it does help see characters as real people, so that we are less likely to create stereotypes. Recognising the extent to which we ourselves are or are not in our characters may also lead to a more complex portrayal.

Exercise 12: Everyday Actions
Nicky Edwards

Aim To improve the clarity with which you describe the actions of your characters.

Method

1 Pick an everyday task from the following list:
 blowing your nose
 using a public call box
 standing on your head
 tying shoe-laces
 putting on a pair of trousers
 cleaning your teeth
 mending a puncture
 having a bath
2 Assume that an English speaking visitor from another planet has arrived. She has learnt the language from books, and knows what the words you use mean, but has never performed any of these tasks.
3 Write 50 words explaining how to perform the task which you have chosen.
4 Follow your own instructions exactly, doing only what is written down. Is it possible to achieve the desired outcome on the basis of your explanation alone?

Note

In the event of any personal injury resulting from this exercise, sue yourself for negligence.

174   *Continuings*

Exercise 13: You Don't Know Me But . . .
Zoë Fairbairns

Aim

To find a character's voice; to write dialogue that is alive and convincing.

Method

1 Imagine you are alone in your home.
2 Now imagine that the telephone rings. You pick it up. The voice at the other end says, 'Is that . . .' (insert some version of your own name here, e.g. Mary Smith, Mary, Miss Smith, Mrs Smith, Ms Smith, Mary Jane Smith, etc.).
  'Yes,' you reply. 'Who's that?'
  The voice says, 'You don't know me,' (insert your name again) 'but . . .'
3 Write the rest of the dialogue. Before proceeding, make a quick, arbitrary choice between A and B.
  If you choose A, then your dialogue must end with you banging the phone down on the caller. If you choose B, it must end with you inviting the caller round to your house.
4 The progression from 'You don't know me . . .' to one or other of these endings must be presented *entirely* in dialogue. Everything on the page must be direct speech. You are not allowed to say, for example, 'Her voice sounded sinister.' If you want the reader to know that the voice sounds sinister, show this in what the caller says . . . 'You don't know me, Mary, but I know you. I know all about you. I've been watching you for some time.'
  Nor should you use any he-saids, she-saids or stage directions. Dialogue only.

Note

If a stranger telephones you, the only way you can form an impression of him or her – and decide whether to hang up or welcome them with open arms – is by listening to what they say and how they say it. Similarly, when writing about fictional characters, you can provide a great deal of information about them – and move the story along – by careful attention to voice.

Does this person speak in perfectly formed sentences? If so, does it sound as if s/he is reading them off a card? Does s/he repeat things? Hesitate? Use conventional grammar? Swear? Take ages to get to the point? Interrupt? Are there any national or regional speech characteristics? Any indications of class, age, occupation? Can you identify the sex? If it is not clear from the pitch of the voice, is there any other way of telling? Can you identify, from what s/he says, what her frame of mind is – nervous, confident, manipulative, desperate, helpful, drunk, threatening, diffident? Might s/he be lying? What speech characteristics might lead you to think so?

You don't know this person. You can't see them, or their body language. Focus on the voice. Deny yourself all props . . . not that there's anything wrong with he-said-furiously, or she-whispered, but you would be amazed how often you and the reader can manage without them if you allow fictional characters to reveal themselves through their own choice and arrangement of words . . . as their factual counterparts do.

Exercise 14: Toning Up the Conversation
Angela Brown

Aim

To make conversation more vivid.

Method

1 How many words can you substitute in place of 'said'? List them.
2 Use *Roget's Thesaurus* and a dictionary to explore all the other possibilities. Examine especially which verbs go with which emotions.
3 Avoid using an adverb if a verb will be more eloquent. Compare: ' "Like my hat?" she said jokingly' with ' "Like my hat?" she joked.'
4 It may be useful to shorten the exchanges between characters

and embellish the use of the verb: ' "I don't intend to remain here any longer," he said' becomes ' "I'm not staying," he snarled.'

Note

There are, however, some wonderful exchanges to be written on the 'He said . . . She said,' pattern. Brian Patten's 'Hair today, no her tomorrow' in *Storm Forces* is a wonderful poem exploiting the breakdown of trust between a couple using the technique. This pattern demands that dialogue should work especially hard to create the tensions, conflicts and ironies of the exchange.

Convincing Dialogue
Valerie Taylor

A convincing dialogue is not how we often imagine. People do not answer each other, or even listen to each other. Conversation does not follow a logical sequence. People often talk in parallels and jump about from one subject to another. Each person has their own voice and unique way of talking. We all carry voices in our heads. Some people are more able to conjure them up, but we have all heard them since childhood. We also have the voices of different parts of our personality which we can use in writing. The authoritarian voice, the masochist's voice, the child voice, can all come from the same person. Equally we have the voices of our parents in our heads, not just the tone but the implicit messages they carry. One way of getting at these implicit messages is to write down actual memories ('Have you seen your face when it's angry') and then write a scene dramatising the implicit message ('Don't be angry, it's ugly').

Notebook work is important for dialogue. If you are working in a group, it is well worth spending time taking down overheard conversations and reading them back to the group. Over a period of time hearing other people's contributions as well as taking down the dialogue, you begin to get a real feel for the way people talk.

Exercise 15: Dialogue in Fiction: Adverbs, Verbs, and Action
Frankie Finn

Aim

To explore the use of adverbs, verbs and action to inform dialogue.

Method

1 Write down the sentence: 'Oh, I do like your dress,' said Jane. The speaker of this sentence could be sending a number of possible messages beneath these words. She could be saying for instance:
  (a) I want you to like me.
  (b) I want you to know that I like you.
  (c) I want you to think I've got good taste.
  (d) I don't know what to say.
  (e) I want you to look at *my* dress.
  (f) I feel sorry for you.
Jot down these interpretations and add two more of your own to the list – (g) and (h).

2 Write down an adverb which you think will best describe the speaker's tone and intention for each of the interpretations. For example:
  (a) 'Oh, I do like your dress,' said Jane *coyly*.
  (b) 'Oh, I do like your dress,' said Jane *enthusiastically*.

3 Repeat the exercise, changing the verb (said) to one which will more accurately inform the sentence. For example:
  (a) 'Oh, I do like your dress,' cooed Jane.
  (b) 'Oh, I do like your dress,' declared Jane.
(Do not use the same word you used in (2) . . . this might be difficult, e.g. for (b) the most obvious verb might be 'enthused', but if you have used 'enthusiastically' for 2(b), try to think of a different verb.)

4 Write down an action to follow the speech for each of the intentions. For example:
  (a) 'Oh, I do like your dress,' said Jane. She smiled ferociously and sat down at Jenny's feet.

    (b) 'Oh, I do like your dress,' said Jane. She reached out and
       touched Jenny's hand.
5 Select one of your action examples from (4). Continue the
dialogue between Jane and Jenny using adverbs, verbs, and
action to enhance the tones and latent meanings within the
dialogue. Choose carefully and appropriately. Of course, it is
not necessary to qualify each part of the dialogue: let some of
the speeches stand for themselves.

Note

Constructing the immediate framework in which to set a
dialogue is a delicate business. An exercise like this, out of
context, is inevitably rather clumsy, but I hope that it brings out
the main points and potential variations. The larger context –
the novel, the story, etc. – is very important; how much you
qualify or do not qualify the dialogue will depend on the general
style of the work and to what extent you have already developed
your characters. Punctuation: an exclamation mark or question
mark can often be the most economical and appropriate
method of indicating the intended nuance.

Exercise 16: Explicit v. Implicit
Katie Campbell

Aim

To add depth and subtlety through implying rather than
explaining.

Method

Go through the text and wherever something is stated, try to
imply it, leaving readers to draw their own conclusions.

Examples

1 Not: 'I was shopping late,' she said. 'I don't believe you,' he
replied.

or: 'I was shopping late,' she said. He didn't believe her.
but: 'I was shopping late,' she said. 'Oh?' he raised his eyebrows.
2 Not: 'The man was fat.'
but: 'The man's shirt stretched across his belly.'

Note

Wherever possible, what is left unstated is more powerful than what is stated. If the reader is given a chance to infer, s/he will be engaged much more in the work than if the whole story is on the surface.

Exercise 17: The Wolf
Christine Crow

Aim

To write, she wants to write . . . Whether the sensation of controlling or submitting to reality is uppermost, everything in writing comes back to the medium of language: what it can be made to do as a means of individual expression, constructing and transforming the writer's and reader's experience in turn.

How easy to forget that words themselves are already veritable treasure-troves waiting to give access to the dialect if not the wisdom of the tribe. Dictionaries and source books can be used not only to trigger new associations but to create new situations for fiction as well.

Method

1 However humble or well known, spend some time tracking down your central image or symbol (*OED* fullest possible version) and, index cards to the ready, noting its etymology, any alternative or conflicting meanings (how revealing, sometimes, the suppressed 'underside' of a concept), together with quotations designed to show its usage in different contexts.
2 Still permitting yourself to be thoroughly obsessive and single minded, continue to hunt your prey in extra reference books

such as Brewer's *Dictionary of Phrase and Fable* where you can creep up on idioms or proverbs from unexpected angles, pouncing in particular on any potential cross-over from literal to metaphorical realms (useful when you come to move the other way round).

3 Widen the hunt yet further to include dictionaries of myths and symbols. Does the psychological structure of what you have written so far appear to link with any, say, classical myth? Rather than write to illustrate a pre-selected myth – myth imprisons as well as liberates, after all – take the plunge first intuitively (thought/emotion at high speed velocity?). Points of similarity or divergence can then be fed in later, illuminating your own particular slant.

4 The lion, if not wolf, lives on assimilated sheep. Imaginative writing being, in other words, an intricate web of echoes of previous voices, take time also to recall any lurking *literary* associations which you may then choose to bring out more explicitly or not according to the way the work deals with its own inevitable 'intertextuality' . . . Your writing is a spider's web where, conscious or unconscious and with all the steps between, your own imagination is now the wolf spider (genus 'Lycosidae' – books on plants and animals also offer countless possibilities through which obliquely to deepen and perpetuate an associative field), to be devoured and revivified by the vampire-like action of reading in turn.

Note

The idea for *Miss X, or the Wolf Woman* (The Women's Press, October 1990) grew, I like to think, from the magical beacon words 'Virginia Woolf' (always one of my most luminous literary lighthouses), giving rise in turn to 'Mary Wolfe', humble but greedily determined narrator, and only then linking with Freud's *The 'Wolf Man'* and a host of wolfish fairy-tales where prey and predator constantly cross and interact. No matter, by some mysterious means or other, 'wolf' had become the main name of the game.

' "Canis lupus", a somewhat large, canine animal found in Europe, Asia, and N. America, hunting in packs, and noted for its fierceness and rapacity . . .'; the harsh, howling vibration you sometimes get on a cello; the constellation 'Lupus', in turn the name of an 'ulcerous skin-disease' as in Webster's *The Duchess of Malfi*, leading in turn to 'lycanthrope', he [sic] who imagines himself a wolf ... Just as a poem can be unashamedly generated by a rhyme, why not a plot around such different lexical possibilities? All is grist to a lighthouse mill. No need to worry, meanwhile, that our true subject or emotion will fail to find a way to speak 'between the lines' when it positively *needs* lines to speak between.

Unexpected rewards already now, then, smiling back from my dictionaries thick and fast (phases of gestation and execution must obviously be allowed to overlap), and by the time of 'to cry wolf' and 'wolf in sheep's clothing' with their hint of writerly themes such as verbal inadequacy and revelation by disguise (is fiction a means to imagine oneself imagining?), my would-be novelistic tongue is hanging out indeed. Mental ... no, index-card note meanwhile to creep back and make Miss X 'wolf' rather than simply 'eat' her 'Mary, my lamb' sandwiches and for Mary Wolfe (fortunately into pun and parapraxis herself) to turn musician – well, would-be musician – finally to howl like a cello in the hills. Then there's the wolf in 'Ceyx and Alcyone' in my translation of Ovid's *Metamorphoses*[1], turned to stone for its ravenous appetite, doubtless sheep as well as heifers and goats ...

The sheep and the goats, 'binary oppositions', the prey and the predator, the scapegoat, the wolf as scapegoat ... Funnily enough, that's what my novel's already about, or was it really the other way round and – give a dog a bad name – language itself provided the theme all alóng? With such potentially infinite material the test is already now to select and cut back ... not to be tempted to try to 'get it all in' or to use the hunt as a substitute for keeping in touch with that precious 'nothingness' – the lone wolf lighthouse of the imagination – with which it all began.

Although no writer can afford to ignore the vertiginous power of metaphor and its divisive cultural persuasions, not all writing uses pun and word play to reveal the vertigo in this manner. However opaque or transparent, words can none the less keep the wolf from the door while we speak to find out what it needs to make us say.

Notes

[1] I have also found the following reference works particularly useful: *Encyclopedia Britannica*; J. G. Frazer: *The Golden Bough* (1922/1963); Robert Graves: *The Greek Myths* (2 vols., Penguin, 1955/1986); Tom Chetwynd: *A Dictionary of Symbols* (Granada, 1982).

Exercise 18: The Elements Game
Julia Casterton

Aim

To squeeze as much as you can out of the meaning of one word. Poems and stories sometimes turn out thinner and less rich than we first imagined them because we've not made each word work at its full strength, and not followed suggestively enough the associations that flow from a particular word.

Method

1 Gather together your dictionary and your thesaurus. Look up the word *water* in each and follow through all the words associated with it.
2 Write all these words down randomly on a page.
3 Now go outdoors, to a river, stream or lake nearby.
   Spend half an hour looking at the water.
4 You can either turn this into a short narrative, or a poem. Your aim is to make the reader feel as deeply as possible the wateryness of water, all the variability in the character of water.

Note

This is good for enriching and deepening our experience of a subject, and for developing our ability to express it. You can go on to play the same game around each of the remaining elements: earth, air, and fire, so that in the end you'll have an Elements Quartet.

Exercise 19: Metaphors
Joan Downar

Aim

To extend the possibilities of metaphor and simile in poetry.

Method

1 Pick out some extravagant examples of metaphor and simile
(e.g. from one of the 'Martian' poets, who include Craig Raine
and Blake Morrison. The term comes from one of Craig Raine's
collections, 'A Martian Sends a Postcard Home' in which the
alien describes things familiar to us in exotic metaphors:

> Mist is when the sky is tired of flight and rests its soft
> machine on the ground.

Elsewhere he describes a hotel bidet as 'half an avocado', and
dogs' feet as 'four-leafed clovers that leave a jigsaw in the dust.')
2 Consider their effectiveness in contributing to meaning, mood,
clarity, etc.

Exercise 20: Rhythms
Joan Downar

Aim

To encourage writers to listen to a rhythmic line. This is a group
exercise.

Method

1 Introduce a line of verse in iambic rhythm.
Iambic rhythm means the line is written in a number of
parcels called iambs. An iamb is an unstressed followed by a
stressed syllable, thus: ˘ ¯
You can have a line with two or more according to the pattern
you prefer. For example in a traditional ballad:

Jăne Wĭlliaṁs hād ă lōvĕr trūe
Aṅd Edwařds wās hĭs nāme,
Whŏse vĭsĭts tō hĕr fāthĕr's hōuse
Hăd wēlcŏme nōw bĕcaṁe. (sic)

Compare this with a modern ballad 'A Staffordshire Murder' by James Fenton:

Ēvĕřy fēar ĭs ă desīre. Ēvĕřy desīre ĭs fēar.
Tħe cīgařettes aře būrniṅg ŭndĕr tħe třee
Whēre tħe Stăffořdshĭre mūrdĕreřs wāit fŏr thĕir ăccōmplĭceš
Aṅd vĭctĭms. Ēvĕry vĭctĭm ĭs ăn ăccōmplĭce.

The number of stressed syllables in the lines is the same but there is more freedom.
2 Count the stressed syllables in the line.
3 Introduce a line with the same number of stresses but any number of unstressed syllables.
4 Compare the difference in sound; the different freedom.
5 Ask group members to write their own example of a strictly scanned line in iambics.
6 Ask members to write an example of a line which is basically iambic with the same number of stressed syllables.
7 Listen to the completed exercises. Discuss which seem easier to write, and why; the difference in effect, and which method might suit different subjects, e.g. for one specific memory of an event it might be better to employ a strict metre; for a more general remembered description a looser rhythmic pattern might be preferable.

Exercise 21: Rhymes
Joan Downar

Aim

To aid the sensitive use of rhyme in poetry when working in a group context.

Method

1 Give each writer three words of one syllable.
2 Write a list of exact rhymes, e.g. brown/town.
3 Write a list of half-rhymes, with either vowel or consonant sounds repeated, e.g. water/nature; feel/dream.
4 Suggest a stanza length of either four, six or eight lines.
5 Use any of the listed words, either whole or half rhymes (it can be varied according to the skills of the group) in a stanza in which only half the lines will rhyme (e.g. abcb, or abcbdb, etc.)

Note

The variations on this exercise are many. It shows the difficulty of rhyming whilst remaining true to what is being said. It also shows the subtle effects of using half-rhyme.

Endings

Finishing

Exercise 1: The Boomerang
Christine Crow

'. . . experience, this thing which was always more than all that could be said about it – and yet in order to know it, you had to be continually trying to say things about it' (Joanna Field, *An Experiment in Leisure*)

Aim

Strange things happen as we near the end of a novel. Finish writing about wolves and there is bound to be a wolf out there in the garden, at the very least a TV programme with just about everything you needed to know before about the real McCoy. Trusting ourselves to judge when the true cut-off point arises, why should we not allow the work still to profit from that extraordinary interaction of 'inside' and 'outside' (let's not say fiction and reality) which invariably takes place as we come up the straits . . .? One last chance at tapping that magical interaction of language, self and external reality, which the act of writing has been preparing so long now and will not stop performing at the arbitrary drop of the conjurer's hat.

Method

1 Bring your novel to its 'natural' ending, celebrating the hard-won pleasure of feeling so many carefully prepared threads 'pull in' at last. What's the betting that this is the moment for the eyes of your wolf at last to stare back in from the window,

causing you a quite different emotion from the heady satis-
faction of bringing a time-consuming structure to a neat, logical
halt?

2 Look back at your writing from this new, revivified standpoint.
Is there some further twist, some more radical, more fantastic or
simply more appropriate event or possibility contained within it
which you have still not quite brought to rest in the light even
now? Change of frame, change of consciousness or conceptual
shift, don't they say? Appearing to puncture the illusion of the
previous fiction, for instance? While this particular gesture is
not always to be recommended it can paradoxically intensify
the illusion of reality by refocusing on the means of
representation.

3 Experiment with the new ending, being ready to sacrifice it if it
really requires a whole new work instead. The true celebration
now is for something different, the *real* work of the future,
already bubbling in the cauldron. The Queen is dead, long live
the Queen!

Note

A particularly unexpected feedback came my own way as I
finished, or *thought* I had finished *The Lighthouse*. No sooner
had Corbet accidentally set fire to the Bell Rock Tower while
making himself yet another cup of tea out there in his little
circular kitchen (too much tea or coffee is bad for the system, so
no wonder *his* novel never gets off the ground), than I heard on
the evening news that the *real* Bell Rock Lighthouse had caught
fire too (at precisely the same moment as I was writing about it,
as it turned out). Was my novel finished? No, of course not.
Thoughts and feelings on the amazing coincidence were already
crying wolf and seeking fictional ways to flood back in, and it
was no more true that *The Lighthouse* was complete than that I
had set fire to the Bell Rock Lighthouse myself(?).

Ending *Miss X, or the Wolf Woman* was not nearly so
dramatic, but yes there was a wolf out there in the garden, not to
mention a lupine programme on TV, just in time at the eleventh
hour to help draw out one last act of turnskin metamorphosis.
Taking reality by surprise, did we say? Believe in the magic but

not the mystique of writing and the boomerang will come back
and amaze you with the power of your own unconscious throw.

Long Echoes
R. M. Lamming

Endings – especially of longer works of fiction – are notoriously
difficult. Sometimes we start out with nothing in mind except
the ending, and one works towards it – only to find that it has
changed completely by the time we get there. Sometimes, there
simply is no ending; the shape of the work is an open curve, and
ending it can feel like cutting the curve short with a sharp knife.

Sometimes, half-way through a novel, and this is particularly
true of some very plotted work, the writer feels forced to
manipulate characters and events to bring about a resolution
that will fit the premises of the story-line.

So what is to be done?

But perhaps first we should ask what is it we want from an
ending. Do we want it to:

Give a message?

Be true to how the writer feels about a certain slice of life?

Ring true to the reader?

Leave the reader uncomfortable, so that the issues in the
book will haunt her?

Cheer her up? Startle her?

Complete the shape of what we have written, so that the
whole has integrity and is not easily dismissed?

Whatever else we want from an ending, it's a fairly safe bet
that we would like it to leave the piece of fiction in the reader's
head, and not wrench it out, or make it disappointingly chuck-
away: we want the ending to establish the whole, and continue
to have power – a kind of echo – in the reader for a long time
after the book has been lent to a friend who forgets to return it.

How, then, can we help ourselves as writers to achieve this?

1 In life, behind every ending there is a forward momentum,
because so far, thank heavens, even in the worst times such as
during the Holocaust, there have always been survivors and
surviving stories that pass the end-point of any particular
people and their stories. Therefore, unless our writing

concludes with the collapse of the entire universe, the ending requires a frame of on-goingness. This may seem obvious, but in some types of fiction it can be tempting to explain everything away, remove all mysteries, bring all story threads to a stable resolution, and even to make negatives/desolation of everything. This, in a sense, collapses the universe – a conclusion which might sound super-dramatic but which actually turns out to be the opposite; it has no resonance. Where nothing is left with potential for exploration, for being wondered about or for development, there can be no echo – or at best, there may be an after-murmur that has very little meaning for the reader since its references are all completely finished and done with.

So it's worthwhile asking have I left some situation open? Something unsaid? Some thread going forward that if not unresolved is at least not quite explored? If some on-goingness enhances endings, have I achieved that?

2 Beware of succumbing to a postscript. Sometimes the 'true' ending is a page or more back, and the writer's anxiety (have I said enough? did I make my point? should I say a tender farewell to these characters?) has added an apologia. This will diminish the power of the true ending – do you want it?

3 A related point: if you have a short, sharp, shock ending, trust it. Don't soften it.

4 And another need for trust – if you find you have an ending that you don't really want, don't tinker with it, seeking for a compromise with what you wanted. First, try out what you have in its pure form, on a couple of people whose taste and insights you generally respect. What you have may well be the 'true' ending – the one that achieves the work's integrity, and provides the strongest echo – while the ending you have fondly nurtured in your head during the course of the writing may not have been an ending at all, but rather an inverted beginning.

5 Unless you are *quite* sure that cash matters most, never let anyone persuade you that a softer/happier ending will sell more copies and that for this reason alone it is the right one. Remind yourself whose writing this is. If you don't respect true endings, you may start to lose your impetus for setting out in the first place. It is (in my view) many times more dangerous to compromise on endings for commercial reasons than on starting points, and especially in fiction.

6 Yet don't be too sure that you've got the ending absolutely right. It may be right in essence, but slightly too cryptic, or a measure convoluted. Again, try it out on those you respect. If no one understands it, think hard: is this the effect you want? If people murmur the word 'contrived', don't be defensive. Listen to them, and then, after waiting a short time, read the work again. If people offer subjective responses, some saying they love the ending and some hating it, take heart, that's probably a healthy sign; and if they offer views as to what happens *next* to your characters – including views that differ wildly from your own, don't be in a hurry to go back to your typewriter and make your ending more explicit: you have set your readers' imaginations working, the echo is working.

Getting it Right
Sue Roe

The end can be such a joyful, transforming, climatic experience if you really have pulled it off, that you will probably end it at least three times. You will keep thinking you have finished. You will rush round to the copy shop and xerox several copies. You will thrust them into the doubtful hands of your most trusted friends, you will draft a letter to a publisher . . . an agent . . . and then you will wake up the next morning and tear the letters up. You will have to make a few phone calls, sheepishly asking if the friends would kindly refrain from opening that package you sent them, because you've just spotted something that needs redoing. Which bit? Well, most of it, really. (Ending it can be quite expensive, what with the xeroxing costs, the phone bills . . .)

But by the time you get to this stage you will have reached the end in essence, if not in fact. That feeling of euphoria is so dangerously related to one of exhaustion that you will not dare to allow yourself to succumb to it until you really have got the bulk of it through the worst. There will be a nasty humming sort of feeling now, at the back of your head, a bit like a hangover. It will probably last about two months. Then you will have to pull it all out again and do the cosmetics: change this, alter that, cut a section here, and – this is always an interesting bit – begin to see what you have said. That humming period can be quite gruelling. The wretched thing's still sitting there on the floor under your desk. It ought to be finished, but it isn't. *Why not . . .?* Just remember this: you will have to live with this feeling for a while. Don't send it anywhere while you still feel like this about it.

One day when you had intended to do something else altogether (the day after you have got out your writing again, and perhaps deleted the odd comma) you will find yourself putting some music on and just sitting with it on your lap. You'll just have a quick flick through and see what you've said. After a while, it becomes quite riveting. I said *that . . .?* The music is beginning to interrupt your reading, and why have you got that bit about VAT in the 1959 section? You have three women characters: their names are Hannah, Anna and Diana. How on earth did that happen? Anna dies in the first section, but Diana bumps into her in Sainsbury's in section three. Hang on: was it Hannah she bumped into? Don't panic. Don't despair. Just get out the Tipp-Ex and a good black biro. Start defacing your pages. Yes, I know, it will be agony but you will have to do it. Go on. Just scribble all over them, until you get it right.

This bit can take some time, but one night you will go to bed with an unusually peaceful, resolved sort of feeling. The next day you will get up and do yesterday's washing up. Then you will ring the gas board, the electricity board, the town hall and British Telecom. You will tell them not to cut you off, because the cheques are in the post. Then you will get out your cheque book and actually write them. And actually post them. You see: you are as good as your word. Then you will go and get your accumulated mail and open all the envelopes, just to see if there are any cheques or exhibitions or invitations or letters from friends. You will answer not only these but all the others. Then you will get out the hoover.

You will hoover the entire house. Even picking things up and hoovering underneath them. Then you will dust everything. Even the things where it doesn't show. You will stand on a chair and pay particular attention to the bits you can't see. You might as well be thorough. Then you will have a bath, wash your hair, repaint your toenails and open the new bottle of perfume somebody gave you for Christmas even though you're not going anywhere. You will stuff the washing machine and switch off the fridge so that it can begin to defrost. Then you will do something really dramatic: you will tidy your desk. It is still only eleven o'clock. This probably means your novel (play, poem) really is finished.

The Problem of Ending
Thalia Selz

The Czech poet, Miroslav Holub, has written short plays which dramatise the results of conflicts, not the conflicts themselves. Presumably, Holub makes clear from the consequences what the original conflict was. His task suggests that of the story writer whose story 'germ', to use Henry James' term, is some event, real or imaginary, suitable for the climax of a story, rather than its beginning. The writer must begin at the end, then, plotting backward from the climax, or denouement, forge the causal chain that forms the story – a device insisted upon by Edgar Allan Poe in 'The Philosophy of Composition' and discussed at length in John Gardner's *The Art of Fiction*, a book which every fiction writer should read.

Suppose, however, that the author wants to plot forward from a climatic event to its results, in order to emphasise theme? Or suppose that the story germ lies in character? How is the author to arrive at a satisfactory conclusion which develops organically out of the story?

Emma, mother of two young daughters, is returning from the market at noon when she sees a young girl struck and killed by a car. Fearful for her daughters who are coming home to lunch across a wide avenue, she rushes back to her apartment, only to hear them squabbling as she opens the door. Emma's relief at their safety is counterbalanced by sorrow when she hears one of the girls yelling at the other that she wishes her sister were dead. Recalling the accident, Emma sinks weeping into a kitchen chair while her daughters, forgetting their silly quarrel, comfort her.

The story ended here until the author realised that the ending was weak and evasive because it did not deal fully with the central conflict underlying the story: chance versus the social structures of human life. The writer added two short lines contrasting the safety of the scene in the kitchen to the ever-present menace of the streets. By evoking the beginning, the end completes a circular pattern which is aesthetically pleasing.

Circling back is a useful device for ending a story. Indeed, it has been said that when you see your beginning coming around again, you are approaching your end. A complete circle is not necessary. A spiral up or down is usually more satisfactory because the reader will feel that something new has been gained. The story about the traffic accident spirals down, but I have read a story about death that ends with an elaborate and delightful funeral ceremony. The story's upward spiral reminds us that even death has its merry side.

Now, how is one to find an ending for the story whose germ is character? If the character is so deeply interesting to you that you are willing fully to explore it, you will arrive at your story's conclusion when you have traced the path to your character's centre.

The story of a charming but weak young man who steals from a strong-minded woman can only conclude in a confrontation with that woman, for what he is really trying to steal is not a material possession but a character trait (her inner strength) which he lacks.

In addition to plotting backward, or forward, or around in a spiral or circle, or tracing one's way to the heart of the labyrinth of character, the writer can search for an end by searching for the story's title. This process seems most useful to the writer who works intuitively, building a story by layering episodes and/or images that seem ('feel') connected. A gifted young woman writer of my acquaintance arrives at her ending by hunting through early drafts of her story for a recurrent word, phrase, or image to furnish its title. Only in this way does she know what her story is about so that she can conclude it. Her solution seems lackadaisical until we remember that the end, and therefore the meaning, of any story is always to be found lurking in the material. The means by which we lure it forth differ only according to the needs of the story and our natures.

Ending Fiction
Ursula Holden

Just as I avoid plotting outlines or naming characters, so I try to avoid worrying about the end of my fiction. I like to think that if I am true to my subconcious the story will curl into itself as naturally as a hedgehog. I usually sense the ending soon after the half-way mark, but things could change until I'm at the last draft. I try to stay fluid in my approach.

Once I dreamed my ending, which was rare and wonderful, though it meant reworking the entire book.

Starting work each morning remains as difficult. I would rather coax a lion bare-handed than feed another page into the typewriter. I keep reminding myself that talent is negligible without discipline, and that with persistence the book will get finished. When I hear my characters chattering to me in my sleep I feel encouraged. They are real people now, which means I have got them rounded, fleshed out.

I liken the last chapter to winning a race. The jockey must crouch right up over the horse's neck, with shortened stirrups, in absolute control. I keep it condensed; I don't think of the reader but concentrate on my own inner guide.

The title comes last, sometimes after discussions with editors and my agent. Like the book jacket, the title is an aspect of selling the book, so their advice is to be respected.

Writing is often compared with childbirth. I know about both. Though writing is the hardest thing I know the rewards are incomparable, despite the long gestation, the isolation and nerve strain.

When I have finished I'm wrecked. Depression and exhaustion alternate with euphoria. I stay in bed, sleeping for hours, no reading, no music. I intend never to put myself through that hurdle again, driving myself to the edge of madness. My healthy diet is ignored. When will my agent get in touch? What will he think of it? The telephone rings . . .

I begin to feel surfeited with chips, ice cream, mars bars and vodka. I start making telephone calls. I switch on the radio, play some tapes. I open a book. I miss something, I need a purpose . . .

And so . . . . .

Out of Context
Helen Flint

I once saw Clive James interviewing Melvyn Bragg on television about his book *The Maid of Buttermere*. He read out a steamy passage which could have easily been lifted out of any bodice-ripper on any airport bookstand. When Clive had finished, they both laughed – see what suave men of the world we are, that we laugh at such things! Clive's obvious question ('How could you?' or 'What on earth are you up to?') was drowned in the audience laughter. But Melvyn came back with something to the effect that if you lift a few sentences out of context what can you expect . . .

Wrong Melvyn!

Never let one sentence or even one word of your book stay there unless you are happy for Clive James or someone even more sarcastic to read it out on television to millions of viewers *out of context*. This is how I write. I too might rip off the odd bodice (or breeches – let's have more breech-ripping novels!) but it would be either in fun or with irony. I would try to embroider into the fabric of that random snatch the thread of meaning I intended. In other words, as Ezra Pound said, your 'language [must always be] charged with meaning.' Otherwise you can never be safe from Clive.

Exercise 2: Editing
Caeia March

Method

Repetition

Take a piece of your writing and photocopy it. Working on the photocopy, first use a yellow felt pen to make a thin coloured 'block' over any word (other than 'and', 'the', 'because',) which is repeated.

Think about the repetition. Are there any repeats you feel you should change? If so, use a *Roget's Thesaurus* to help you. If not, why not? Are you deliberately using repetition for rhythm?

Does it work? Could a word of the same syllable length give you the same rhythmic effect? Or one with the same first letter? Do you want a rhyme? Does rhyme give you more power here, or less? Try more than one version and read it aloud to yourself.

Speech

Do the voices of the speakers sound very different? Using different light-coloured felt pens (so that you can easily read through the colours) block in the words or phrases that each speaker uses more than once.

What is there to notice about the patterns? Do some speakers talk in 'questions'? For example, 'Well she would, wouldn't she?' 'Life's like that, innit?' When you read these patterns back to yourself do they sound real?

Try changing the patterns in the voice of one speaker. What happens? Re-read some passages from one of your favourite books in which a favourite character is talking. Are there any noticeable words and phrases, questions, circular endings (wouldn't it, didn't they?)?

Imagery

Using a photocopy of your work, read it slowly to yourself. Take any sentence in which you feel there could be a picture/image embedded in the words. Concentrate on the picture/image. Don't change the sentence on the photocopy at this point. Instead, on a separate piece of paper write down the first two or three words that come up *now* from the picture/image in your mind. Is there a colour connected with this? Write it down on the spare paper. Is there a shape? A feeling/emotion? A sound? A smell? A taste? What else in your life conjures up a connection? Now return to the photocopy with the original sentence. Does it convey the depth of the picture/image, the quality, the richness? Is it already complete or do you now want to modify it? If you do, then try out the new versions on the spare paper. Do not change the photocopy until the modified versions are exactly what you want. Keep all the versions for the time being.

Rhythm

Taking any other sentence, think about the length and rhythm.
Read the chosen sentence aloud to yourself from the photocopy.
Tap out the rhythm with your hand on the table or chair where
you're writing. Is the rhythm sad, angry, hard, soft, long, slow,
fast, short, comforting, upsetting? What else if none of these?
Does this rhythm carry out what you want from the original
sentence? Do you want to modify the original sentence, e.g. two
short instead of one long, one medium length instead of one or
two short ones? Would one word do? Try several versions on the
spare paper. Don't write on the photocopy at this stage. Speak
all new versions out loud to yourself.

Experimenting with alternative layouts

At this point you may find that several alternative layouts,
patterns and sequences are occurring to you.

Assuming you have an edited photocopy of the original
work, and spare papers with several rewrites and trial versions,
take scissors and glue and a clear space such as a table, worktop
or ironing board. You can then work on several sheets of new
A4 at the same time, which gives you continuity.

Using a felt pen label the lines in the right order. Label them A
to Z or numerically but don't confuse page and paragraph
numbers which is all too easy when you have a long section of
work to rearrange.

Cut the photocopy and rewrites up into chunks, lines and
single words as necessary. Without glue place the passages and
lines in their new order(s) on clean paper. (Offcut paper is
available from most paper merchants; and some offices will give
away their scrap A4, used on one side.) A stapler will hinge the
pieces temporarily, in case you are interrupted during this
process; stapled sheets can be cheaply stored in A4-size
polythene food bags through which you can read.

Working towards the final draft in this way can be very
satisfying, and very flexible. For me, it's the physicality that
appeals: the handling of pieces of writing, the feel of the paper,
the steady growth of two to twenty sides of finely worked-on
product.

Note

'Editing' can take a long time: breaking through the barriers between words/paragraphs/lines/sections/stanzas in our heads. It is also useful work that can be done at any stage between bouts of other writing.

Publication

Confessions of a Fiction Editor
Sarah Lefanu

In Muriel Spark's *A Far Cry from Kensington*, kind Mrs Hawkins, editor at Mackintosh & Tooley, regularly offers tea, biscuits and advice to new and aspiring authors. There is one young man who has written a large novel about nothing in particular. When Mrs Hawkins advises him to try again, this time more concisely, and with a particular subject matter, he insists on talking at length about other noted novels – large and about nothing in particular – most of which Mrs Hawkins has not read.

I don't think there are many editors nowadays who are as generous as Mrs Hawkins to aspiring writers, particularly ones who have written large novels about nothing in particular.

But then The Women's Press does offer certain advantages, to staff and authors alike, over Mackintosh & Tooley. The publishing director, for instance, does not rely on astrological charts for the running of the business. And although we don't agree to see, or speak to, all aspiring writers who contact us, once we have taken on an author we like to have as much personal contact with her as possible. Within a small company like The Women's Press there is little room to duck responsibility. I think this works to an author's advantage, although not necessarily to that of the editor. We don't have someone like Mackintosh & Tooley's Colin Shoe, whose particular job it is to protect the staff from the righteous wrath of authors. 'We can't have our staff upset,' he says, and appeases the author with a large lunch.

A publisher has certain expectations of an author who wishes to submit a manuscript, just as an author has expectations of a publisher. The first expectation is that the author has chosen to submit her work to us because she thinks it might be suitable for our list. This doesn't mean that she has to have read – and be able to quote from – fifty per cent of our books. A couple of hours in a bookshop is enough to give a general idea of how publishing houses differ one from another. Assuming that The Women's Press has been chosen for a good reason, I shall now describe how my ideal author submits her first novel to us, and how we deal with her submission.

She should first write a letter that briefly describes her novel and why she thinks it might be of interest to us in particular. She should give any relevant biographical information, which might include details of previous publications, or experience which is used as a basis for the novel, or anything which she thinks has a bearing on her work.

The letter should be simple and straightforward. I can think of nothing that turns me off more than someone telling me that I must publish their work because of its striking originality and/or incomparable profundity. What often goes with this self-evaluation is page after page of explanation of the finer points of the manuscript. The heart of the editor sinks like a stone. I think immediately: 'This author shows no distance from her work. It's not likely to be much good. And if she allows me no freedom to make up my mind about it, then she's likely to bully the reader as well. No thanks.'

With her letter she should enclose a synopsis. Some authors prefer to send this first letter to a named person, and ring up for the name of the managing director or a fiction editor, but it is perfectly all right, and safe, to address it to the submissions editor.

The fact that an author doesn't have an agent is neither here nor there. Too much time can be wasted by a beginning writer trying to find an agent for herself, and she may get demoralised by being turned down. Having an agent doesn't guarantee publication, and there's no point in getting demoralised before you've even started.

First, then, a brief letter and a synopsis. If the synopsis gives the impression that the novel might indeed be suitable, then we usually ask for two chapters, sometimes three, which should be sent in with return postage. At least one editor, sometimes two, looks at these. At this stage I see all the science fiction submissions, and any of the general fiction submissions that the managing director or the submissions editor think I might be interested in. (There are four editors at The Women's Press, and between us we have quite a wide range of interest.)

It is enormously advantageous to the aspiring author to submit a clean and attractive manuscript. Not only is it much easier to read, but it indicates a professionalism and pride in her work that I find I respond to. If *she* thinks her work is worth that effort, then *I* am prepared to think so too. Double spacing, indented paragraphs and wide margins are the traditional requirements; nowadays word processing offers a wide range of layouts, and I'm quite happy to read single-spaced manuscripts as long as there is a lot of empty space around each paragraph. But if manuscripts have been word processed they should be printed in high, not draft quality, and I don't know a single editor who is willing to read a manuscript on unseparated sheets of continuous feed paper.

It is at this point that the first major decision is made. Do we want to see the whole manuscript? Of the 50 or so books we publish a year, about half are fiction titles, and as we actively seek fiction from black and third world writers, from science fiction and crime writers, we do turn down a considerable amount of fiction that doesn't fall into any of those categories. This does not mean that it isn't worth publishing, simply that it isn't right for us. If there is something striking about the two chapters we've read, then we ask to see the whole manuscript.

But it is very difficult to define what quality it is that we're looking for, that makes me say, yes, I must read the whole of this novel. A dull or dreary opening paragraph puts me right off. Whereas, for example, I find it impossible to resist: 'Someone threw a stone at me this morning.' (Ursule Molinaro's *The New Moon with the Old Moon in her Arms*); 'Irrational behaviour is rarely frowned upon if it is traditional.' (Judy Allen's *Bag and Baggage*); ' "Do you have a boyfriend?" asked the analyst almost right away at the first interview. "Certainly not," I replied sharply, "And nor do I want one, if that's what you think." ' (Christine Crow's *Miss X, or The Wolf Woman*).

Each of the examples above made me want to read on. But this is probably enough to paralyse any beginning writer, which is not what I mean to do at all. (Indeed the first two are previously published writers, not that previous publication counts for as much as many people think.) It is notoriously difficult to start a work of fiction, and the advice of many writers is just to start somewhere, anywhere at all. Beginnings can always be scrapped, reworked, or even written for the first time at the end. This is one reason why I never recommend that an author submits an unfinished novel: the ending is in a real way contained in the beginning, and if the ending is vague and woolly then the beginning is likely to be, too. Which means that the chances are greater that I won't be sufficiently impressed to want to see the rest. Another reason is that it unnecessarily increases an editor's workload: she has to read the resubmission as well as the first submission before deciding whether she wants to see the whole work. And yet another is that it is impossible to tell from an unfinished manuscript how much editorial intervention will be required.

If we ask to see a whole manuscript it should be sent in as soon as possible with, again, return postage. It will then be read either by an in-house editor, if the material we've already seen suggests to us that there is a high possibility we will take it on, or if it is less clear, we send it to an outside reader and ask for a detailed report. The reader will give her assessment of the book's potential, pointing out strengths and weaknesses and making suggestions, where she thinks appropriate, for editorial intervention. At Mackintosh & Tooley the readers invariably, and sorrowfully, find they cannot recommend the books for publication. At The Women's Press they can, and do.

We see a lot of good and interesting work, but not all of it is suitable for our list. In such cases we try to recommend another publishing house for the author to try.

The ideal working relationship between an editor and an author is one in which they are both in complete agreement about what needs to be done to the manuscript (and the author goes away and does it in three days!). I used to take on manuscripts that required (in my opinion) a fair amount of work, but the increase in the number of books we publish and the resulting increase in the number that I am editorially responsible for means that I now do that very rarely. In some ways this is a shame as I enjoy working closely with an author on her book, but I just don't have the time to do it (non-fiction is a different matter). My role is more like that of an alert and deliberately irascible reader: picking up inconsistencies, querying ambiguities, noting parts of the story that I feel need expanding, or condensing. Then I will ask the author for her response. Sometimes she feels that my query is a good one, and wants to rewrite accordingly, sometimes not.

So I react to what is there on the page, rather than what might be there if the author did such and such. And there is little general advice that I can offer beyond practicalities, such as be as ruthless as you can bear with your own work and cut out all the padding. A 500-page first novel, even if it is about something, rather than nothing, in particular, will not be viewed with a great deal of sympathy (I am personally in favour of short novels, the shorter the better).

General advice remains general, and all too often does not apply to particular work. For example, the presentation of credible human relationships is widely thought to be important; but then the protagonist of Rhoda Lerman's *The Book of the Night* spends a considerable amount of time as a small white cow, and that of Carol Emshwiller's *Carmen Dog* as a golden setter. Fast-paced action and a gripping plot? Olive, in Lisa Greenwood's *The Roundness of Eggs*, spends a lot of her time sleeping and dreaming in her attic. There are, in fact, no hard and fast rules that will guarantee quality of writing.

A novel can be about anything, can have as many or as few characters as the author wishes, as many or as few 'events', as much or as little dialogue. What is important is a sense that every word has purpose and meaning. I want to be made to feel that if I skip a single word it will be my loss. If I find that I'm skipping whole chunks of it, then I know that I'm not likely to get to the end of the manuscript.

This is not to say that we only take on work that we consider word perfect. What would happen to our jobs as editors if that were the case? But we are not likely to be interested in work that doesn't show a striving towards that, a manuscript that calls out to be cut by a third. But, even although finally we might decide against a work for other reasons (on a commercial, yes, commercial assessment, say), we would always give careful consideration to a work in which it looks as if the sentences have been considered every-which-way until the words seem to live on the page in the only possible combination.

It is enormously pleasurable to read a manuscript from an unknown writer and to say, yes, this is wonderful, it is just right for us and we must publish it. And while we have never, so far as I know, perpetrated a mistake of the magnitude of that committed by Mrs Hawkins' colleague, Connie, who failed to correct 'blind man' to 'blond man' on page one of the proofs, thereby making the whole novel virtually incomprehensible, nonetheless what takes place between acceptance of a manuscript and eventual publication is fraught with pitfalls and dangers. But that is quite another story!

Publishing Poetry
Sue Stewart

Poetry publishers can't usually afford to put money on a wild card, so poets need first to built up a good track record with the poetry magazines. *The Writers' and Artists' Yearbook* carries a list of the main ones; a more comprehensive list is available from the Poetry Society (see 'Useful Addresses, pp265–271).

You can also consult many magazines at the South Bank Poetry Library at the Royal Festival Hall in London. Do buy or consult magazines before you send work to them, to make sure they publish your type of work. It's best to send three or four poems at a time, with a short covering letter, and always with a stamped addressed envelope. If it's a quarterly magazine, as most are, you'll probably have to wait up to three months for an answer. Don't be put off by a rejection: just send your poems somewhere else. When you've had around 15 poems published in reputable magazines, you can then write to a publisher, asking if they would be prepared to consider your manuscript, and giving a list of all the magazines who've published your work. (For details of poetry presses, see 'Writing Poetry' pp90–100.)

Guidelines for Women Writing for the Theatre
Lizbeth Goodman

This article is intended for a wide variety of women who may be writing (or hoping/planning to write) for any area of the theatre, including performance art and comedy/cabaret. A list of useful contacts (names and addresses of all groups and organisations mentioned herein) is given in the 'Useful Addresses' section at the end of the volume.

By way of introduction, I should say that I do not believe there are any hard and fast guidelines for all women wishing to write for the theatre (or people wishing to do anything). Personal objectives, personalities, talents and circumstances will, of course, vary from individual to individual, and for some, this will make my suggestions ineffective.

Furthermore, I should explain that my approach is rather materialistic. This is more to do with the politics of theatre production and the politics of theatre-as-industry than with my own personal politics. Like it or not, the theatre is seen as an industry by those with power to offer jobs and commissions, so a materialist approach seems the most useful way, in such a short space, to address the issue of women writing for the theatre. It is crucial that we make available basic information about the ins and outs of theatre politics; I hope that, by making the mechanisms of theatre production more accessible, the process will be de-mystified, and may thereby seem less personally alienating to would-be playwrights.

To begin with a bald statement: it is difficult to get plays read and produced. This is true for men as well as for women, and is perhaps more true for working-class women and men, or for women and men living outside the prosperous south east of England. The standard set of personal-political connections and 'networking' strategies which apply to most businesses and careers also apply to the theatre. This is complicated by the innately creative (and personal) nature of playwriting, an activity which takes place largely in private, well outside the very public spaces of the rehearsal room and stage. But even for playwrights with 'the right connections', living in or near London, with another source of income to support them through the hard times, it is difficult to get new plays read and produced. There are many reasons for this, but most stem from one (predictable) common denominator: lack of resources.

The theatres are hard put to keep themselves running these days, and very few can afford to pay 'literary managers', whose primary job it is to read manuscripts. The Royal Court Theatre has an excellent literary manager (Kate Harwood), and it is no coincidence that the Royal Court has an outstanding record of producing 'new work' (i.e. plays by little-known writers), and also of producing work by women. Other theatres' records are not so exemplary: it is well known that the RSC and the National have had very few productions of plays by women on their high-profile stages. In fact, even Caryl Churchill (arguably the best-known and most successful woman playwright in Britain today) has not been produced by either of the 'Theatres National', and Sarah Daniels is the only feminist playwright to have been given a full-scale performance at the National (*Neaptide*, in 1986). The situation for women directors has been slightly better: Deborah Warner has been tremendously successful at both the RSC and the National. Still, one woman does not an effective 'equal opportunities' make.

This is not an attack against the Theatres National; like all businesses, they operate according to business principles: considerations such as marketability of names as commodities, the characteristically British evasion of anything smacking of feminism (or most political/ideological stances, unless advocated by very well-known 'safe bet' men). All this, coupled with the workings of the insidious old boys' network, results in the observable situation that, to put it mildly, the mainstream commercial/subsidised sectors are not the most progressive contexts for women's work in the theatre.

To sidetrack for just a moment into matters political: though the policies of the commercial and subsidised theatre sectors have not on the whole been supportive of women, this is, I believe, due not so much to the misogyny or conservatism of particular individuals, but rather to structural faults, i.e. the entire system was set up by and for men. We are dealing less with an outright policy against promoting women, than with an unstated but largely operative preference for supporting the status quo, 'the norm' (i.e. for replicating a system in which the roles, and the role models, are traditionally male). Without proper funding to hire new people, to institute pro-women policies (whether they include positive discrimination or equal opportunities clauses or not) and to commission new work, the system is unlikely to change.

These are important points, and each new writer will need to remind herself of them from time to time. But for most women just breaking into theatre writing, these are academic issues. It is more practical to start with the basics: where to send a play, or who to talk with if you are thinking of writing a play (or scripting some comedy sketches, or devising a theatre piece, or working on performance art work). And before any of these issues arise, the all-important question must be addressed. That question (probably the most frequently asked of all playwrights, and in all playwriting workshops) is: how to begin writing?

There is no one answer to this, but a different answer for each individual writer. Some writers begin with ideas, and then flesh out characters. Some begin with one character (perhaps modelled on themselves or someone well known) and then begin to construct a reality for that character. Some writers begin with issues, or with political energy behind them; some begin with phrases or ideas that stick unusually in the mind. Some begin by researching a certain historical period or geographical area; others by observing life around them in the present. The processes are as individualised as are the writers.

To take an example from my own experience in the area of comedy writing: some friends and I were recently writing sketches for the Footlights Women's Revue, and were throwing out ideas of 'what we find funny'. All manner of ideas came up: the usual collection of 'feminine hygiene' ads and voice-overs on soap powder commercials, etc. But one woman related a line, just one line, which she had overheard in a conversation between two other women on a train: one woman said to another: 'I like her all right, but she does have rather a lot of facial hair.' Now that is not an inherently funny line, but months later, I still laugh every time I think of it. Partly I suppose it is because it sounds so ludicrous out of context: it is so difficult to imagine who might say such a thing, and why; it also calls up all kinds of stereotypes of 'the beautiful' and 'the feminine' which are untrue to most women's natural body shapes and functions. But more to the point, it was just plain silly. We never found a way to work that particular line unobtrusively into a sketch. But it got us all laughing, and changed the tack of our thinking, and was thus indirectly inspirational to a great many of the sketches which were eventually written for that show.

However you begin writing for the theatre, it is important to keep in mind the characteristics of theatre writing which distinguish it from other forms of creative writing. Writing is often a lonely business, and theatre writing is complicated by the nature of its eventual medium. It is difficult to visualise the proportions for a play, the dimensions, the number of characters, when you have no idea what kind of space your play might eventually be performed in, the age and abilities of the performers cast, or indeed who is likely to make up your audience. These considerations affect the work of established writers as well as first-time playwrights.

I offer one simple and flexible guideline: start small, with minimal cast numbers (and perhaps multiple roles per performer), minimal sets and props, etc. This, some might argue, necessarily limits your scope of vision from the outset. Perhaps. But it also teaches you to write within practical limitations. When you are a Churchill, you can expand your cast list, and the theatre will build a revolving stage and hire in someone to write a libretto. Meanwhile, as in most endeavours, start small and work your way up. This is the general rule for theatre work intended for performance to adult audiences, in theatre spaces.

One way to get around some of these considerations is to write for younger audiences (as in Theatre in Education) or even to write for younger performers (as in Young People's Theatre, which is sometimes directed at teenagers, and sometimes written for them to play in as well). These are viable options for women, or anyone, wishing to write for the theatre, and should not be underestimated either in terms of their artistic validity or their political importance (the images represented by and for young people will certainly play a part in shaping the future generation and its forms of representation). It is true that young people are a very demanding audience; writing for them is a very demanding job, but a rewarding one. At the same time, it should be remembered that, on the whole, theatre writing in TIE and YPT is not among the best-paid (or most publicly profiled) of writing areas in the theatre.

Alternatively, some writers find community theatre work most rewarding. This can be an excellent way to start writing and to become more involved in your own community: the actors are generally members of a given town or area, and the play is usually written, or adapted, with that community in mind. Ann Jellicoe, one of the first successful women playwrights of our time, and now the acknowledged expert in Community Theatre, has written all about this form of theatre writing, detailing its strengths and also warning of its demands.[1] These options are not mutually exclusive; in fact, many writers begin with one kind of writing and move to something completely different. It can take a long time to find your own voice, and the space in which it sounds out strongest.

Once any writer has found a form or style or intended audience and has actually begun to write, the next crucial factor is getting feedback. This is where many of us find the most obstacles. For those who have written something but do not know how to go about getting someone to read it, whether it be a complete script, a few scenes, or just some ideas for a possible play, I suggest some very basic approaches: the best place to start is at a women writers' workshop, if you are fortunate enough to live near one. There are several excellent women's workshops in London, including one based at the Drill Hall (check your local telephone directory, or write to your Regional Arts Association or city/district council for contacts in your area). If you are not so lucky, you could try sending scripts to a workshop for a written response, but this may not be as helpful as face-to-face criticism. You might try a mixed workshop, as there is very likely some creative writing group in operation nearby, or try a women's centre or women's group of a non-creative kind; the women who attend may not be experts on women's writing or on the theatre, but some will very likely show genuine interest in your work, and may offer valuable comments as well.

If you are interested in more 'academic' responses, most universities, colleges, and polytechnics have some facilities for drama, whether it be a proper course or department, or one or two individuals with an interest in theatre. You need not be enrolled in any course to take advantage of these resources. Ring or write to your local campus, whatever it may be, and ask for the drama department. If there is none, ask for the English department (which there is very likely to be) and then ask the receptionist for the name and number of one of their staff with an interest in theatre. Contact this person, and ask if you might send them some work, or meet to discuss your work. Do not be discouraged if the reply is negative (people are busy, and teachers and lecturers these days especially so). Try again with someone else.

College drama societies always need new work, and often have funds available for production. Find out the names of the drama societies near you, and write to the presidents or administrators offering material. If they accept, you may find the lag between acceptance and performance unduly long, but remember that while you are dealing with students, they are dealing with exam schedules and college bureaucracy in finding the funds for your play. If you can sit this out, you may well see your play performed. Your fee will be negligible, but the experience gained can be very valuable indeed.

Alternatively, contact one of the following organisations set up precisely to encourage and nurture new writing talent (addresses at end of volume):

The Women's Playhouse Trust, which regularly runs playwriting workshops and discussions, as well as producing plays.

The New Playwrights' Trust, an organisation set up for new writers, where you can gain access to lists of other 'new writers' in your geographical area, or to writers (female or male) with similar interests. The NPT keeps a file of plays by its members (if you file yours, it will be read and commented on by members of the trust).

The Theatre Writers' Union, with branches all over the country, comprising hundreds of playwrights of varying degrees of experience: to join, you need only have written and produced one full-length play (and you may attend meetings, with permission, even if you are not a member: attending a meeting is an excellent way to meet people who might like to read or discuss your work).

The Playwrights' Agency, which provides a current listing of plays (staged or unstaged). To be entered into that listing or index, you need only send them in a typescript of your work (published plays are listed automatically). Entry in, and access to, the index is open, free of charge to anyone who has completed any form of drama for stage, radio or television.

If you do not feel ready to plunge in by sending out your play to strangers (of whatever status), there is also the option of beginning your public career by 'coming out' with a rehearsed reading, before you take the step to full stage production. Organisations which specialise in doing readings of 'new work' include an organisation called Player–Playwrights ('dedicated exclusively to try-outs of new scripts') and The Playwrights' Co-operative ('in which playwrights take responsibility for presenting their own work'): these are mixed groups, but are positively orientated towards the work of new writers, and not known to be antagonistic towards women's work. A reading can be very instructive in that it costs very little or nothing to put on, and so generally requires no production team or company backing, but allows you as the playwright to hear your own words spoken. If you wish, you may have the option in a reading of interrupting in order to direct the performers in some way which might be instructive to you, and thereby to experiment with your own play as it is read by others. This often helps new writers to find flaws in their work, and also to see the strengths: rewrites which follow may well shape a text up for positive consideration by companies seeking work for production. Several young women playwrights began their career with rehearsed readings, notably Jacky Kay (author of *Chiarascuro* and *Twice Over*), who began and is still best known as a poet, and who broke into writing for the theatre with readings of her plays at the Gay Sweatshop's Times Ten Festivals.

Such festivals are worth looking into, as are the theatre listings pages in *City Limits*, *What's On London* (or your regional equivalent), *Time Out*, and *The Stage*, where various awards and incentive schemes for new writers are periodically listed. Sarah Daniels and Charlotte Keatley are two of many successful young women who won such awards early in their careers. Look especially for the Verity Bargate Awards, the Mobile Playwriting Award, and the George Devine Award. In terms of funding for new writing, the Arts Council offer writers bursaries of various kinds. Unfortunately, most require the writer to be attached to a company, and/or to be based in London, but there may well be a scheme which suits you (details available from the Arts Council); also enquire from Greater London Arts, if you reside in or near London, or from your local regional arts association. In addition, some theatre companies need writers in order to qualify for such bursary schemes, so be on the look-out for local groups advertising for writers; there may be a fee written into the contract for you.

When the time comes to submit a play for production, there are several avenues to try. The New Playwrights' Trust and The Theatre Writers' Union both publish 'calls for plays' in their monthly newsletters. Small fringe companies often advertise in this way. A women's multi-media production company called Vera also occasionally advertises for scripts, or on behalf of companies seeking scripts. If you are very new to the theatre, it may be best to begin by submitting scripts to small fringe companies: if they take on your work, you will (in most cases) have more access to the rehearsal process, and thereby the maximum chance of treating early projects as learning experiences.

The next step is sending scripts to middle-scale and large-scale companies and venues. The Royal Court is very good about reading and commenting on new work. The Theatre Royal, Stratford East also has a good reputation for this. Venues like the Albany Empire (where the Second Wave Young Women's Project is based) not only encourage new writing, but sometimes give awards, or offer productions with readings. The Oval House, Kennington has an excellent reputation for taking women's work (and particularly lesbian work), as does the Drill Hall. It is, as always, best to address work to an individual rather than to a company: to the literary manager if there is one, or to a director or an administrator. Contact names for each company and venue are listed in the major theatre directories (updated annually).

Several wonderful feminist theatre companies are worth looking into; their grants are small and they are unlikely to be in positions to commission new work, but their interest will be genuine and if they like your work they may put you on the road to making the contacts you will need to break into production. These include: the Monstrous Regiment, the Women's Theatre Group, the Gay Sweatshop (Women's Company), Siren, Scarlet Harlets, and Trouble and Strife, among many others. Such companies are located in all the regions, and may well have a place for you as member of a producing team, management committee or writing/devising collective.[2] It is worth taking a day out to look through the listings in *The British Alternative Theatre Directory*,[3] where companies are described along with the kind of work they do, and whether or not they accept unsolicited scripts.

Finally, there are (actual) horror stories of people sending out scripts, never to hear about them again. This is inevitable in any field, but it is a special problem in the theatre, where funds are currently so tight, and readers so few and far between. Always keep a copy of anything you send, and always enclose a stamped addressed envelope with sufficient postage for return of your script. If you have not heard after three weeks, ring the theatre/company/individual to whom you sent the script. If more time elapses with no reply, contact The Theatre Writers' Union, who are expert in handling such problems and, when necessary, in intervening to settle disputes.

I have so far touched on the how to's. There are experts at all the organisations I have mentioned who can guide you in the right direction, given your own objectives and style of work. For further support, critics and academics have written several valuable volumes on 'women and theatre' and 'feminist theatre', which I list in the references. These are worth reading, or glancing at, as the mere knowledge that we are not alone, and that our work is taken seriously, can inspire the confidence to keep writing.[4] I suggest that new writers read interviews with established playwrights and performers, like those I list, since most writers experience similar struggles in the early years.[5]

My last suggestions are the most important of all, and, though obvious, are often overlooked. The first: read plays by women. Study their structure and style. Determine what it is you have to say that has not been said before. Build on the work of other women, giving credit where credit is due. And most importantly, go to the theatre. There is no better school for playwriting than the theatre itself.

Here, I want to touch briefly on the 'whys': why it is important that women should write, and keep writing, for the theatre. These are the simplest answers: because we have things to say that need to be said. Because we have ways of seeing, and saying things which are not available to men (and I mean that in a positive, non-essentialist way); because we have ways of working with each other, and with men, which can enrich the experience of working, and thereby translate both the process and the product into something new, liberating and authentic to our own experiences – individual and collective.

In conclusion

When I set out to write these 'guidelines' I thought I would include separate sections on 'advice for women writing for the "mainstream" ', 'advice for women writing in small (low or unfunded) companies'; 'advice for women writing in colleges or universities'; and 'advice for women writing freelance'. Instead, my advice for all women writing for the theatre is the same: hang in there. The odds are against us, and are getting worse all the time. The vast majority of artistic directors, producers, and critics (not to mention the sponsors) are men. Since the theatre itself is in such a perilous position – due to the funding problems I have described and the so-called 'solution' in the turn towards sponsorship – it is a unique time to put ourselves out on a limb and write for the theatre.

All that said, this is a good time for women to be writing. Every time is a good time for women to be writing. The politics of funding develop and change without regard for our personal lives and values; what we can do is inscribe our lives, our voices, ideas, thoughts and values, into the fabric of this society. That in itself will make a difference. Writing, even without performance or production, can make a difference.

When we go one step further and get our words enacted on stage, we take our vision into the third dimension, and affect people in that way that only live theatre can. This is why women's work in the theatre has so long been labelled 'subversive': a term which is meant to be derogatory, but which can equally well be interpreted positively, for it can so easily be reclaimed, re-viewed, and re-presented. If women's theatre, and even the act of women working in the theatre (or women *working*) is 'subversive', it is positively so in the sense that it challenges cultural norms and creates an active alternative to the malestream. That can only be a good thing.[6]

The bald statement again: it is difficult to break into writing for the theatre. It is not impossible. Not by a long shot. Now for the optimistic ending: we can redefine the possible, and restage it, so that eventually, politics may take on board the questions of our personal and political agendas. Many rejections come with each acceptance, and the encouragement of women writers and directors and performers and producers and technicians – in the face of mounting political and financial difficulties for the theatre as a whole – may be the most valuable resource we can offer each other. With the confidence which such encouragement brings may come the end reward of successful entrance into theatre writing as a career.

Good luck.

Notes

1 Ann Jellicoe, *Community Plays: How to Put Them On*, Methuen, London, 1987.
2 Key Women's Theatre Groups include: Gay Sweatshop (Women), c/o Kate Owen, PO Box 820, London NW1 8LW; the Monstrous Regiment, c/o Rose Sharp, admin., 123 Tottenham Ct. Rd. London WIP 9HN; Siren Theatre Co., c/o Jane Boston, 223B Graham Rd., London E8 1PE; and the Women's Theatre Group, c/o Kathleen Hamilton or Jenny Clarke, admin., 5 Leonard St., London, EC2A 4AQ.
3 Robert Conway and David McGillivray, eds. *The British Alternative Theatre Directory*. (London: Conway McGillivray, 1989, republished annually.)
4 See Helene Keyssar, *Feminist Theatre*, MacMillan, New York, 1984; Janet Brown, *Feminist Drama: Definition and Critical Analysis*, Scarecrow Press, Metuchen, NJ, 1979; Lynda Hart, ed., *Making a Spectacle: Feminist Essays on Contemporary Women's Theatre*, The University of Michigan Press, Ann Arbor, 1989; Elizabeth J. Natalie, *Feminist Theatre: A Study in Persuasion*, Scarecrow Press, Metuchen NJ, 1981; Sue-Ellen Case, *Feminism and Theatre*, MacMillan, NY, 1988; Michelene Wandor, *Carry on Understudies: Theatre and Sexual Politics*, Routledge and Kegan Paul, London, 1986; Michelene Wandor, *Look Back in Gender*, Methuen, London, 1987; Lesley Ferris, *Acting Women: Images of Women in Theatre*, Macmillan,

London, 1990; Susan Bassnett, *Magdalena: International Women's Experimental Theatre*, Berg Publishers, Oxford, 1989; and Morwenna Banks and Amanda Swift, *The Jokes On Us: Women in Comedy From Music Hall to the Present*, Pandora, London, 1987.

Also see the collected 'Plays by Women' Series (in seven volumes, eds. Michelene Wandor and Mary Remnant) and the 'Lesbian Plays' Series (in two volumes, ed. Jill Davis) put out by Methuen.

5 See interviews collected in Susan Todd, ed., *Women and Theatre: Calling the Shots*, Faber and Faber, London, 1984; and those I conducted for *New Theatre Quarterly*, vol. VI, nos. 21–3, 1990.

6 See Karen Malpede, ed., *Women in Theatre: Compassion and Hope*, Limelight Editions, New York, 1985; Helen Kirch Chinoy and Linda Jenkins, eds, *Women in American Theatre*, Crown Publishers, New York, 1981; and Kathleen Betsko and Rachel Koenig, *Interviews with Contemporary Women Playwrights*. Beech Tree Books, New York, 1987.

Pictures in the Mind: Commissioning Radio Drama
Caroline Raphael

'I like radio because the pictures are better.' Whether or not a precocious six-year-old actually said that to her mother, it is a statement worth considering when starting to write for radio.

Writing for radio is about using sound to create worlds in the listener's imagination, to excite, turn and twist, romance and sadden the mind. The power of radio is that the listener has offered you, the writer, their mind to take over for a short period in a way that no other medium (except perhaps the novel or short story) can. I know the cliché that the joy of radio listening is that you can cook a meal, bath the kids or drive up the M1 at the same time, but it is wonderful to be told by an appreciative listener that actually they were so enthralled that they *stopped* what they were doing and just listened!

It is difficult to analyse what makes a successful radio play, although every day of the week I and my fellow editors have to do just that. It is not simply two people at a microphone talking. Of course dialogues, indeed monologues, are broadcast and are successful. But radio is most appealing and beguiling when it is active and not static. A good radio script can move between place and time, between interior thoughts, narrative and dialogue with consummate ease. More to the point, if these devices tell the story well no one ever questions them.

On radio a talking fillet of fish can help a widow come to terms with the sudden death of her husband.[1] People on radio talk to themselves endlessly and are never committed for it! The past can become the present, the secret thoughts of a character yours, at the switch of a dial. Unable to face the loss of a close friend, a young woman sees the walls of her room move in, while outside her window an orchestra plays requiems.[2]

Radio is a magic carpet; we have the production budgets to take the listener anywhere you choose to go; why then are so many plays I receive set in a living-room in outer suburbia? For some the choice of ways in which to tell the story is bewildering. Writers wander spellbound like a child let loose in a toyshop. What excites me is the script that shows that the writer has not just considered the story they are telling but *how* that story will be told aurally. For precisely this point, we do not consider unsolicited material originally written for another medium. Take away the stage directions, the camera directions, or set details and you are *not* left with a radio play.

For example, three acts set in the kitchen, dining-room and bedroom may offer some visual excitement on stage but on radio they could sound tedious. There is no appreciable acoustic difference between such settings. And radio does not work at its best when it is in scenes or acts in the traditional sense of the word. We need no stage hands, no intervals for costume changes – our transformation scenes can outdo any pantomime. But you do need to consider how you move from one 'scene' to another for this will control the pace and style of a production. Slow gentle fades out of scenes will tell the listener one thing, sharp cold cuts on the end of a sentence or sound effect quite another. Are we to dovetail 'scenes' or to cut or fade to silence giving the listener time to reflect on what has just passed? If one has to compare media it is more helpful to think of radio in terms of film or music rather than the theatre. How to express such requirements in your script when you have no experience of radio often causes writers anxiety and indeed may put them off writing for radio at all. Your producer will provide the technical jargon; at this stage just explain 'in your own words' how you *feel* it should sound, what the emotional effect should be. Use the vocabulary of film or music if that comes easily.

Do not have too many people in each scene – if they do not speak how will the listener know they are there – and you will find it impossible to establish their presence. One pair of feet sounds much the same as another so a character needs lines to take him or her into and out of the action. Consider varying the length of sequences as, particularly in radio, it is a superb way of quickening tension. Equally there is nothing as tedious as a piece in which each episode takes an equal amount of time. While stage directions are useful at production stage, in the end the action must be reflected in the dialogue: 'Rebecca picks up her briefcase and leaves the office pursued by a bear' will mean nothing if someone at sometime does not refer to what has happened. A quick direction as to time of day and setting is most helpful. I should say at this point that one of the most difficult things to achieve is the giving of information in as natural a way as possible. Signposting, as we call it, can be excruciatingly obvious and you need to consider what is actually necessary for the listener to know. A silly example, but a character greeting someone in the park with: '. . . and what a lovely red dress with black spots' is not only unnecessary but can destroy the pictures in the listener's mind if they have imagined the character in peach. (Of course, should the key to the mystery be a red dress with black spots then so be it, but such a bald statement is still not acceptable.)

Other small points to watch: the sounds of people going up and down stairs, in and out of cars or making cups of coffee are not interesting sounds, and if it is essential for someone to make the aforementioned cup of coffee do make sure they have something interesting to say while they do it, or cut it. You would be amazed how long it takes for a kettle to boil – it is redundant, meaningless, air time, and is too long for a pregnant pause. Equally it is often not necessary to start a scene with someone coming into a room and shutting a door. Why not start with them in the room?

Sound effects and music are enormously important but need to be chosen with care and economy. They can be essential, along with dialogue, for establishing period and place, and they have obvious emotional overtones. They can, if used skilfully, become another character. A murderer never speaks but we hear the bell on his bicycle as he rides past the children playing in the street.[3]

For some writers the mystery is not how you write a radio play but how you get it considered for broadcast. Radio is a flourishing market for new writers and has been for a long time, so it is disturbing that it is occasionally still considered a no-go area particularly by women, lesbian and black writers. Our record in producing plays by such writers is not as good as it could be but it is still better than much mainstream theatre, film or television.

Radio Four currently broadcasts five new plays a week, two soaps (*Citizens* and *The Archers*) and a 30-minute series or serial; and on Radio Three there is one slot for original writing, Drama Now. This is besides a dramatised serial of a classic novel, a short story each morning on Radio Four and other original prose readings on Radio Three, not to mention assorted dramatisations, adaptations and abridgements across the board. Radio Five began in August 1990 and broadcasts drama for children and young people. Just concentrate on the drama alone and you will appreciate this amounts to a unique showcase for writers. We think of ourselves as the National Theatre of the Air.

We have many more stages than the edifice on the South Bank and, on many an afternoon, a larger audience than the National could dream of. At the moment independent local radio produces little drama. Radio Clyde is a notable exception and LBC produces a 60-minute play or serial once a week – the effect of the Broadcasting Bill on radio drama in the independent sector has yet to be experienced.

The administrative and editorial centre of the BBC Radio Drama Department is in London but half the producers actually work at the BBC in Edinburgh, Belfast, Cardiff, Birmingham, Bristol, Manchester and Sheffield. If you live near one of these centres do consider sending material to them. It is their brief to develop the work of writers living in their regions and there is no doubt it is easier for them to have a productive dialogue with a writer living close by than it is for us in London.

Any writer who does not have an existing relationship with a producer, or a suitable name in mind, can submit material for Radio Four or Radio Three to the Literary Manager at Broadcasting House, London. They will arrange for the script to be assessed centrally or passed to a producer, as appropriate. All material sent to London is acknowledged and registered on a central computer. Short stories should be sent direct to the reading Editor. Radio Five material should be sent direct to the Editor, Children and Youth Drama and will then be passed on to the most suitable producer. Radio Five does not consider unsolicited, unpublished short stories or novels for its reading slots but does consider original drama for the seven to tens (at twenty-five minutes), ten to thirteens and Young Adult material (at thirty minutes).

It is a simple and effective process but it does take time – months rather than weeks. After waiting such a time I appreciate how dispiriting it must be if you receive a standard rejection letter. We simply do not have the resources to enter into detailed correspondence with everyone. It must make sense for us to devote our time to writers who we feel are likely, at some time, to have work broadcast. We are here to nurture talent but we are not a writing school. When a script comes in I am looking first and foremost at the quality of the dialogue. Help can be given with story-lines, structure and characterisation but I cannot rewrite dialogue. Your play may also be rejected because the theme is over-familiar.

If you are a regular listener to radio plays you may already have a good idea how our output is organised. While radio can offer immense freedom to the writer there are, obviously, some restrictions. All plays on Radio Four and Five have to fit a particular time slot (writing to time is a skill in itself) and the subject matter and style have to be appropriate for the time of day and listener expectations of that slot. I hate to be too specific about what sort of play is acceptable when quietly and carefully, over the years, we have encouraged the listener to accept and enjoy more complex and provoking pieces while still balancing the output to include pieces that are pure entertainment.

But, for example, an explicit and possibly violent play on Radio Four about rape within marriage at 45 minutes might cause problems. Our only 45-minute slot is on Wednesday afternoons and this topic is more suitable for evening listening. Our only suitable evening slot, however, is 75 minutes or 90 minutes. Having said this I *can* envisage an afternoon play on this theme, it simply depends on *how* it is treated. It could be argued, of course, that three-quarters of an hour is not long enough to do justice to such a complex issue.

The slots on Radio Four, for original writing, can be generally defined thus:

Afternoon Play: one 45-minute and one 60-minute play a week. A wonderful collection of plays, a lucky dip of romance, thrillers, kitchen sink, social realism and fantasy. Certainly the best slot for writers new to radio to consider.

Thirty Minute Theatre: one play a week on Tuesday afternoons. Covers much the same range of material as Afternoon Play but it is deceptively difficult to write a successful piece at this length. Can also work as a less narrative based piece focusing, for example, on a particular moment in time, an encounter, a turning point. Perhaps closer in form to the short story.

The Monday Play: 75 minutes or 90 minutes with an evening placing. The plays tend to concern more complex emotional and political issues.

Saturday Night Theatre: again 75 minutes or 90 minutes. More than any other slot the emphasis is on story-telling, although increasingly the way in which the story is told is becoming more interesting and beginning to reflect trends in cinema rather than Shaftesbury Avenue.

One of the joys of writing for Radio Three is that there are less stringent time restrictions within the slots. The main slot for new writing is Drama Now which covers almost any length from say, twenty minutes to – exceptionally – two hours.

What makes a play Radio Three and not Four? One basic definition is that it will make more demands on the listener in terms of form and subject. In the past Radio Three has introduced listeners to new plays by Samuel Beckett, Howard Baker, Harold Pinter and Caryl Churchill, as well as international dramatists in translation, all of which, in some way, made one reassess the nature and purpose of drama.

Listen to radio plays. There are regrettably few radio plays in print but even if they were more readily available nothing could substitute the experience of listening. A radio play only fully exists in the mind of the listener, in the unique pictures it conjures in the imagination.

Notes

1 *Kedgeree Grief*, Tina Pepler, Afternoon Theatre, Radio Four, 17 July 1986.
2 *Dusty's Story*, Hattie Naylor, Thirty Minute Theatre, Radio Four, 21 November 1989.
3 *The Past Becomes The Present*, Sally Worboyes, Afternoon Play, Radio Four, 26 March 1987.

The address of the script unit is: Script Unit, Radio Drama, Broadcasting House, London W1A 1AA. Please address Radio 5 material to the Editor, Radio 5 Drama. Please always enclose a stamped addressed envelope and a short synopsis.

How to Sell – and How Not to Sell – Screen Drama
Jill Foster

There are not many rules in selling screen drama. There is no great mystique either – just common sense, realism, research and some courage. There are only two things to consider: how best to present what you have to sell and to whom you should try to sell it.

If you are reading this, you are very likely a writer as yet unestablished and without an agent. Where do you start? You can try to find an agent but, as new writers cost a lot in time and money, there is a limit to how many unpublished writers an agent can handle. I will therefore assume that you are on your own. What you have to do is exactly what the agent did when she first set up in business: study your market, decide on those producers and companies whose work seems most in accord with yours and make contact with them.

First, study your market – watch television and read some appropriate publications: the *Radio Times* and *TV Times* are good guides to who has produced and directed what and disclose basic information like the typical lengths of programmes. There are other publications which are good sources of information, such as *Broadcast* and *The Producer*. With the advent of all the independent companies there is a bewilderingly wide choice, which is why some initial research is essential. You may decide to approach a director or a leading actor or actress, instead of a producer. The advantage of being an unrepresented beginner is that you can send out ten scripts at a time if you can afford it, whereas it is unethical for an agent to scatter a writer's work without giving reasonable time for a response.

Compiling a list of people to approach is not difficult; advising on how you should make that approach is, because so much depends on their preference and your courage. Should the first contact be a telephone call? Would it be better to write or to send a script? In my view, you should telephone first – and keep it short: 'My name is —. I have written a 60-minute comedy thriller. May I send it to —?' You do not need to speak to the producer or head of department and will probably get more help from a secretary, assistant or script editor. One call can elicit a good amount of information: the producer is in mid-production and will not be able to consider anything else until the end of filming; the producer is at Cannes and is then going on a six-month sabbatical; the producer hates comedy thrillers and is never going to produce another in her life; the producer is just about to start production on a new series and wishes to encourage new writers; this office cannot help you, but so-and-so is especially interested in new comedy/drama writers, etc. If your offer to send a script is turned down, use the occasion for gleaning further information: ask when you *can* send material, or what kind of material is being sought, or if the person you are talking to can recommend someone else for you to approach. Be brief and businesslike. Whether the response is positive or negative, make sure you keep a record of those you approach and the information you receive; it is easy, after the first ten calls or so, to forget who told you what and you may very well wish to do follow-up calls later. If it is agreed that your script will be read, keep your covering letter short, your approach simple and your script (let them see a full script initially) easy to read.

Do Not:

tell them you can write better material than most of today's writers;
bother with character breakdowns, premises, synopses, outlines, etc. Think of the person who is on the receiving end: they do not know you from Eve, they will have a hundred other approaches from would-be writers and all they want to know is whether you can write a script;
give them a 'crit' of your work: 'I'm enclosing my hilariously funny comedy . . .';
tell them how brilliant your friends think your work is;
try and attract attention by writing gimmicky letters, enclosing a lock of hair or lying through your teeth;
start your letter with 'Hi Jill' to someone who is a total stranger;
underline any part of your script in red;
enclose press cuttings;
send scripts in draft quality typeface;
spend money on expensive binding – a loose-leaf script in a clear plastic pocket is easiest to handle;
put in illustrations or plans, unless they are essential;
try to do the director's job by giving detailed camera directions;
try to do the casting director's job (only use actor's names as indications of type);
itemise precisely which pieces of music you want as background to scenes.

Do:

refer to your telephone call;
say clearly on the front page what you are sending: 30-minute pilot comedy, 60-minute drama series script with six storylines, etc;
put your name, address and telephone number on the front page;
number your pages.
Good luck!

Television Drama: Who the Piper, Which the Tune?
Jane Harris

Writing television drama has always been a dangerous and potentially destructive business for writers; and women writers have their own history of problems and perils which I shall return to later – chiefly because of misled, misguided expectations combined with the effects of savage competitition in an industry in which the stakes for all involved are exceptionally high. The rewards can be dazzling; but the attendant punishment and pain far outstrips them.

Writing television drama in the 1990s embodies all this and more besides. The new franchises are due to be distributed across the board; the BBC faces the end of its charter in 1996; Satellite broadcasting, the Broadcasting Bill, the creation of Channel 5 and looming technological changes – all coalesce to make for a nervous industry in a state of flux and uncertainty. Great opportunities lurk on the horizon, we are told; what they will consist of is an unknown quantity for everyone, especially the writer.

There are certain imperatives which the current climate necessitates for the struggling woman writer. It is vital to glean information from all available sources by reading publications and trade journals, viewing programmes, chatting to those in programme-making who will make themselves available to discuss the nature of the industry and the organisational changes that are taking place in television.

In pragmatic terms, in order to write and find a home for the development and possible production of a script, all guidelines must be regarded with the maximum amount of distrust and scepticism. And in one sense there are as many methods of approach to be explored as there are individual producers in the industry. There are, however, certain elementary matters on which general advice can be given and I outline below some basics borne of experience and an amalgam of opinion garnered from across the television drama industry.

The first great irony of the business is that unsolicited scripts – those which arrive unaccompanied and uncalled for on the editor's desk – tend, of course, to be treated with a mixture of hostility, exhaustion, cynicism and irritation from overburdened executives and producers, with too much to read and assess. Yet there is a point in every executive's or producer's life at which the unsolicited script reveals the new talent, the new voice for whom everyone in the industry is seeking with such desperation.

Which home can it seek with impunity? There are stages through which any script can move – in the world which recruits talent and seeks it for television writing this can mean the writer making her way through radio, theatre and literary agencies. Or it may mean that the writer manages to discover individual producers to approach. Individual producers housed for a time in the BBC or elsewhere usually have the opportunities, inclination and supporting staff (script editors, for instance) to read unsolicited scripts. Submitting a script to the head of a drama department who is rarely involved in the direct business of seeking day-to-day material for production is a mistake. Heads of department will only re-direct that material into the labyrinth of the television company where they eventually find their way to a reader with no axe to grind. Readers are talented creatures, patiently sifting through enormous quantities of material but they are not directly involved in production concerns. It is not their job to decide (as a rule) where a script may best be placed. It is their job to read, assess and evaluate the quality of the script before them and return their opinions to source.

It is the business of the writer – preferably through an agent but often on their own – to try to discover names and places likely to be favourable to their submitted work. A telephone call can help, and manuals like the quarterly *Spotlight*, which list names and institutions in the industry as a whole, are useful.

Presentation can be a vexed question for writers, and those to whom they submit their work. Writing a script in the dark, without a commission, is an essential prerequisite for recognition and production. All the treatments, outlines and synopses cannot replace the full-blown script to illustrate the writer's abilities; but this is at the very beginning of a writer's history and there are many producers who will be ready to assess the strength of an idea from an outline or treatment. Though these are difficult to write, read and evaluate, they are used increasingly as a form of presentation. They represent the art of telling a story simply and concisely whilst retaining the distinctive flavour of the writer's voice. Probably the best combination for a new and aspiring writer is to submit a script with an outline of the story attached to it. During the evolving career of any television writer there will be countless occasions when a treatment or outline may be called for as a document which encapsulates the next episode, the new 60-minute play concept, a thirteen part series. With a body of established work in existence this becomes a different proposition.

I should add here that fragments of scripts are never helpful: a few pages of undeveloped story and dialogue make for an unsatisfying experience for all concerned. They tell the reader next to nothing and do a disservice more often than not to the writer's abilities and ideas. It may be courteous on the writer's part to write a letter first, asking whether a script can be submitted for a reading, as, in the harsh realities of a competitive world, an unsolicited script invites rejection. Again, once the writer is more established – perhaps with an agent doing the asking – relationships are altered and the request, one hopes, is directed more specifically to available openings.

On the heels of this thought comes the trying issue of 'slots'. The submission of a 90-minute screenplay to the head of series or an idea for a three-part serial to the producer of 60-minute studio plays frequently occurs, wasting time and doing precious little to help get a commission. As does the submission of 10-15 or even 30-minute scripts to a company which has no such transmission times in its schedules, unless they are specified in the accompanying letter as being samples of the writer's work. Information is not hard to gain – reading the *Radio Times* and *TV Times*, and *watching* programmes provides a good indication of the expectations of different channels.

Increasingly, poorly presented scripts with ragged typescript or faint printout from a word processor are unacceptable. There *is* a reluctant acknowledgment from all those who have been in this industry for any length of time that miracles occasionally emerge from dog-eared illegible chunks of paperwork – and certainly high-powered packaging and presentation can only momentarily disguise a weak project. Nevertheless, whatever resources can be mustered for submitting a well-spaced, easily read script, should be. And this does not mean a script encumbered with technical directions; it is not the writer's job to deploy these. The simplest layout is best.

For those who gain a response in the jungle of submissions where stamina and persistence can count almost as much as talent in the early stages of a writer's career, the issues of commissioning and the subsequent development process arise.

Here, a word about selection, which usually implies many rejections. Writers can be rejected for a multiplicity of reasons, many of which have nothing to do with the writer's ability. If this is frustrating, there is solace – the 'subjective factor'. The judgment of individual producers and television executives is borne out of the constant search through large quantities of script work and the trying and testing of material on the screen, but nonetheless individual judgments are fallible, and are shaped by innumerable constraining and influential factors. These include the existence of similar or even identical projects, and scripts already in development or production; the balance (in terms of mood, style, context and substance of story told) of offerings to be transmitted in any given season or even year of television drama; the paramount matter of *cost* (a script set in the Brazilian rainforest during the 1790s will be a problem); and, for independent producers trying to make their own way, the pressures of the industry at large which they both resist and succumb to at different times of the day, week and month. Battling to retain a sense of self-worth as a writer is a condition of survival and success: stamina counts.

Once a commission has been achieved through the good offices of an enthused producer – probably the most common way in which a commission occurs – then begins the loosely termed process of 'development'. Moss Hart, the great American lyricist once coined the immortal phrase, 'There is no writing in this business – only re-writing.' Writers in television not only need to be able to accommodate the demand for re-writes from all quarters (executive producers, producers, directors, and script editors amongst others), but should ideally harbour a positive relish for re-writing as a physiological urge. It becomes increasingly clear that the most successful writers are those of whom this is true. And this should not be a process of deference, submission, or intimidation to which the writer is subject (although, of course, it frequently can be); it should be one in which the writer is committed to presenting a first draft whilst mentally advancing into the second, third, fourth on her own terms. However arduous and exhausting the battles can be and however crass and demoralising the demands and those who make them may be, the fundamental reality remains the same. Writing for television is in its best sense collaborative; in its worst, destructive and painful. Above all it is collective. The writer is primary (there are many who would beg to differ) but, however primary, the script is the essential contribution into a collective process and much suffering is endured by those writers who do not make this assumption before they engage with television drama.

It is vital to remember that the industry as a whole has a rapacious need for new talent, better scripts and exceptional ideas. This, in turn, means a need for writers who can bring fresh energy and a unique independence to the job, who can both accommodate and rise above the exigencies and pressures of the industry: a tall order indeed. Writing itself though, as an occupation, is the tallest of orders when taken as seriously as it must be.

This brings me to women writers. The practical questions of how to submit work and to whom, which transmission slots to aim for and what kind of presentation is most effective are general to all writers of the species. Yet the practicalities, the approach, the marketing, the pursuit and refinement of style and content are all enormously coloured and shaped by social and political factors that are frequently special to women. Women's lives, and therefore their emotional writing and production of scripts, are dominated by their roles as nurturers in the home and at work, and by the infinite demands of domesticity. This has been the subject of many millions of words over the past decades but it is still necessary to raise it here. For not only does it govern the amount of work that women are able to achieve in any arena – in writing television drama, it gives special leanings to much of the content and the choices that women make. There is a tendency in women's writing towards intimate, emotional and domestic subjects, which is hardly surprising given that these are familiar arenas, and ones we have actively been encouraged to explore. There is a need for all this in television drama. But how are we to promote the scripts by women that are bold, international in perspective, dynamic, complex (in the best sense) and in which the personal and political – in their most comprehensive meaning – are meshed?

How are we to discover more women writers, and in particular encourage that energy to break boundaries, flout conventions, sharpen perceptions and make the altogether tougher choices about story and style displayed by some women's writing, in an industry that is little inclined towards such encouragement as a primary concern?

The building and development of a good script is a difficult task, the process of marketing, seeking and finding the right programme maker or executive and the right opening for the script is harder. At last, too, the stamina needed to live and work with it through to production with all its disappointments, hazards, and problems can never be over-emphasised; so it is almost an irony that the actuality of seeing your own work on the screen carries with it such an impact. Once tasted, never forgotten, it embodies a level of seduction for any writer that few other experiences can match.

So: back to the drawing board, back to the script, word processor, ancient typewriter, pen and paper – the various means by which writers find their way through their story. Back to planting the bum on the seat of the chair which the old saw says is the essence of all writing. Back, too, to the story that each writer most passionately wants to tell: whether it be comedy, melodrama or a factual tale, whatever the genre or form, conviction and obsession is what drives through the strongest television script. The demands of the industry which fluctuate almost hourly need to be considered, but in the end must be thrown aside if an original work is to be given the true vitality that will ensure its appearance on the screen.

Writing Treatments for Film and Television Drama
Jill Hyem

With the increasing number of co-productions, and companies and independent producers trying to obtain financial backing, a writer can find herself spending most of her working hours writing treatments rather than the actual screenplays. The two require very different skills.

A treatment is basically a selling document. It will be seen not only by the potential producer and those who are to be involved creatively, but also by hard-headed business people whose criteria can be very different and whose reading capacity is often severely limited.

Before you start, make quite sure that you know what market you are aiming for, e.g. a glossy family series; a studio-based play; a thriller serial with a foreign location; a gritty human interest film with social content; a twice-weekly soap; a comedy series.

The length of a treatment can vary considerably depending on whether it is to be a one-off screenplay or a series, whether it has a large number of characters and how complicated the story is. The last treatment I wrote for a film was 24 pages and for a television series (of eight episodes) 35 pages. For a single episode in a series it would obviously be much less.

Unfortunately it is impossible to write a good treatment off the top of your head. This means you have to work out all the characters and story-line(s) in some detail before you can start. The first rule, whether it is an original idea or a dramatisation, is know your story thoroughly.

There are no absolutes about the form a treatment should take so long as it provides all the information required and gives a flavour of the style intended. After much trial and error I have, however, found that the following formula is the most successful and the one that also makes the task of writing the proposed screenplay/pilot episode easier if it is commissioned.

1 *A brief synopsis* of the idea, written in a selling style which will make people want to read on.

2 *Expand on idea*. Give any background or research details which will lend the idea authority. Say why it would make such a brilliant screenplay/series. What is fresh and original about it? Emphasise its attractions for that particular market, e.g. its fascinating locations; its comparative cheapness; its social relevance; its universal appeal.

3 *Style*. Some notes on how you would treat the subject, e.g. black comedy, concentrating on the psychological viewpoint of a certain character, aiming for documentary detail and authenticity.

4 *Characters.* A general piece about the characters. How they will contrast with each other. How they will appeal to young as well as old. How the leading role will attract a big name. How the parts will offer challenging roles for women, black actors, whatever. How the lead could, without much social engineering, be played equally well by an American!

5 *Character biographies.* A detailed biography of all the main characters.

6 *Story/story-lines.* If it is a series idea you are trying to sell you will need to provide a detailed breakdown of the first episode and the stories of subsequent episodes in more general terms. If you are envisage the project as an ongoing series you should indicate further story possibilities, e.g. 'By the end Janet has got over Tom's death and plans to take over the business where he left off. The problems she encounters could provide plenty of mileage in a subsequent series.' For a one-off screenplay you should give a detailed breakdown of the story.

A treatment should be well presented on A4 paper with a clear heading to each section. Some writers go to extraordinary lengths with photographs and expensively designed covers. Fine if the content is equally impressive, but people are not fooled by this sort of dressing up. At the end of the day it is the idea that you are selling.

Words Into Pictures: Writing Television Documentary
Caroline Spry

Writing for television, other than drama, almost seems like a contradiction in terms. After all, doesn't television consist of pictures, and people speaking? However, there is a role for writers generating ideas, researching and writing treatments for documentary material.

This article assumes that you are a freelance writer who has ideas for programmes and who wants to get these on to television.

Channel Four and to a lesser extent BBC and ITV commission independent producers to make programmes. Commissioning editors, who deal with such areas as current affairs or arts, are responsible for Channel Four's output. A mixture of commissioning editors, executive producers and series editors have this function at the BBC and ITV.

A brief run through a hypothetical example of a programme proposal will illustrate the process of commissioning.

Assume that you have spent much of your life watching television mega-documentary series in which 'great men' expound their theories on Civilisation or the Ascent of Man week after week after week. You think that this is all very interesting but where are the women? The time must be ripe for a 26-part Women's History of the World or Women and Culture: Sappho to Alice Walker. But how do you go about realising this modest proposal?

There is no single path to success in television; often several different routes have to be tried. However, whichever path you follow the first step must to be get someone in television interested in your idea. To achieve this you need something on paper, so start by writing a short but fascinating outline. This should indicate the essential elements that you want to cover in your series. It is a good idea to pick out a few details which will act as appetisers to those television executives who are desperate for good stories and insights. It is also useful to put forward an argument for why you think your proposal is important; why the series has to be made.

Most of the people you will approach with the outline spend large parts of their day snowed under by bits of paper like yours, so it is an essential rule at this stage to keep it brief but eye-catching.

Try to make it as easy as possible for them to grasp your idea.

Your target for the outline is an executive in television who is in a position to commission your series for the slots in the schedule that s/he controls. There are two possible routes to this person: direct and indirect.

It has always seemed reasonable to me to assume that anyone who wants to be involved in making television should actually watch a lot of programmes. You need to understand how television is constructed, what is being made and what is being watched.

Let us assume that all of this is obvious to you; you are square eyed and steeped in television culture. So you will be watching enough of it to identify programmes which seem to bear some resemblance to the content or format of your idea. You may notice that Channel Four is doing a series in the Another Long Version of the Ascent of Man genre. You at least know from this that there is someone at the channel who is interested in the format of your programme. Content of course is a different and a more difficult matter.

Once you have identified your programme area you can either ring up the channel and ask which editor commissioned it, or you can approach the production company who made it. Their name will be at the end of the programme and you can contact them through the Independent Programme Producers' Association (see 'Useful Addresses').

At some point you will have to get together with a production company who will translate your idea to the screen. You need to feel confident that they will be people you will be happy working with and that they are interested and sympathetic to your ideas. You may need to meet several companies before a mutual understanding is reached. The producer and director will help you sharpen your outline and present it to the appropriate commissioning editor. If, however, you have decided to go it alone at this stage, you will have to send the outline with a covering letter directly to him or her. You then wait, wait, and wait. It will sometimes take quite a long time (sometimes months) for any response other than an acknowledgment. This is usually not sloth on the editor's part; there is always an overwhelming number of proposals to read and think about, meetings to have and programmes to deal with. You may be lucky and hear very quickly but be prepared to have great patience.

Let's assume that your proposal has found its way to the one commissioning editor in Britain who has a remit for your kind of programme and is interested in the subject matter. You will be invited to meet and discuss the series. If all goes well – you agree on the substance of the project and the editor is committed to moving forward with it – you will probably be commissioned to develop the project further. If you have not already linked up with a production company the editor will suggest various people for you to meet. It is important that you enter into a formalised agreement with your production company. However nice you all appear to be and however well you get on, the stresses and strains of television can often lead to misunderstanding.

Once the development commission is finalised you will go off and research your subject matter for a number of months and then write it up, in conjunction with your director, into a treatment for the series. This will contain a lot of detail about the content and form of each of the programmes. At the same time your producer will have prepared a budget based on what you have written. Your treatment will then go back to the commissioning editor who will decide whether the project is still of interest and whether there is sufficient money to produce it. The final decision may not be immediate, especially if it is part-way into the financial year and your editor has spent all his or her budget.

If the series goes ahead your involvement will depend on what you negiotate with the editor and production company. You may be very involved, even to the extent of presenting and interviewing; you may write the commentary; or you may want to take a back seat.

Television production is a collective process involving a lot of people. It may well seem strange, indeed frustrating or unsatis-factory seeing your ideas translated into pictures. On the other hand, the added visual and aural dimension can illuminate what may otherwise be difficult concepts.

Writing Non-Fiction
Jo Campling

Do not write a single word of your book, especially a professional or academic book, until you have discussed your ideas with a sympathetic publisher. This is very important. Otherwise you have no guarantee that your book will be accepted, that you have clearly defined your aims and your market, or even that the market exists in any substantial way. A good publisher will help you to clarify all this and will indicate at this early stage whether she is interested, and will advise on the proposal, potential market and world limit for the book. Feminist publishers, on the whole, are very generous in this respect and will, where appropriate, suggest alternative publishers.

The proposal

Most non-fiction books are commissioned on the basis of a four to five page proposal and sometimes a sample chapter. Always begin your proposal with a marketing statement which should cover your aims, the market for the book and deal briefly with the competition (in order to indicate how your book will be different from existing books on the subject and, by implication, better!). This will also help you to clarify what it is you want to do and should always be completed before moving on to the more conventional part of the proposal: the structure of your book. Take this chapter by chapter, clearly outlining the main points to be covered in each chapter so that the publisher and assessors have a good idea what the book will be like. Indicate clearly at the end of this section the approximate number of words you require. For example, academic and professional books can range from between 50,000 and 100,000 words and there are obvious implications for pricing, print runs, etc. Complete your proposal with brief CV details which highlight your credibility as an author. New authors should not be deterred at this stage if they have no publications, but should seek a personal meeting with their publisher.

The process

A number of proposals are rejected at this stage, but certainly in the case of the list for which I am responsible, 'Women in Society' (WIS), never with a rejection slip or formal letter. Honest and constructive advice is always offered and, in most cases, suggestions as to how the proposal could be improved. The revised proposal is then sent out to assessors for comment. WIS, for example, has a number of assessors worldwide who give very generously of their time to support other women authors. A marketing assessment of the proposal is also sought to determine potential sales of the book. Remember, a book is a long-term, international product. For example, all WIS books appear in the North American markets and some of the books I have been responsible for publishing are already entering their second decade of life, in new editions. Books conceived now are likely, if successful, to be around in the next century! Once the assessments have been received and any revisions discussed, if the project is accepted, a contract will then be issued.

The contract

As an author, I never read my own contracts but as a publisher I always advise authors to do so. It will contain vital information on your advance, royalties, completion date, word limit, etc. Make sure that you also discuss other issues, such as the print run, whether the book is to appear in hardback or paperback, the possible price, international sales, publicity and your right to be consulted on jacket design. Some standard contracts contain an 'options clause' – which commits you to offering your next work to the same publisher but with no obligation on the part of the publisher – which, whilst they do not stand up in court, it is as well to strike out. Do feel completely happy with your contract and your publisher before you sign.

The book

A similar system of advice, discussion and support should operate throughout the writing process. Once your first draft is completed your book will normally be sent to readers for comment. This can prove invaluable in helping you to achieve a second and sometimes third perspective on what you have written before your book is finally typeset. You should be involved throughout the publication and publicity schedule. It's great fun, very hard work and, in its most effective operation, great sisterhood.

Going Public
Rosalind Brackenbury

I do not believe that anyone writes for their bottom drawer. Writing is also about being read. But publication can happen at many levels.

The first time you read your work to a group of friends and fellow writers, it is going public. Read it aloud, send it to people, find out about and use methods of going public locally. Use local papers and radio stations. Do not beat yourself with not being this year's Booker prize-winner. Think of your writing as a lifelong apprenticeship, not as an instant spurt to fame. Make long-term plans and devise short-term goals. Do not confuse the two.

Never give up. Buy lots of brown envelopes and keep sending your work out. Write elegant looking letters to publishers and include enough stamps for them to answer. Do not send out dog-eared manuscripts with coffee and tear stains on them. Make sure there is always a piece of your writing out there somewhere, being read.

Waiting to hear from a publisher can feel as painful as waiting to hear from a lover. So it is worth developing a strategy to get past this. Do not put all your eggs in one basket, and never confuse your publisher with your lover. It is, however, reasonable to expect good treatment, and not to be kept waiting for months on end. We are human, after all, and writing is very close to our hearts.

Do not pretend that rejections or negative criticism do not hurt. Tell a friend or fellow writer how you feel. Remember: a writer is someone who writes, not someone who makes the Sunday supplements or wins prizes.

Move on past failure and success alike. Drink the champagne, throw the parties, cry on somone's shoulder – but get back to work. Easier said than done? *This* is the point of building the daily relaxed habit of writing, so that it is simply what you do, whatever else is going on.

A Wider Audience
Moira Monteith

It is important that we do all we can to increase audiences for today's writers, not that we increase the number of writers. There are already too many writers chasing too few readers. Although the real writer will always emerge without coaxing, it is not so easy to encourage new readers into existence. Charles Osborne, former Literary Director, Arts Council

Such a comment sounds patronising but it echoes a general sentiment. Shouldn't we concentrate on reading the best writing? Is there any point in publishing little booklets that perhaps only a few people will ever read? There are several responses to such an attitude, which I think is not only discouraging but also mistaken. First: who defines the 'best' or the 'real' writer? Then, only a few people anyway read much of what is published. I believe the average readership of a scientific paper published in American science journals is six. Readership and value should not be rigidly equated. Also, with the advent of desktop publishing, everyone who wants to publish will. There is no point regretting the numerous publications that will blossom and flourish – or those which will subsequently wither and perish. It is possible, even probable, that the more people write the greater our potential readership becomes. As we write we become more interested in how other people have written, how they have managed to put across an idea similar to one of our own.

We might become a society where virtually everyone bequeaths one book to the next generation, as I have heard they do in Iceland. My grandfather wrote a small book entitled *Football and Other Games in Heybridge*, a history of (male) sport in a village, and sold it in aid of the local football club. I doubt whether any copies exist now outside his immediate family but we are very pleased to possess them. I only wish my grandmother had written something as well.

Writing has many functions and being published by a notable publishing firm is not the only option, though few would deny its attraction. Publishing is part of a line of communication. Dale Spender has suggested that novels are really communication between women, when you consider the number of female novelists and the fact that the majority of readers are women. Women's publishing firms have been able to make this line even more direct. Such communication can also be achieved in writing groups, particularly if a group works towards a publication or a performance. Performance poets are fashionable at the moment, and I hope the fashion lasts. A performance might be just for members of a writing group and their friends, or for a wider audience. Apart from anything else, performance sharpens the will to revise and redraft.

Some schools are pleased to have writers perform. If you do this on a regular basis you may even be able to consider charging a fee, particularly if this can be subsidised by Regional Arts Council groups, the Poetry Society, etc. Show the head-teacher or head of the English department the kind of work you might read. Sometimes a performance is more varied for the pupils if two or three writers read their work. If you do visit a school to read remember to gauge your material to the age group. Apart from anything else you will be encouraging younger writers who are still at school. Associations – such as NAWE (Northern Association for Writers in Education) and VAA (Verbal Arts Association): Writing, (See Useful Addresses pp 267, 270) – exist to promote such practice. They publish newsletters and hold workshops for writers, teachers and lecturers.

Having suggested alternative forms of publication, possibly I shall be accused of a negative approach to publication, of a 'many are called but few are chosen' attitude. In reality few writers are published by any well-known publishing firm, or by any lesser-known firm with national outlets. I would never suggest that people should not try for publication by such firms, rather that they should look for alternative publication at the same time. For too long publication has been the prerogative of a small, select group of people – often extremely talented, but not always so. (Pick up a selection of books from a second-hand bookshop and you often wonder why some of them were ever published.) I think we should concentrate on sustaining and building up our own audiences and readership, so that 'publication' – in the sense of having a public voice for our writing – can be available to everyone who wishes it.

The possibilities:

1 Decide on your audience and maintain alternatives. You can try for commercial publication and/or small local presses and/or a performance. You can choose to keep some work, perhaps in slightly altered form, for members of your family to receive subsequently.

2 Plan the publication: don't rely on a casual 'opportunity knocks' approach.

3 Build your 'publications' with others.

'It was Only a Dream' or 'How to Explain to Aunt Prudence'
Sylvia Kantaris

Dear Aunt Prudence,

I'm sorry to hear that you are so shocked by my book. Please believe me that I did not intend it to shock. I honestly did not have 'intimate relations' with the local butcher in *real* life, and when I mentioned his 'porky fingers' it was a poetic metaphor for sausages (which don't really have much pork in them these days, do they?)

My lawful-wedded was also a bit perplexed, and thought it likely that I had really been 'getting up to tricks' in the sauna with the vicar, but, as I explained to him, it was 'only a dream'. In fact, all the poems you consider 'lascivious' are only funny dreams I had. (We all have funny dreams sometimes, don't we? I expect even Mrs Whitehouse has them sometimes?)

No, my mother has not read my book, and so is not shocked. She doesn't normally read poetry, so there was no risk. In any case, she knows about 'poetic licence' because I took the precaution of telling her about it. Please be sure that anything you find 'unseemly' has nothing whatsoever to do with my real life. I should hate you to think otherwise. The poem about the glut of gooseberries is real enough, unfortunately. I seem to be forever picking and pickling gooseberries again, this season. Do you have the same problem? I put it down to the Greenhouse Effect, myself, rather than 'green fingers'. (The reason that reviewer called some of my poems 'seedy' was no doubt due to the fact that there are a lot of seeds in gooseberries.)

My dear aunt, steer clear of books by a woman called Fiona Pitt-Kethley. The latest reviewer said she was 'anxious to shock the pants off your maiden aunt in Tunbridge Wells'. Isn't that *appalling*? I certainly don't read such things, myself – though perhaps she is as respectable as I am, and only dreamt the poems.

The shocking four-letter words you mention were a shock to me, too, believe it or not. Please do bear in mind that it was a 'character', not I, who used such words. I read about her and that equally seamy male character in a tabloid, so I thought I'd have a go at dramatising their sleazy speech, if you see what I mean. Of *course* she is not me, Aunt. We call these things 'poetic masks' in the trade. Nobody in poetry 'walks naked' like those nudes you saw on the beach in Spain.

Yes, I'm sure you're right that books like mine should carry a government health warning to protect the young. Children are far too direct, these days, as I've found in schools where I have been doing workshops in order to earn a few pence. They use words such as you and I would never use, and not only in the state sector. The headmistress of a renowned private school (no names named) was as concerned as you about the 'tone' of some of my poems, but the children were not. So one can only place one's hopes in the new generation, cannot one? Naturally, I normally have to slum it in comprehensives, so it is indeed possible, as you suggest, that some of their public-sector slang has inadvertently crept into my poems, for the purpose of satire. Yes, I'm sure you are right when you say that, had I called the book 'Silver Linings', it would have been more tasteful. I did toy with 'Golden Harvests' for a minute, I must confess.

Still, 'Man is such stuff as dreams are made of', and I suppose woman is too? What do you think, Aunt? You know how much I value your astute comments. Indeed I do agree that there is a subversive element in all forms of creative writing, and that the fate of Salman Rushdie proves it. Unlike you, I don't agree that the answer is to turf all Muslims out of Britain and to burn the Koran in public. (Which reminds me that a local High Anglican priest condemned me as a 'heretic' recently, because I said, in public, that instead of a certain four-letter word used of female genitalia, 'We need a new word, clean as amethyst . . .')

No, Aunt, you can be sure I am not 'milking the government' in order to finance what you see as 'obscenities'. Social Security is a thing of the past, I'm afraid, and poetry does not attract private sponsorship. Any suggestions . . .? Which reminds me to tell you that the poems you saw as 'Marxist' were not intended as such. They were simply meant to be ironic. However, as the poet T. S. Eliot said, every different reader's different interpretation of a poem is equally valid, and as valid as that of the author. So you see, poets also embrace your own principles of democracy and freedom of speech.

For other reasons, Ogulu agrees with you that I should never have taken up poetry. He says it is ruining our marriage. I never dreamt to see the day when you and he would be on the same side, but he's a bit under the weather since he was made redundant, and says that if I'm going to spend so long sitting at a table I might at least have something to show for it, such as a best-selling novel. Unfortunately, every time I try to write a novel, it turns into a poetry sequence instead. In any case, remember that 'unmentionable' best-seller you were so furious about that you burnt it to ashes after reading the first chapter?

Incidentally, I am currently considering writing a very nice sequence called 'Matters of the Heart' and dedicating it to you. It will have to be privately hand-printed in a limited edition in order to be worthy of you, which is a problem (because highly expensive) so I'm afraid it may take rather a long time for me to scrape the money together, which is a pity because I had your golden wedding anniversary in mind. I've already written the first sonnet, which starts: 'A better heart than thine was never known.' Ah well! I suppose I'll just have to write the best-selling novel first! In the meantime, do take care not to over-exert yourself pruning the rose bushes on the terrace. I'm about to start another sonnet entitled 'My aunt still beautiful amongst the roses' but I shan't tell you anything more yet because I want it to be a surprise gift, bound in pigskin, with gold-leaf inset lettering. So keep your fingers crossed that I can earn enough with my 'pot-boiler' to be able to present you with your just deserts before we *both* turn into leaf-mould! I do hope you will now understand my dream poems in the way they are meant to be read.

Ogulu and the children send you their love, along with mine. Your devoted niece,
Verity xxx

Appendix

Joining a Writing Workshop (1)
Carole Satyamurti

Why do we write? No doubt everyone who writes would answer this question in a different way, but I would guess that most of us would say in one way or another that we want to communicate with other people. Yet usually the people for whom we are writing are unknown and invisible. We send off our work, and in the fullness of time it comes bouncing back to us; or, if we are lucky, it gets accepted and published. But we rarely know why the work is rejected, or how it is received by other people if it is published. We cannot learn in any precise way from our failures and successes. Joining a writing group or workshop can be one way of obtaining valuable and detailed feedback on our work.

Perhaps you are not sure whether what you are doing is 'proper' writing at all? Women particularly can fall prey to an inner voice that undermines them, tells them that what they write must be rubbish and how dare they think otherwise! Joining a writing group can give you confidence. If only you can take the initial step, you will find that the other people in the group are not somehow special, but pretty much like you, with an interest in writing, and in learning how to do it better.

Or perhaps you feel that you would like to write, but can't seem to get round to it? A writing group can be a stimulus. If you are going to get the most from it, you have to produce work for that meeting once a month, or once a fortnight, even if you write nothing else.

The format that works best for a writing workshop, in my

experience, is as follows. Each person brings enough copies of their work to enable everyone in the group to have one. In order for discussion to be useful, it has to be detailed – even down to talking about commas and spacing perhaps – and this is just not possible unless you can see the work on the page.

It is helpful if someone takes responsibility for keeping an eye on the clock, so that the available time is fairly divided between those who have brought work to present. Without this, as time runs out, those who have not yet read may become tense and distracted, and may leave the workshop upset that they have not had a hearing.

The person who has written the piece to be discussed reads it aloud; everyone else thinks about it, perhaps reading it again to themselves, and a discussion follows.

Sometimes it works well for the author to stay silent at first, so that the others have to interpret the piece as best they can, without having the benefit of knowing what the author intended. In that way, the group has no more to go on than would the readers of a magazine, who of course have no explanation to guide their reading. For the author, this is a useful test of whether what s/he has written is comprehensible, ambiguous or downright obscure. When you feel that the group has totally misinterpreted what you have written, it is very tempting to put them right at once; but to restrain yourself can be instructive! Before the allotted time is up, though, the author should join in the discussion, respond to points people have made, clear up any misunderstandings, say what s/he was trying to achieve in the writing and perhaps evaluate the criticisms.

Everyone who comes to a workshop should bring work they are, in principle, prepared to change. Although your impulse may be to bring the work you feel most pleased with, it will probably be more useful to you to present something you have doubts about – something on which you want reactions to which you are ready to respond if you feel they are helpful ones. Seasoned workshop hands will have come across people who seem to have brought their work merely to get applause. They respond to criticism with quick dismissal, or even hostility, and the rest of the group feels frustrated – although serious discussion of a piece of writing is always a useful learning exercise, whatever the reaction of its author. Alternatively, a person may disarm criticism by saying, 'well I only wrote this for myself; it doesn't matter if it doesn't get across to other people' – to which a suitable response might be, 'why bring it to a workshop then?'

This may seem harsh. To write down a personal problem, in the form of a poem perhaps, can, after all, be a very effective way of dealing with it. I think, though, that a distinction needs to be made between writing that is *primarily* private and therapeutic, and writing which, though it may have therapeutic side effects, is primarily intended to communicate – to someone, if not to everyone. A writing workshop can only deal effectively with the second kind, because it is concerned with helping its members to write better, to express themselves more vividly, more strongly, and it can do this only with writing which is genuinely in the public domain.

Normally, people will want to bring to the workshop writing they have initiated themselves. But sometimes it can be fun for the group to set itself a particular exercise for next time – to write on a given theme, for instance; to write something based, however loosely, on a particular picture; or to write in the voice of an inanimate object. It can also be good, occasionally, to do exercises in the workshop – for example, to write a 10-minute poem incorporating a line taken at random from an anthology; or to use five words chosen 'blind' from the dictionary. Such exercises do not appeal to everyone, and they can seem nerve-wracking to contemplate, but people are often surprised at how much they are able to achieve in 10 minutes, when they are used to staring into space all morning and only coming up with a line or two.

I have heard it said that writing groups have a natural lifespan – that after a year or two they become too cosy and predictable. People bring work they know the group will like, and the meetings become occasions for mutual congratulation. I do not think that this is inevitable, though. Being thoroughly at ease with other members may, on the contrary, enable one to take risks and try new things. But if cosiness does threaten, then inviting new people to join can help to stave it off.

Everyone feels nervous the first time they attend a writing workshop. There is the fear of criticism, ridicule or scorn even; fear that the other people will be much better than you are; fear that you will be an embarrassment or a liability. It is worth bearing in mind, until reality allays your anxieties, as it probably will, that your writing is not all you bring to the group. You also bring your honest and sensitive reaction to other people's work. So even if you have doubts about the worth of what you have written, you can still feel that your response to what you hear will be of value.

Joining a Writing Workshop (2).
Amryl Johnson

Writing is, can be, a very lonely business – even with the cat sitting on your shoulder! Joining a writing workshop may work for you. Ring the office of your Regional Arts Association or look for advertisements of local classes and groups. Local newspapers and libraries are good places to look.

In a writing group you will find yourself working with a group of people who share the same interest in writing as yourself. The format will vary from group to group. There may be a group leader. A published writer may be employed to lead the workshop, or the group may have been created by someone like yourself who is just beginning and wants to learn the craft with others just starting out. A writing group may work well for you if you need an incentive. Often, you will be asked to write a poem, scene, story or synopsis for the next meeting. Call it a deadline if you wish.

Writing is a craft. I know the terror of uncertainty, the lack of confidence many beginning writers face. It takes a while for us to come out of our closets, to admit to ourselves and others that we write. In submitting our work to strangers, we reveal ourselves. We stand naked, allowing our imperfections to be scrutinised. It therefore saddens me when writers talk of phrases like 'crap!', 'what rubbish!' and 'why on earth did you bother?!' being directed at their work, more often than not by the person leading the workshop. This is not constructive criticism. If the brusque, dynamic approach spurs you on, starts the adrenalin pumping, fine. If, however, you experience and continue to experience terror every time you submit a piece to your group, my advice? Get out. You have not failed. You are not being over-sensitive. The format, quite simply, is not for you.

You still feel you would like to work with others? Many regions have more than one writing workshop. Why not try another? If for any reason this does not leave you any happier, you still have not failed. You may have met others in the workshop of the same mind as yourself. Why not get together with them and start a small group of your own? Or join together with a group of friends. Shape your group the way you choose. Inject variety into it by looking at new publications. Discuss them as a group. Look at the way a particular writer's work has developed over the years. Analyse the style. Make it fun.

Get your group recognised by your Regional Arts Association. If there is no other group of the same kind in your area, they may well offer some financial assistance. Get books from the library about the craft of writing. Read any article you can lay your hands on. Read and discuss. Read, discuss and write. Write. Write. And Write.

Do you have any published writers living locally? Ask them to come and talk to your group. Ask your Regional Arts Association for help with funding. Keep your ear to the ground for 'Writers in Residence' in your area.

Finally, once you are established, why not share what you and the group have created by giving a public reading? And don't forget the booklet!

Good luck!

Notes on Contributors

Gillian Allnutt is ex-poetry editor of *City Limits* magazine and author of *Spitting the Pips Out* (Sheba, 1981), *Lizzie Siddall: Her Journal (1862)* (Greville Press, 1985) and *Beginning the Avocado* (Virago, 1988). She is co-editor of *The New British Poetry* (Paladin, 1988), and tutors creative writing in Newcastle upon Tyne where she lives.

Janet Beck studied drama at Hull and went on to work in Theatre In Education and Youth Theatre. She developed her first play in conjunction with The Soho Poly Theatre, and currently works for the Brent Arts Centre and teaches video and drama. Together with Cheryl Robson, she is a director of the London-based Women Writers' and Directors' Workshop.

Rosalind Brackenbury is the author of eight published novels and two volumes of poetry, the latest of which, *Making for the Secret Places*, appeared with Taxus in 1989. She is a regular columnist for the magazine *Resurgence*, and a tutor in creative writing for the extra-mural department of Edinburgh University.

Jeannie Brehaut was born in Toronto, Canada, and came to Britain when she was 19. She is a contributor to The Women's Press women writers' notebook *Delighting the Heart* (1989), and a selection of her poetry is published in the lesbian anthology *Whatever You Desire* (Oscars Press, 1990). She has also contributed a short story to *More Serious Pleasure* (Sheba, forthcoming), and has a first novel currently in progress.

Angela Brown is a tutor in creative writing, working with university adult studies classes and community groups. Whilst her real love is poetry, she squeezes in frenetic bouts of writing in fields as diverse as trade journals and arts reviews for local papers. Her hobbies include folk and circle dancing, and attempting to cultivate organically the garden of the inner-city vicarage where she lives with her industrial chaplain husband, two sons and a ginger cat.

Katie Campbell's plays have been performed in a variety of venues, including BBC radio, and as part of the Royal Shakespeare Company autumn festival (1988 and 1989). Her journalistic credits include *The Times*, *The Women's Review of Books*, *Mail On Sunday*, *Guardian*, *City Limits*, *Time Out*, *New Statesman*, *She*, *Company*, *Women's Review*, *Literary Review* and *Writer's Monthly*. Her collection of poems, *Let Us Leave the Believing*, is published by Aquila and Quarry Presses (1989), and her collection of stories, *What He Really Wants Is A Dog*, by Methuen (1989).

Jo Campling is the publisher of a number of academic and professional lists, including Macmillan's 'Women In Society'. She won the 1987 Pandora award for the most positive contribution to the image of women in publishing, and runs numerous publishing workshops. She is visiting fellow at the Centre for Research and Education on Gender at the London University Institute of Education.

Julia Casterton is author of *Creative Writing* (Macmillan, 1986), and teaches literature and writing at the City Lit in London and for the Open University. She is development editor for the magazine *Ambit*, and her poems and reviews have appeared in a number of international publications. Her collection of poems, *That Slut Cleopatra*, was published in 1988 (Turret Books).

Gladys Mary Coles' poetry has appeared in seven collections, including *Liverpool Folio* (Duckworth, 1984), and *Leafburners: New and Selected Poems* (Duckworth, 1986), and has won several major awards. She has written a biography of Mary Webb and edited two editions of Mary Webb's verse. A new biographical and critical study of Mary Webb is forthcoming from Seren Books. She is a tutor in creative writing in the department of continuing education at Liverpool University, and manager of Headland Poetry Publications.

Christine Crow's first novel, *Miss X, or the Wolf Woman*, was published by The Women's Press in 1990. She is honorary reader in French literature and a fellow of St Leonard's College at the University of St Andrews. Her critical writing has focused mainly on the work of the French poet and thinker, Paul Valéry.

Maxine Davies is a counsellor and psychotherapist and tutors journal writing in London. She has worked as a senior social worker, and was an executive officer with the GLC Women's Committee Support Unit. Her published writing has been mostly in the form of letters and articles, which have appeared in the Open University and National Extension College *Newsletters*, the GLC Women's Committee *Bulletins*, the *Radio Times*, the *Observer*, the *Association of Child Care Officers' Journal* and the *British Association of Social Workers' Newsletter*.

Joan Downar has three collections of poetry, *The Empire of Light* (Peterloo, 1984), *From the First World* (Poetry Nottingham, 1985) and *The Old Noise of Truth* (Peterloo, 1989), and has won a number of prizes both for her poetry and her short stories. She writes a weekly column on amateur theatre for the *Nottingham Evening Post*, and teaches creative writing in adult education at Loughborough University.

Nicky Edwards is the author of two novels, *Mud* (The Women's Press, 1986), and *Stealing Time* (Onlywomen Press, 1990). She teaches creative writing in London, and at the University of East Anglia.

Zoë Fairbairns' published novels include *Benefits* (Virago, 1979), *Stand We At Last* (Virago, 1983), *Here Today* (Mandarin, 1984) and *Closing* (Methuen, 1987). She has taught creative writing at the Arvon Foundation, the City Lit, Morley College, the Hen House, Silver Moon Women's Bookshop, in schools and in both men's and women's prisons. Her latest novel, *Daddy's Girls*, is forthcoming from Methuen.

Gerrie Fellows was born in New Zealand and trained as a painter at the Middlesex Polytechnic and Central School of Art and Design. Her collection *Technologies and Other Poems* is published by Polygon Press (1990), and her poetry has appeared in numerous anthologies and journals as well as on television, particularly in Scotland where she now lives.

Frankie Finn's first play, *Collecting Leaves*, was performed by the Mouth and Trousers Theatre Company in London in 1982, and her novel, *Out On The Plain*, was published by the Women's Press in 1984. She is currently teaching writing in Dartmoor Prison, and training (part time) to be a psychotherapist.

Helen Flint has two novels in print, the most recent of which is *In Full Possession* (Heinemann and St Martin's Press, 1989). Her first novel, *Return Journey* (Heinemann, 1987), won a Betty Trask award. Her poetry has been published in anthologies and magazines, including *Doors: Into and Out of Dorset*, a Dorset-based magazine which she has also edited.

Jill Foster began her working life as an actress at the age of 12, from which profession she retired at 17. She has been a literary agent for 21 years, and has run her own agency for 13. While her agency deals with most media, her specialisation is film and television.

Lizbeth Goodman wrote her PhD on 'British Feminist Theatre Since 1968' at St. John's College Cambridge, and is a lecturer in Literature at the Open University, working both in Literature/Drama and in Women's Studies. She has worked as an artistic director and producer for the Cambridge Footlights Women's Company and for the Better Half Women's Theatre Co-operative, for whom she has also written. She is co-organiser of the forthcoming conference 'Theatre Under Threat: The Economics and Politics of British Theatre Production', and has compiled a collection of interviews with women playwrights, performers, directors, theatre administrators and critics.

Rahila Gupta is a freelance journalist, writer and activist, and currently works as a publications officer for a housing organisation. She has contributed to *Right of Way: Prose and Poetry from the Asian Women Writers' Workshop* (The Women's Press, 1988), *Charting the Journey: Writings by Black and Third World Women*, (Sheba, 1988) and *Balancing Acts* (Virago, 1989).

Sue Habeshaw is co-author of seven books in the *Interesting Ways to Teach* series (Technical and Educational Services, 1984–90). She is a lecturer in literary studies at Bristol Polytechnic, and also teaches study skills, co-counselling and counselling.

Caroline Halliday has contributed poems and short stories to various anthologies, and is author of the collection *Some Truth, Some Change* (Onlywomen Press, 1983). She combines writing with working as a management consultant, and until recently ran a lesbian creative writing class in London. She is a co-mother, and is currently co-editing an anthology of creative writing from lesbians around the subject of children.

Valerie Hannagan was brought up in France. She came to Britain to train as a teacher, and began to write out of a desire to bring her French and English sides together. She has written a family history, poems, short stories, and literary criticism, and is currently working on a thesis on the French writer Monique Wittig.

Jane Harris began her career in the theatre, training in television by making films for BBC Drama. She then joined Kestrel Film Productions, where she was involved in assisting with the making of such films as *Kes* and *Family Life*. She spent part of the 1970s and 1980s travelling and working in Mexico, North America and Canada. She returned to London in 1986 where she became a script editor for BBC Television Drama. In 1988 she became Script Executive for BBC 1 and 2 films. She is a single parent, and has a passion for history, politics and all movies that move.

Elizabeth Hawkins began writing as a freelance journalist, and became increasingly interested in writing for children through her three sons. Her books include *Supermum* (Van Dyke, 1977), *Johnny's Shipwreck* (Macdonald, 1988), *Climbing Clare* (Macdonald, 1988) and *Henry's Most Unusual Birthday* (Andersen, 1990). She teaches classes on writing for children in London.

Ursula Holden began writing seriously at the age of 43 and is the author of 12 novels, the most recent of which are *Tin Toys*

(Methuen, 1986), *Unicorn Sisters* (Methuen, 1988) and *A Bubble Garden* (Methuen, 1989). Born in Dorset, she spent part of her childhood in Egypt, and served in the W.R.N.S. during the second world war. She has three daughters and lives in West London.

Jill Hyem has written over thirty radio plays, and was co-originator of the daily radio serial *Waggoners' Walk*. In the past 10 years she has worked extensively for television, writing a number of single plays and contributing to many successful series and serials. She was co-author of the BBC award-winning *Tenko*, and co-creator of London Weekend Television's *Wish me Luck*. Her theatre work includes *Post Mortems* and *Equal Terms*. She was a founder member of the Writers' Guild Women's Committee, and has tutored for the Arvon Foundation and London Media Workshops.

Amryl Johnson was born in Trinidad and came to Britain when she was 11. Her stories and poems have appeared in a number of anthologies, and she is the author of two collections of poetry, *Early Poems by Amryl Johnson* (Sable Publications, 1982) and *Long Road to Nowhere* (Virago, 1985), and a travel-biography, *Sequins for a Ragged Hem* (Virago, 1988). She works as a creative writing tutor in adult education and in schools.

Julia Jones has written over 50 original plays and films for television, including *Back of Beyond*, *Still Waters* and the prize-winning *Devon Violets*, as well as novel and story adaptations for adults and children. Her dramatisation of Jenny Nimmo's *The Snow Spider* won a 1989 Bafta award and a prize at the New York Television and Film Festival. She has written extensively for radio, and her stage plays *Country Ways* and *The Garden* have been performed at the Hampstead Theatre and Bristol Old Vic.

Sylvia Kantaris has published five collections of poetry, the latest being *Dirty Washing: New and Selected Poems* (Bloodaxe, 1989). She studied French at Bristol University, and wrote MA and PhD theses on French surrealism at the University of Queensland in Australia. She has worked as a tutor for the Open University and the Arvon Foundation, and in 1986 was appointed Cornwall's first Writer in the Community. She was awarded the Honorary Degree of Doctor of Letters by Exeter University in 1989.

R. M. Lamming was born in the Isle of Man and educated in Wales and at Oxford. She has published short stories and two novels, *The Notebook of Gismondo Cavalleti* (Cape, 1983), which won the David Higham First Novel Award, and *In the Dark* (Cape, 1985). She is a tutor for the Arvon Foundation.

Sarah Lefanu is a commissioning editor at The Women's Press. Here she writes about her role as fiction editor, but she is also responsible for some non-fiction publishing. She has co-edited two anthologies of fiction, *Despatches from the Frontiers of the Female Mind* (The Women's Press, 1985), and *Colours of a New Day: Writing for South Africa* (Lawrence and Wishart, 1990), and is author of *In the Chinks of the World Machine: Feminism and Science Fiction* (The Women's Press, 1988).

Eugenia Liroudia studied film and video at the Stavrakos Film School in Athens, the London International Film School, and the London College of Printing, where she was awarded a BA. Born in Greece, she has worked as an editor and director for Greek television, and has written, filmed and edited various 8mm and 16mm films, including *The Disguise of Absence*, which was screened at London's Riverside Studios in 1989. She teaches script-writing for film and video at the Drill Hall Arts Centre in London.

Caeia March was born in the Isle of Man and grew up in industrial South Yorkshire. She graduated from London University in 1968, and currently divides her time between London and Cornwall. Her stories and poems have been published in various anthologies, and she is the author of three novels, *Three Ply Yarn* (The Women's Press, 1986), *The Hide and Seek Files* (The Women's Press, 1989), and *Fire! Fire!* (The Women's Press, forthcoming). She came out as a lesbian in 1980, and is currently recovering slowly from myalgic encephalo-myelitis and working on a new novel, a collection of short stories, and a collection of poetry.

Kara May has written numerous plays for the theatre and for BBC radio. Her most recent children's books include *Knickerless*

Nicola (Macmillan, 1989) and *Horrible Henry and the Headless Ghost* (Hippo, 1990). She is a tutor in creative writing at Goldsmith's College.

Christian McEwen was born in London, and grew up in the Borders of Scotland. She has been living in the States for the past 10 years, first as a student, and currently as a writer working in conjunction with the Teachers and Writers Collaborative in New York. She has contributed poems, stories and reviews to a range of publications, and is editor of two anthologies, *Naming the Waves: Contemporary Lesbian Poetry* (Virago and Crossing Press, 1988), and *Out the Other Side: Contemporary Lesbian Writing*, (with Sue O'Sullivan, Virago and Crossing Press, 1988).

Ursule Molinaro has published 10 novels, the most recent of which are *Positions with White Roses* (The Women's Press, 1988) and *The New Moon With The Old Moon In Her Arms* (The Women's Press, 1990). Her short stories have been published in various international collections, anthologies, newspapers and magazines. She has written plays for the stage, translated novels, stories, plays and film titles into English, and has published a number of works of non-fiction, including *A Full Moon Of Women: 29 Word Portraits Of Notable Women From Different Times and Places + 1 Void Of Course*, (Viking Penguin, 1990).

Moira Monteith is senior lecturer in the Department of English at Sheffield City Polytechnic. She has published articles on Ursula Le Guin, Doris Lessing and Marge Piercey, and is editor of *Women's Writing: A Challenge to Theory* (Harvester, 1986).

Caroline Natzler's short story collection, *Water Wings*, is published by Onlywomen Press (1990), and she has contributed stories to a number of anthologies and magazines. She works part time as a local authority solicitor, is a member of a lesbian writers' group, and teaches writing at the City University and Goldsmith's College.

Rebecca O'Rourke has been involved in the worker writer movement for many years. A founder member of 'Women and Words' (Birmingham, 1979), she has worked for Centerprise

Community Publishers, and is currently a part-time women's education worker. She writes fiction and criticism. Her most recent publication is *Reflecting on The Well of Loneliness* (Routledge, 1989), and she has a new collection of short stories, *Dead Men Don't Rape*, nearing completion.

Caroline Raphael studied drama at Manchester University and went on to become assistant director at the Nuffield Theatre, Southampton. She has worked at the Royal Exchange Manchester nd as director at the Bristol Old Vic. She joined the BBC Radio Drama Department in 1984, and in 1990 became the first Editor of Children and Youth Drama & Features, Radio 5. She is married and has a son.

Joan Riley was born in St Mary, Jamaica, and now lives in Britain. Her first novel, *The Unbelonging*, was published by The Women's Press in 1985, her second *Waiting in the Twilight*, 1987, and her third, *Romance* in 1988. She has worked as a tutor for the Avon Foundation and is currently working on her fourth novel.

Michèle Roberts has published five novels, the most recent of which is *In the Red Kitchen*, (Methuen, 1990). *A Piece of the Night* and *The Visitation* are both available from The Women's Press. Her poetry collections include *The Mirror of the Mother* (Methuen, 1986), and she has also published short stories and essays in numerous anthologies. Her play, *The Journeywoman*, was premiered at the Mercury Theatre in Colchester in 1988.

Cheryl Robson was born in Australia and studied drama at Bristol before working for the BBC. She was literary manager for the Bristol Express Theatre Company from 1988 to 1990, and is currently studying for an MA in playwrighting at Birmingham University. Her play, *O Architect*, was performed at the New End Theatre in 1989. Together with Janet Beck, she is a director of the London Women Writers' and Directors' Workshop.

Sue Roe's poems and short stories have appeared in *Writing Women*, *PEN New Poetry 1*, *The Scotsman* and *The Printer's Devil*. Her novel, *Estella: Her Expectations* was reissued by Harvester (1987), and she is author of *Writing and Gender:*

Virginia Woolf's Writing Practice (Harvester Wheatsheaf, 1990).
She is a regular reviewer of fiction and criticism and is a
contributor to *Delighting the Heart: A Notebook by Women
Writers* (The Women's Press, 1989). She has recently completed
a second novel and is currently working on a third.

Carole Satyamurti has two collections of poetry, *Broken Moon*
(Oxford University Press, 1987), and *Changing the Subject*
(Oxford University Press, 1990), and has contributed poems to
numerous anthologies and magazines. She was winner of the
1986 National Poetry Competition, and teaches at the Polytechnic of East London and for the Arvon Foundation.

Thalia Selz is writer in residence at Trinity College, Hartford,
Connecticut. Her short stories have appeared in various
anthologies and magazines, and have won several major
awards. She also writes articles and book and film reviews.

Joanna Scott is the author of three novels, *Fading, My
Parmacheene Belle* (Ticknor and Fields, 1987, and Bodley
Head, 1988), *The Closest Possible Union* (Ticknor and Fields,
1988, and Bodley Head, 1989) and *Arrogance* (Simon and
Schuster, 1990), and is currently working on a fourth. She has
won a number of awards for her writing, and has taught a range
of creative writing courses at university level.

Caroline Spry is deputy commissioning editor for Independent
Film and Video at Channel Four television. She was trained at
the London College of Printing and Royal College of Art in film
and television photography, and worked as a documentary
camera operator before becoming an independent producer.
She was co-founder of the Cinema of Women, a feminist film
and video distribution network, and at Channel Four has been
responsible for commissioning a wide range of women's work,
including the *In the Pink* and *Women Call the Shots* seasons, and
the gay and lesbian series *Out On Tuesday*.

Sue Stewart's poetry has been published in numerous magazines, in *Four Ways* (Phoenix Press, 1985) and *Delighting the
Heart: A Notebook by Women Writers* (The Women's Press,
1989). She has compiled *Big World, Little World*, an anthology
of contemporary poems and other writings on green issues for

children (Macmillan, forthcoming), and teaches creative writing in adult education and in schools. She is a member of the Council of Management of the Arvon Foundation and the Southern Arts Literature Panel.

Valerie Taylor has written since the age of 11, and has completed two novels and published poems. She has taught creative writing and worked in adult education for over 10 years, where one of her specialist areas is Afro-Caribbean Literature.

Sue Teddern's feature articles have appeared in a wide range of publications, including *Radio Times*, *Guardian*, *Mizz*, *Time Out*, *Company*, *Options*, *Woman's Journal*, *Prima*, *19* and *Ms London*. She teaches feature journalism at the National Council for the Training of Journalists and the City Lit. She has written drama for radio, and is currently working on comedy scripts for television.

Maria Tolly's most recent albums/cassettes are *Voices* and *Up To Here*. She has performed her songs internationally, including concerts in Cuba, Belgium, the Netherlands, the German Democratic Republic, Czechoslovakia and the USSR. She won the 1983 GLC Song for Peace Competition, and is currently combining her early work in theatre as an actress, performer and writer with her singing and song writing.

Lisa Tuttle has had more than 60 science fiction, fantasy and horror stories published in magazines and anthologies on both sides of the Atlantic. She is the author of four full-length novels, including *A Spaceship Built of Stone* (The Women's Press, 1987) and *Gabriel* (Sphere, 1987, and Tor, 1988), the non-fiction *Encyclopedia of Feminism* (Longman and Arrow, 1986), and *Heroines: Women Inspired by Women* (Harrap, 1988). She is the editor of the horror story anthology *Skin of the Soul* (The Women's Press, 1990).

Valerie Windsor's radio plays have won a number of major prizes, including The Society of Author's Pye Award and the Giles Cooper Award. Her stage play, *Effie's Burning*, was performed at the Library Theatre Manchester in 1987 and as a platform production at the National Theatre. She writes for

Mersey Television's *Brookside* (Channel 4) and is a regular tutor for the Arvon Foundation.

Sally Worboyes has worked in Youth Theatre, and has written for radio and television. She has been a member of the Riverside Studios Writers' Group since 1983. stage plays read publicly there.

Sheila Yeger's most recent radio play, *Yellow Ochre*, was broadcast on BBC Radio 4 in 1989. She has also written for television, and her theatre plays include *Self Portrait* (Theatre Clwyd and Derby Playhouse), *Geraniums* (commissioned by the Royal Shakespeare Company), *Alice and Other Reflections* (Soho Poly and national tour) and *Watching Foxes* (Bristol Old Vic).

Bibliography

Aiken, Joan, *The Way to Write for Children*, Elm Tree Books, 1982.

Ascher, Carol, Louise DeSalvo, and Sara Ruddick, editors, *Between Women*, Beacon Press, 1984.

Ash, William, *The Way to Write Radio Drama*, Elm Tree Books, 1985.

Asian Women Writers' Workshop, *Right of Way: Prose and Poetry*, The Women's Press, 1988.

Baldwin, Christian, *One to One: Self Understanding Through Journal Writing*, M. Evans, 1977.

BBC, *On Camera: How to Produce Film and Video*, BBC, 1984.

Beddoe, Deirdre, *Discovering Women's History*, Pandora, 1983.

Beja, Morris, *Film and Literature*, Longman, 1979.

Bernikow, Louise (ed), *The World Split Open: Women Poets 1552–1950*, The Women's Press, 1979.

Bradshaw, Jan and Mary Hemming (eds), *Girls Next Door: Lesbian Feminist Stories*, The Women's Press, 1985.

Brande, Dorothea, *Becoming a Writer* (1934), Papermac, 1983.

British Film Institute, *The BFI Film and Television Yearbook*.

Brooks, Cleanth, and Penn Warren, Robert, *Understanding Good Writing*, Dobson, 1956.

—*Understanding Poetry*, Holt, Rhinehart and Winston, 1976.

Browne, Connors and Stern (eds), *With the Pain of Each Breath: A Disabled Women's Anthology*, Cleispress, 1985.

Brownjohn, Sandy, *Does It Have To Rhyme?*, Hodder and Stoughton, 1980.

Bruner, Charlotte H., (ed.), *Unwinding Threads: Writing by Women in Africa*, Heinemann, 1983.

Caputi, Jane, and Mary Daly, *Webster's First New Intergalactic Wickedary of the English Language*, The Women's Press, 1987.

Casterton, Julia, *Creative Writing: A Practical Guide*, Macmillan, 1986.

Chamberlain, Mary, (ed.), *Writing Lives: Conversations Between Women Writers*, Virago, 1988.

Chambers' Thesaurus, Chambers, 1986.

Chester, Gail, and Sigrid Nelson (eds), *In Other Words: Writing as a Feminist*, Hutchinson, 1987.

Cobham, Rhonda, and Merle Collins (eds), *Watchers and Seekers: Creative Writing by Black Women*, The Women's Press, 1987.

Couzyn, Jeni (ed.), *Bloodaxe Book of Women Poets*, 1987.

Deen, Rosemary and Marie Ponsot, *Beat Not the Poor Desk*, Boynton Cook, 1982.

Dickson, Anne, *The Mirror Within*, Quartet Books, 1982.

—*A Woman in Your Own Right*, Quartet Books, 1982.

Dinesen, Betzy (ed.), *Rediscovery: Three Hundred Years of Stories by and about Women*, The Women's Press, 1981.

Doubtfire, Dianne, *The Craft of Novel Writing*, Allison and Busby, 1981.

Elbow, Peter, *Writing with Power*, Oxford University Press, 1981.

Evans, Christopher, *Writing Science Fiction*, A. & C. Black, 1988.

Fairfax, John, and John Moat, *The Way to Write*, Elm Tree Books, 1981.

Fairfax, John, *Creative Writing*, Hamish Hamilton, 1989.

Farrell, Kate, and Kenneth Koch, *Sleeping on the Wing*, Vintage Books, 1981.

Field, Syd, *Screenplay: The Foundations of Screenwriting*, Dell Publishing, 1984.

Fuller, Cynthia (ed.), 'Modules on Women's Literature and History', National Extension College 'Workbooks'.

Gardner, John, *The Art of Fiction*, Vintage Books, 1985.

Gates, Henry Louis, 'Authority, (White) Power and the (Black) Critic' in *Cultural Critique*, Autumn 1987 issue.

Gauthier, Xavière, *Is There Such a Thing as Women's Writing?*, Mass. Press, 1980.

Gensler, Kinereth, and Nina Nyhart, *The Poetry Connection: An Anthology of Contemporary Poetry with Ideas to Stimulate Children*, Teachers and Writers Collaborative, 1978.

Giannetti, Louis, *Understanding Movies*, Prentice Hall, 1975.

Grahn, Judy, *Another Mother Tongue*, Beacon Press, 1984.

Green, Jen, (ed.), *Reader, I Murdered Him: An Anthology of Original Crime Stories*, The Women's Press, 1989.

Grumman, Joan, *Woman as Writer*, Houghton Mifflin, 1978.

Hennessy, Brendon, *Writing Feature Articles*, Heinemann, 1989.

Hull, Gloria, Patricia Bell Scott, and Barbara Smith, *But Some of Us Are Brave*, The Feminist Press, 1982.

Jelinek, Estelle C. (ed.), *Women's Autobiography*, Indiana University Press, 1980.

Kaplan, E. Ann, *Women and Film*, Methuen, 1983.

Kenyon, Olga *Women Novelists Today*, Harvester, 1988.

—*Women Writers Talk*, Lennard Press, 1989.

—*Women Writing World Wide*, Pluto Press, 1990.

Kelsey, Gerald, *Writing for Television*, A. & C. Black, 1990.

Kitchen, Paddy, *The Way to Write Novels*, Elm Tree Books, 1981.

Koch, Kenneth, *Wishes, Lies and Dreams*, Harper and Row, 1970.

—*Rose, Where Did You Get That Red?* Vintage, 1973.

Land, Pat, and Zrzowski, Sue, (eds), *In Our Experience: Workshops at the Women's Therapy Centre*, The Women's Press, 1988.

Lannin, George, and Robie Macauley, *Technique in Fiction*, St Martin's Press, 1987.

Lee, Hermione (ed.), *The Secret Self: Short Stories by Women*, J. M. Dent, 1985.

—*The Secret Self 2: Short Stories by Women*, J. M. Dent, 1987.

Lefebure, Molly, *The Bondage of Love: A Life of Mrs Samuel Taylor Coleridge*, Gollancz, 1986, 1988.

Manguel, Alberto (ed.), *Other Fires: Stories from the Women of Latin America*, Picador, 1986.

Martin, Rhona, *Writing Historical Fiction*, A. & C. Black, 1988.

Meulenbelt, Anja, *For Ourselves: Our Bodies and Sexuality*, Sheba, 1981.

Methuen/BBC publications, *Best Radio Plays*, Giles Cooper award winners, published annually.

Miller, Casey, and Kate Swift, *The Handbook of Non-Sexist Writing*, The Women's Press, 1981.

Miller, William, *Screenwriting for Narrative Film and Television*, Columbus Books, 1988.

Minot, Stephen, *Three Genres*, Prentice Hall, 1988.

Monteith, Moira, (ed.), *Women's Writing: A Challenge to Theory*, Harvester, 1986.

Muir, Anne Rosse, *A Woman's Guide to Jobs in Film and Television*, Pandora, 1987.

Nichols, Grace, *The Fat Black Woman's Poems*, Virago, 1984.

Olsen, Tillie, *Silences*, Virago, 1980.

Padgett, Ron (ed.), *Handbook of Poetic Forms*, Teachers and Writers Collaborative, 1987.

Paice, Eric, *The Way to Write for Television*, Elm Tree Books, 1981.

The Penguin Book of Caribbean Verse in English, 1986.

The Penguin Book of Women Poets, 1978.

Progroff, Ira, *At a Journal Workshop*, Dialogue House Library, 1975.

Rainer, Tristine, *The New Diary: How to Use a Journal for Self-Guidance and Expanded Creativity*, Angus and Robertson, 1980.

Rich, Adrienne, *On Lies, Secrets and Silence*, Virago, 1980.

Roberts, Ellen, *The Children's Picture Book*, Poplar Press, 1982.

Rule, Jane, *Lesbian Images*, Crossing Press, 1982.

Scott, Diana (ed.), *Bread and Roses*, Virago, 1982.

Sellers, Susan (ed.), *Delighting the Heart: A Notebook by Women Writers*, The Women's Press, 1989.

Silverberg, Robert, *Robert Silverberg's Worlds of Wonder*, Gollancz, 1988.

Smith, Barbara (ed.), *Home Girls: A Black Feminist Anthology*, Kitchen Table Press, 1983.

Stablefold, Brian, *The Way to Write Science Fiction*, Elm Tree Books, 1989.

Sternberg, Janet, *The Writer on her Work*, Norton, 1980.

Stillman, Frances, *The Poets' Manual and Rhyming Dictionary*, Thames and Hudson, 1966.

Strunk, W. and E. B. White, *The Elements of Style*, Collier, 1982.

Tate, Claudia (ed.), *Black Women Writers at Work*, Oldcastle Books, 1985.

Trease, Geoffrey, *The Young Writer*, Nelson, 1961.

Turner, Barry (ed.), *The Writer's Handbook*, Macmillan, 1989.

Tweedie, Jill, *In the Name of Love*, Granada, 1980.

Ueland, Barbara, *If You Want to Write*, Graywolf Press, 1987.

Washington, Mary Helen, *Any Woman's Blues: Stories by Contemporary Black Women Writers*, Virago, 1980.

Walker, Alice, *In Search of Our Mothers' Gardens*, The Women's Press, 1984.

Walker, Barbara, *The Women's Encyclopedia of Myths and Secrets*, Harper and Row, 1984.

Weldon, Fay, *Letters to Alice on First Reading Jane Austen*, Coronet, 1984.

Willis, Sue Meredith, *Personal Fiction Writing*, Teachers and Writers Collaborative, 1984.

Wilson, Robin Scott (ed.), *Those Who Can: A Science Fiction Reader*, New American Library, 1973.

Woolf, Virginia, *A Writer's Diary* (1953), Triad Panther, 1978.

Writers' and Artists' Yearbook, A. & C. Black, published annually.

Writers Market (US), Writers' Digest Books, published annually.

Yeger, Sheila, *The Sound of One Hand Clapping: A Guide to Writing for the Theatre*, Amber Lane Press, forthcoming.

Useful Addresses

Apples and Snakes
489a New Cross Road
London SE14 6TQ
0181 692 0393
(Puts on regular performance poetry events. Welcomes cassette tapes and
biographies of new poets.)

Arts Council of England
14 Great Peter Street
London SW1P 3NQ
0171 333 0100

Arts Council of Northern Ireland
MacNeice House
77 Malone Road
Belfast BT9 6AQ
01232 385200

Arts Council of Wales
9 Museum Place
Cardiff CF1 3NX
01222 376500

The Arvon Foundation
Totleigh Barton
Sheepwash
Beaworthy
Devon EX21 5NS
and
Lumb Bank
Hebden Bridge
West Yorkshire HX7 6DF
and
Moniack Mhor
Moniack
Kirkhill
Inverness IV5 7PQ
Information from Totleigh Barton: 01409 231338
(Runs residential writing courses at its three centres throughout the year.
A number of grants are available to those on low incomes.)

British Film Institute
21 Stephen Street
London W1P 2LN
0171 255 1444

Drill Hall Arts Centre
16 Chenies Street
London WC1E 7EX
0171 631 1353
(Runs a number of writing and women-only workshops.)

The Fawcett Library
London Guildhall University
Old Castle Street
London E1 7NT
0171 320 1189

The Feminist Library
5 Westminster Bridge Road
London SE1 7XW
0171 928 7789

New Playwrights Trust
The Interchange Studios
Dalby Street
London NW5 3NH
0171 284 2818

The Poetry Library
South Bank Centre
Royal Festival Hall
London SE1 8XX
0171 921 0600
(The library has an up-to-date collection of small magazines publishing new
writers, as well as details of competitions and courses.)

The Poetry Society
22 Betterton Street
London WC2H 9BU
0171 420 9880
(Offers a wide range of services including a 'Critical Service' for poets, a
National Poetry Competition, quarterly newsletter, and advice and
information.)

Regional Arts Boards:
Eastern Arts
Cherry Hinton Hall
Cherry Hinton Road
Cambridge CB1 8DW
01223 215355

East Midlands Arts
Mountfields House
Epinal Way
Loughborough LE11 0QE
01509 218292

London Arts
133 Long Acre
London WC2E 9AF
0171 240 1313

Northern Arts
9-10 Osbourne Terrace
Newcastle upon Tyne
0191 281 6334

North West Arts
Manchester House
22 Bridge Street
Manchester M3 3AB
0161 834 6644

South East Arts
Union House
Eridge Road
Tunbridge Wells TN4 8HF
01892 507200

South West Arts
Bradninch Place
Gandy Street
Exeter EX4 3LS
01392 218188

Southern Arts
13 St Clement Street
Winchester W023 9DQ
01962 855099

West Midlands Arts
82 Granville Street
Birmingham B1 2LH
0121 631 3121

Yorkshire Arts
21 Bond Street
Dewsbury
W Yorks WF13 1AX
01924 455555

Scottish Arts Council
12 Manor Place
Edinburgh EH3 7DD
0131 226 6051

Society of Authors
84 Drayton Gardens
London SW10 9SB
0171 373 6642
(Offers members a range of services, including legal advice.)

Ty Newydd Creative Writing Centre
Llanystumdwy
Gwynedd LL52 0LW
01766 522811
(Residential writing courses.)

Women's Art Library
Fulham Palace
Bishop's Avenue
London SW6 6EA
0171 731 7618

Writers' Guild of Great Britain
430 Edgeware Road
London W2 1EH
0171 723 8074
(TUC-affiliated trade union for writers.)